CHASING SHADOWS

T0315412

Miles Johnson is an award-winning investigative journalist for the *Financial Times* who covers organised crime and financial corruption. In over a decade at the *FT*, he has worked as a correspondent in London, New York, Madrid and Rome. For his work covering the Italian Mafia he was nominated for British Foreign Reporter of the Year at the 2021 British Press Awards. *Chasing Shadows* is his first book.

'As breathless, complex and on-the-edge suspenseful as the finest thriller fiction – but it's all real, which makes it truly extraordinary' Lee Child

'A terrific and utterly absorbing account of the murky and lethal connections between transnational organised crime and global politics. Enthrallingly and lucidly written with great authority and expertise, it is a classic of its kind' William Boyd

'Read this powerful book by Miles Johnson right now. It will make you realise that what we call terrorism is actually drug trafficking, what we call politics is organised crime and what we call peace is just a truce between mafias' Roberto Saviano, author of *Gomorrah*

'A truly impressive book that takes the reader deep into the dark underbelly of global money laundering where Hezbollah, Russian arms traders, the Italian mafia and Colombian drug lords meet. This *McMafia* for a new age is vital for understanding the black cash networks that have funded wars and terrorism across the Middle East' Catherine Belton

'Gripping … Part geopolitical essay, part toothsome slice of true crime … [a book with] humour, tension and pathos' *Daily Telegraph*

'Johnson has recreated the most private of criminal moments, including dialogue and even thoughts. He has opened a window on the narco-terror nexus that most observers knew very little about ... Johnson's writing gallops along' *Guardian*

'Reads like a first-rate thriller. [A] vivid expose of the murky world of transnational crime ... the overall narrative is so compelling and well-presented' *Spectator*

'A page-turner that criss-crosses borders and time zones, told in brisk, episodic, non-linear chapters' *Irish Independent*

'This is an extraordinary story of improbable but lethal connections across continents. Miles Johnson writes with verve and insight about ruthless men and the terrible consequences of their crimes' Fergal Keane

'This book is like being inserted deep into the secret heart of the global criminal economy, where mafiosi, terrorists and traffickers are all on the same side. It's compelling, visceral and highly readable' Oliver Bullough, author of *Moneyland*

'Holy Mackerel, what a story! Miles Johnson exposes the interlocking worlds of terror and drugs with verve and drama in this tale of truck bombs, arms deals, political assassinations, undercover cops and several tonnes of cocaine. *Chasing Shadows* is an astounding true-crime epic that puts us in the room as a Calabrian mob boss whispers to his mistress, a Lebanese militant plots to set the world on fire, and a US agent races to expose it all' Dan McCrum, author of *Money Men*

'This astonishing and cinematic rollercoaster of a debut will bring Miles Johnson's talent into the brilliant light. Delivered with trademark verve and precision, it achieves that rare and precious thing that is the goal of all great reporting: it reveals the world to itself' Alex Perry, author of *The Good Mothers*

'*Chasing Shadows* is a fascinating journey into the intersecting worlds of politics, terrorism and organised crime. Miles Johnson adopts a narrative technique reminiscent of the late John le Carré, while telling a true story. The result is an impeccably researched book, which is also a pleasure to read' Federico Varese, Professor of Sociology, Sciences Po and global organised crime expert

'*Chasing Shadows* offers a captivating glimpse into the complex world of international intrigue. This skilfully written thriller intertwines the compelling stories of three distinct men whose fates are undeniably linked. With its engaging prose, well-structured plot, and memorable characters, *Chasing Shadows* provides a thought-provoking look into the darker aspects of humanity and the high-stakes realm of drugs, terrorism, and power. Readers will find themselves fully immersed in this fascinating tale from start to finish' Eliot Higgins, author of *We Are Bellingcat*

'*Chasing Shadows* is a true-crime work of international intrigue as gripping and suspenseful as any novel you'll read this year' Harlan Coben

CHASING SHADOWS

A True Story of Drugs, War and the
Secret World of International Crime

MILES JOHNSON

The
Bridge
Street
Press

THE BRIDGE STREET PRESS

First published in Great Britain in 2023 by The Bridge Street Press
This paperback edition published in Great Britain in 2024
by The Bridge Street Press

1 3 5 7 9 10 8 6 4 2

Copyright © Miles Johnson 2023

The right of Miles Johnson to be identified as the Author
of this Work has been asserted by him in accordance with the
Copyright, Designs and Patents Act 1988.

All rights reserved.
No part of this publication may be reproduced, stored in a
retrieval system, or transmitted, in any form or by any means, without
the prior permission in writing of the publisher, nor be otherwise circulated
in any form of binding or cover other than that in which it is published
and without a similar condition including this condition being
imposed on the subsequent purchaser.

A CIP catalogue record for this book
is available from the British Library.

ISBN 978-0-349-12867-2

Typeset in Bembo by M Rules
Printed and bound in Great Britain by
Clays Ltd, Elcograf S.p.A.

Papers used by The Bridge Street Press are from well-managed forests
and other responsible sources.

MIX
Paper | Supporting
responsible forestry
FSC
www.fsc.org   FSC® C104740

The Bridge Street Press
An imprint of
Little, Brown Book Group
Carmelite House
50 Victoria Embankment
London EC4Y 0DZ

An Hachette UK Company
www.hachette.co.uk

www.littlebrown.co.uk

For Flora

Contents

Book Three

Prologue

The Cousins

Beirut, October 1983

At the crack of dawn on a quiet Sunday morning, two men in their early twenties climbed on to the roof of a tall building and took out their binoculars.

Most of the hundreds of American soldiers inside the barracks below were still fast asleep. On Sundays the base woke up later than normal. The Reveille had been pushed back an hour to 6.30 a.m., and the tired marines were looking forward to a break. Later that day they were going to enjoy a late brunch.

The two young men up on the roof overlooking Beirut international airport knew all this already. The barracks, home to American soldiers on an international peacekeeping mission, had been under surveillance for months. Their team had studied everything about their target, spending hours noting the exact times when the food and water trucks arrived and making sure to remember the vehicles' colour and make.

The Americans were already on guard. Six months before that Sunday morning, on 18 April 1983, a van packed with two thousand pounds of explosives had driven into the US embassy in Beirut. The blast tore through the building, its façade spewing twisted metal and black smoke before collapsing. In total sixty-three people died, including most of the Beirut staff of the CIA and the agency's top Middle East analyst. Nothing, however, could have prepared the sleeping marines for what was about to hit them.

A bright yellow nineteen-tonne Mercedes-Benz truck approached the entrance. A similar truck regularly passed the airport to deliver water and would not have given the guards any immediate cause for suspicion. But earlier that morning the real truck had been ambushed and replaced on its route with an exact replica. At around 5 a.m. the operative chosen to drive the vehicle received his final blessings, said some prayers and drank several cups of sweet tea.

At 6.22 a.m. the truck crashed through the sandbags at the guard posts. A duty sergeant had spotted the Mercedes beginning to accelerate, crunching through the barbed wire outside the compound. He started to scream. 'Get the fuck outta here! Hit the deck! hit the deck!' Seconds later, a bright orange-yellow flash ignited in the grille of the truck and a huge explosion ripped through the barracks. It was the largest non-nuclear explosion ever detonated, the force equal to between fifteen and twenty-one thousand pounds of TNT.

The blast was so strong it caused the four-storey reinforced concrete structure to collapse. The marines sleeping close to the blast died instantly. Others were woken by their windows bursting, shards of glass flying through the air, doors smashed off hinges and ripped paper floating across the room like confetti. The first reaction of those still alive was that it had been a Scud missile attack, or a heavy artillery hit. Those who could still walk stumbled outside into hell. Mangled body parts were strewn across the base. Bodies – some writhing in agony, some already dead – were covered in a thick grey dust.

A marine commander rushed to send a message to Washington: 'Explosion at BLT 1/8 HQS ... Building collapsed ... Large numbers of dead and wounded.'

Outside, one marine's body, still in its sleeping bag, had been impaled on the limb of a tree. Teams of rescuers tried to save anyone still alive underneath the wreckage. They began digging with shovels, picks, sledgehammers, axes. They used blowtorches to cut through the steel reinforcement rods in the concrete, scrambling to reach the cries for help and harrowing groans.

And sitting on the rooftop nearby, watching the unfolding chaos through their binoculars, were the two men. Below them a mushroom of smoke rose in the morning sun.

The blast killed 241 US servicemen and left countless others wounded. It was the largest loss of life suffered in one day by the US marines since the Battle of Iwo Jima in 1945. Their mission complete, the men climbed down from the roof and disappeared into the chaos of Beirut.

BOOK ONE

BOOK ONE

1

'The Navy SEALS of the DEA'

Virginia, January 2014

One of the first pieces of advice Jack Kelly ever got as a young Drug Enforcement Administration agent in New York was to quit before he was thirty. 'Son,' an older colleague told him, 'you are fearless now, but after a few years in this job you will be done. You will be cooked by the time you are twenty-nine.'

Jack remembered the night he first considered that he might be getting too old for this. It had been close to midnight, and he was drinking alone in a dank, dimly lit bar called Hogs & Heifers. And three hours earlier two heroin dealers had tried to crush him to death with a car.

It had started as a routine surveillance operation. Jack, who back then still wore his hair in a ponytail, was alone in an unmarked BMW M3 in plain clothes. Close by were two other DEA agents in another vehicle. They were there to observe a mob-connected heroin dealer in Little Italy. The suspect had walked into a social club and returned to the street holding a silver cooler bag, handing it off to two younger men sitting inside a nearby car.

Jack's supervisor was excited. It was a big bag – as much as a kilo of heroin. Enough to make it worth taking a risk. Over the radio he instructed Jack to follow the two men and, if possible, to arrest them. Other agents would arrive shortly afterwards to provide back-up. The suspects drove away, and Jack followed, trying to hang as far back as possible. They stopped, and Jack parked about five feet in front of them. Slowly, he began to walk towards their vehicle.

There were thousands of things Jack Kelly should have been thinking about as the man in the car panicked and slammed his foot on the pedal. He should have been thinking about how he was seconds away from his legs being crushed. He should have been thinking why he had stupidly left his badge dangling round his neck when he approached the vehicle. He should have been thinking about where the hell the promised back-up was. He should have been thinking about how quickly he could draw his Glock. He should have been thinking about how bullets can change direction when they hit a windscreen, and whether he risked hitting a civilian if he opened fire. He should have been thinking about all of those things, but in that split-second he could only think about one thing: he couldn't believe this was happening to him on his birthday.

Jack was about to be trapped. The car was on course to ram into his body, smashing him into the back of his own BMW. But the driver had pushed down on the pedal too hard, sending his car spinning out of control and into the oncoming traffic. At that moment, Jack's colleagues screeched down the street, crashing into the side of the dealers' vehicle. After they made the arrest they did Jack a favour, dropping him off at Hogs & Heifers rather than making him come in to do the paperwork. It was his birthday, after all.

Drinking alone at the bar, it hit him for the first time: he couldn't keep doing this for ever. Since that encounter with the BMW, more than a decade had passed. Jack had been an agent in the DEA for over fifteen years and was long over-due a posting to headquarters. It promised to be a calmer time in his life, pushing papers from a quiet desk in an office in Arlington, Virginia. Boring, perhaps, but after years on the streets Jack needed it. Then he got a phone call from Derek Maltz.

Maltz was the Special Agent in Charge of the DEA's Special Operations Division, an elite unit based near Chantilly, a small town outside Washington DC. From the outside, the SOD, as it was known, looked like the regional outpost of a life insurance company. But hidden inside the three-storey brown brick building, located between the Lee-Jackson Memorial Highway and Dulles International Airport, rows of DEA agents were busy studying a multilingual cacophony of wire-taps, telephone metadata and intelligence. And it was from there that Derek Maltz was busy building one of the most audacious experiments in American law enforcement history.

Jack had first met Maltz when he was a kid agent on the streets of New York in the 1990s, working wiretap cases against organised criminals. Maltz had been the boss of the New York Drug Enforcement Task Force. It was there that Jack had learned how to run wiretaps, follow money and build cases. Maltz knew a good drug cop when he saw one, and the man he wanted to join him in Virginia was John 'Jack' Kelly.

From the moment Jack had left his childhood home in suburban New Jersey for the DEA's training camp at Quantico
in his early twenties, he had leapt into the job like a man
possessed. Back then, living in a small apartment in Hell's
Kitchen, he would be available on his beeper at any time of
day or night. Older agents would switch off and go home to
their families. For Jack there was no raid he wouldn't volun-
teer for, no informant he wouldn't meet on a weekend in the
middle of the night, no surveillance post he wouldn't man for
hours on end. Quickly, he was noticed by the DEA hierarchy,
gaining a reputation first as 'a worker' and then, as time went
on, as a talented and driven investigator: a 'case maker' who
could go after dangerous and complex criminal gangs.

Shaven-headed and muscular, Jack had lifted weights or
gone for a long run almost every day of his adult life – no
matter where he was or how many hours he had worked.
Some might have considered him a health obsessive. But Jack
also loved to drink red wine. He wasn't running because it
was respectable. It was a visceral need, a release valve for
an immense, sometimes overpowering nervous energy that
would build and build inside him ever since he had been
a child. Missing a single day would cause him to suffer
migraines or become dizzy.

It had made him the type of agent the DEA bosses loved.
But it had come at a cost. Five years in the DEA was like
twenty in a normal job. More than fifteen years in, Jack was
burned out, exhausted. A posting to a desk job would have
done him a world of good. When Maltz called him up about
the job at the SOD, he warned him this was going to be different from anything he had ever done before. And Jack had
little idea about what sort of cases he was going to be working
on. It didn't matter – he couldn't resist.

*

Jack was going to be placed in the Counter Narco-Terrorism Operations Center, the part of the SOD that coordinated all DEA investigations and intelligence linked to the overlap between drug cases and terrorist financing. Jack's new job, according to Maltz, involved two seemingly simple mantras: 'putting the pieces of the puzzle together' and 'keeping the bad guys off the streets'.

Each time one of Maltz's hand-picked recruits arrived in Virginia he would take them into his office to give them a pep talk. They weren't in a field office in Miami, Baltimore or New York any more, Maltz warned them. He had brought them to the SOD to pursue complex international operations involving connected drug cases, weapons trafficking and terrorism. This was going to be a different ball game.

Maltz's office was packed with mementoes from his long career in law enforcement. Being a drug cop was in his blood. His father had run the New York Drug Enforcement Task Force, the oldest of its kind in America, before he had. Colleagues would joke that Maltz had been taken on surveillance operations by his dad while he was a kid.

Hanging on the walls were framed front pages from the *New York Daily News* on the day after the attacks on the World Trade Center. Maltz's brother, who was in the US air force, had died in a helicopter crash during the invasion of Afghanistan. The trauma of 9/11 and his brother's death had marked him. In his mind, taking charge of the SOD was his chance to do his bit.

Maltz's screensaver was a photo of him on top of a cartoon desert island surrounded by sharks. It was meant as a light-hearted reminder of what Maltz called 'the nature of the beast': the daily inter-agency political battles that came with running a maverick operation like his. He wanted his recruits to be aggressive, but also smart: 'You got to stay focused on what you are doing and worry about the security of the country and the world,' he would tell them as he pointed at his screen. 'Don't worry about the sharks, just don't go swimming. And if you go swimming – be careful!'

Maltz would take new recruits into his office and pull out a large box of commemorative coins, emblazoned with the insignia of different US law enforcement, military and intelligence agencies, which he had been given as gifts when he had visited them. Maltz would clatter the coins onto the table, spreading them out. Then he would bang down a large, red metal apple he had been given as a parting gift from the New York Drug Enforcement Task Force.

'OK,' Maltz began in his thick New York accent. 'You were all really good agents, working overseas or in different DEA offices. Now you are here in SOD. And you are coming here with a goal.'

He would jab his finger at the shiny red apple. 'This is you on your first day. Your goal is you want to get to the apple, that is what you are trying to do.' Next, he pointed at the shiny coins. The coins, he said, represented land mines scattered across the Washington DC Beltway, bureaucratic and political IEDs blocking their path. 'If you come here with all your tough-guy, aggressive attitudes and try and run through to get to your goal you are going to hit one of these. You are gonna blow up, and you are never gonna recover.'

It didn't take long for Jack to get what his new boss was talking about. He could immediately see that Maltz had got his hands on a powerful machine, one that he was determined to use to maximum effect. The SOD was an elite DEA division whose work was largely secret. It had a staff of three hundred and collaborated with more than twenty different US government law enforcement and intelligence agencies to pursue multi-jurisdictional drug cases using cutting-edge surveillance technology.

It had almost all happened by historical accident. Before 9/11, the DEA was viewed by many in the US government as, in the words of Maltz, 'a little old drug agency'. Since being founded in the 1970s to fight the war on drugs, the DEA had grown into eighty-three offices in sixty-two countries, creating a vast network of sources and information reaching into the international criminal underworld. In 1994, the SOD had been launched to allow the DEA to find a more effective way of sorting through the huge quantities of information, tips and leads that were generated by its investigations.

Then, in 2006, the year after Maltz had arrived in Virginia as Special Agent in Charge of the SOD, the US passed a little-known federal statute known as 21 U.S.C. § 960a relating to what the DEA had long called narco-terrorism, or the interconnection between terrorist groups and drug traffickers. Before then, if the DEA was going to go after criminals abroad, such as cocaine cartels in Latin America, it had to prove they were conspiring to move narcotics into the US. Now a drug deal conducted anywhere in the world that involved a transfer 'of pecuniary value to any person or organisation that has engaged or engages in terrorist activity' could become a case for US law enforcement. All of a sudden, the 'little old drug agency' seemed to have almost universal jurisdiction.

At around the same time changes to US law in the wake of 9/11 were smashing down information barriers between US intelligence and law enforcement agencies. The DEA was formally admitted into the United States intelligence community and was given access to some of its most powerful tools. The Special Operations Division was now supercharged, and Derek Maltz had the authority to go after some of the biggest, most frightening bad guys on the planet.

The first of these major cases came in 2007 when DEA agents took down Monzer al-Kassar, a Syrian-born arms trafficker known as the Prince of Marbella, who had been linked to the hijacking of the *Achille Lauro* cruise ship by the Palestine Liberation Front in 1985. The DEA, using informants posing as Colombian paramilitaries wanting to buy weapons, arrested al-Kassar in a risky sting operation in Spain. He was extradited to the United States and sentenced to thirty years in prison. Rival agencies were shocked by the audacity of what the DEA had pulled off.

Then, in 2008, the DEA decided to go even further. Maltz went to a meeting at the White House between senior DEA leaders and top national security officials. Juan Zarate, President George W. Bush's national security advisor, brought up the name of an infamous arms trafficker born in the former Soviet Union called Viktor Bout. No one had been able to lay a glove on Bout for decades. Maltz and the other DEA bosses took it as a direct challenge: go out there and bring him in.

Before that day, Maltz had never even heard of Bout. But he soon learned that people in the US intelligence agencies had been dancing around him for decades. Many believed Bout, who operated under the protection of Moscow, was untouchable. What could a bunch of drug cops do when the best and brightest of US intelligence had failed? Then, out of nowhere, as Maltz proudly described it to his recruits, 'little old DEA comes in under the radar and – *boom, boom, boom*'. Just like that, the DEA arrested Bout in an undercover sting in Thailand. Perhaps they even shocked themselves at what they had managed to pull off. The whole operation, from the conversation in the White House to Bout in handcuffs, took just seven months.

Seemingly overnight, DEA agents Maltz had brought to the SOD, who had spent their careers arresting drug dealers on the streets of Baltimore and the Bronx, were chasing Bond villain-esque supercriminals. The early success of this new, turbo-charged policing operation meant the SOD's budget was expanded, giving it new resources to pay informants and to spend on safe houses, security and flying agents around the world.

But this transformation was making some people uneasy, and Maltz knew it. Some of the DEA stings provoked full-blown diplomatic incidents. The Russian government was outraged that the US had arrested Bout and tried to block his extradition. Defence attorneys started to complain that the DEA was wildly overstepping its jurisdiction. Some said its elaborate overseas stings were nothing more than entrapment: some had ensnared people with no links to drugs or terrorism. One lawyer quoted in a *Time* magazine article dubbed the SOD 'the Navy SEALs of the DEA'. It was meant to suggest an agency pushing the limits of its authority. Even Bout took a shot from prison: 'The DEA have become worse than drug dealers. At least drug dealers have ethics.'

None of this seemed to concern Maltz very much. He was proud of the SOD and its daring operations, and took the 'Navy SEALs' jab as a compliment. If his outfit was pissing people off, then good. It showed they were getting things done.

Divorced and in his forties, Jack lived with his two cats in a condo in a town about fifteen minutes away from the SOD office. Each morning, he would drive to work in his Jeep Wrangler to the sound of the Stone Temple Pilots and arrive at a desk surrounded by mounting stacks of papers and sprawling wall charts piecing together international criminal networks.

When other agents would go out for lunch at local chain restaurants, Jack would bring his own food and eat at his desk. Some of his colleagues immediately labelled him an oddball. He sometimes wore a MIT T-shirt in the office, even though he hadn't attended the university, leading some bosses to assume he had. Even though life at the SOD was meant to give agents a better work–life balance, many still headed out to the nearby bars each night. Jack mostly wouldn't go, aside from the evenings when someone was retiring after twenty-five years of service. More often than not this would involve some heavy drinking, the DEA bag-pipers blasting out a version of 'Auld Lang Syne', and Maltz delivering a raucous, profanity-laden leaving speech.

Maltz had asked Jack to take a closer look at what, on first glance, seemed to him like one of the more obscure areas on the SOD's list of international targets: tracking criminal networks linked to Iran and Hezbollah, the Lebanese terrorist group and Shia political party that had been sponsored by Tehran as a proxy force since its birth in the early 1980s.

Before arriving in Virginia Jack barely knew the difference between a Sunni and a Shia, let alone the complexities of Iranian and Lebanese history. But he threw himself into his job as ferociously as he had done back in New York.

Sat in his paper-laden mess of a cubicle, Jack could soon tell that this area had potential. Using the information coming in from informants and agents around the world, Jack's job was to coordinate investigations into these networks: being 'an eye in the sky', as it was called. On weekends Jack would wake up early, drink his morning coffee, and then hit the gym before spending hours working on open-source research.

The closer Jack looked, the more wiretap transcripts he studied and the more reports he read, it became clear to him that something deeply troubling was happening. It was like being at the centre of a panopticon watching cash, drugs and guns moving across borders. Jack's investigations started to show connections between criminal organisations which sometimes had little idea themselves of how enmeshed they were. A drug cartel in Colombia could be shipping cocaine to Mafias in Europe, who in turn laundered their money through Middle Eastern banks holding cash for rogue regimes. Those sanctioned governments could then use the funds raised on the international black market to purchase bombs and weapons.

The DEA had picked up numerous leads about Iran and Hezbollah exploiting these networks to circumvent US sanctions. Governments like Iran still needed to procure hard currency and arms as before, but now increasingly had to turn to criminal schemes to source them. To do this they used procurement agents or 'super facilitators' – cells that operated in the shadow dimension of international arms and drugs trafficking.

It was a murky world where it was hard to know who was doing it for the money and who was working for a higher cause. Jack could see some targets were freewheeling entrepreneurs profiting from the global criminal free market, delivering hard-to-source items such as helicopter parts or stealthily moving illicit funds across borders. But others seemed more closely integrated into Hezbollah and Iran's undercover operations. Some of these super facilitators, the DEA believed, appeared to be communicating with some of the top officials in the Lebanese organisation.

Early on, Maltz had told Jack that if he was going to get traction in other agencies he would have to come up with a project codename. Jack had been reading *In the Garden of Beasts* by Erik Larson, a book about William Dodd, the American ambassador to Germany who had warned Washington of the dangers posed by Hitler in the 1930s. Dodd had named his speaking tour after Cassandra, the Trojan princess who was fated to never be believed but whose prophecies were eventually proved correct. Jack had become convinced the new breed of criminal he was tracking was a threat not yet properly understood – and needed to be attacked urgently. So he came up with a name: Project Cassandra.

By 2014, Jack Kelly was working harder than ever. Thousands of miles away from his cubicle in Virginia a bloody civil war had exploded in Syria. He could immediately sense its impact rippling out across the global criminal underworld. Bashar al-Assad, the Syrian dictator, was unleashing horrific violence against his own population, using chemical weapons on civilians. And it seemed like no one knew exactly how to respond. War fatigue had long replaced the post-9/11 sense of purpose that had inspired the SOD's early swashbuckling foreign sting operations, and the US economy was still reeling from the global financial crisis.

As Western politicians hesitated, Hezbollah and Iran quickly moved to ensure the Assad regime did not collapse. If an unfriendly new government took power in Damascus, then Hezbollah risked being cut off from its Iranian sponsor and losing its ability to move people, money and weapons through Syria.

Intelligence was showing that some of the criminal procurement networks that Jack was tracking had gone into overdrive to supply weapons for the conflict. He now had more targets than ever before. Some of these super facilitators appeared to be moving material that could make chemical weapons into Syria. For Jack, it was like looking inside a hall of mirrors of globalisation, revealing the disfigurement of an international order that suddenly felt like it was breaking apart.

There was one man out there who was likely at the centre of it all: the end user. His name was Mustafa Badreddine, and he was a legendary Lebanese terrorist who had been dispatched to Damascus to lead Hezbollah special forces fighters in support of Assad. Everyone knew that thirty years before it was Mustafa who had executed the deadly attack on the US marine barracks in Beirut, watching through his binoculars from the roof of the nearby building.

A bunch of DEA agents were never going to get close to a guy like Mustafa. He was a ghost, a phantom who had evaded the world's most determined intelligence agencies for decades. But Jack knew that they could at least go after some of the people sending weapons to people like him and others supporting Assad in Syria. They just needed the right leads.

One morning a colleague stopped by Jack's desk and asked him what he knew about a Lebanese businessman by the name of Ali Fayad. They ran Fayad's name through a database. He appeared to be an important international arms dealer who was selling weapons to Damascus.

DEA undercover informants working in West Africa had picked up information that Fayad was now selling weapons being used by Hezbollah to fight in Syria. The informants, Jack's colleagues told him, were slowly working to set up a large arms deal with him that they could secretly record to gather evidence.

The SOD now had what appeared to be a top-level target in its sights. After several preliminary meetings, the informants had got the arms dealer to agree to meet them in a hotel in the Czech Republic. The sting operation was on. Jack and a team of agents were flying out to Prague, and they were going to bring Fayad in.

2

'Elias Saab'

Damascus, 2014

Somewhere in Syria, a middle-aged man wearing spectacles, green military fatigues and a camouflage-print baseball cap roused his fighters for the battle ahead. 'You are up to the challenge,' he told them, shaking a fist with a large blood-red agate ring on one finger. 'May holy God bless your deeds.'

The Americans didn't know exactly when Mustafa Badreddine had slipped across the border into Syria, but they knew he was there. At the start of the Syrian civil war in 2011, Hezbollah's leadership denied any of its men were even in the country. As the first body bags began to be sent back to Lebanon, the funerals were held in the dead of night so as not to attract attention. By 2014, it was an open secret: Mustafa, one of the most wanted men in the Middle East, was in Syria. Exactly where, nobody knew. Rebels reported spotting him commanding groups of elite Hezbollah fighters waging urban warfare near the Lebanese border. US spies believed he was in the capital, Damascus, brokering crisis meetings between the Syrian and Iranian governments as they scrambled to prop up Assad's teetering dictatorship.

Even Mustafa's enemies – and he had many – had to admit that he wasn't just good: he was one of the best. For more than three decades he had presided over one of the longest uninterrupted sprees of bombings, assassinations and kidnappings the world had ever seen. And he had always managed to slip away. The truth was, officially at least, Mustafa barely existed. Since his youth, he had carefully avoided being photographed, and had never been issued a passport in his own name, nor a driving licence. There was no record of him ever holding a bank account. There was no record of him ever having entered or left Lebanon. He had paid no taxes, owned no property.

He was a man with many faces. Before leaving for the war in Syria, he had been cocky, brazen. Mustafa, some said, could zip through the crowded streets of Beirut alone on his scooter, a black baseball cap pulled low on his head and dark sunglasses covering his piercing eyes. At other times, he travelled in heavily guarded convoys of SUVs, barking instructions down multiple mobile phones at once.

Now in his early fifties, his closely trimmed beard, once jet black, had turned grey. Mustafa had one last mission left in him, and it was going to be the most difficult he had ever faced. The instructions from Hezbollah's leadership were clear: protect the Syrian dictator from the insurgency at all costs.

By March 2014, Bashar al-Assad himself had started to lose hope and considered leaving the country. Rebel militias were positioned not far from the gates of the Presidential Palace, and top officials in the regime were scrambling to send their families into hiding. The anti-Assad fighters – a mix of the Free Syrian Army and Sunni jihadists – had seized large parts of Aleppo, in the far north. Syria's second city was now encircled by government battalions, Iranian forces and Hezbollah fighters under Mustafa's command. He knew the fate of the dictator would likely be decided on the barrel-bombed streets of Aleppo. Should the rebels seize full control, Damascus would be next.

With the Syrian army unable to regain lost territory, the regime had unleashed sickening violence on its own population. A year earlier, it had attacked the opposition-controlled suburbs of Damascus with Sarin nerve gas, inflicting an agonising death on hundreds of civilians. By using chemical weapons, Assad had wantonly crossed what a year earlier President Barack Obama had pledged would be a 'red line'. But international retaliation for the crime was minimal. Hundreds of thousands of Syrians had now died in the fighting, and millions more were fleeing the country.

Syria, some warned, would become Hezbollah's Vietnam. Mustafa was a killer who had murdered hundreds of people since he was a teenager. But men like him claimed they murdered in the name of a just cause: defending his land from Israeli attacks. Now he was sending young men to die in a bloody sectarian quagmire, fighting in the name of a loathed Arab dictator.

Some of the men Mustafa had started out fighting with in the 1980s said his war was a betrayal of the movement's founding principles. Those who kill children in Syria, the former Secretary-General of Hezbollah warned, 'will go to hell, and cannot be considered martyrs'. But Mustafa believed Assad could not be allowed to fall. For decades, the Assad regime had served as a bridge between Tehran and Hezbollah. This bridge had to be defended; defended from the hordes of Islamic State fighters who were pouring like tar from city to city; defended against the Free Syrian Army, parts of which were being trained and supported by the Americans. And most of all defended against falling to a new regime that could go on to strike a deal with Hezbollah's enemies, leaving it stranded in southern Lebanon and cut off from Iran.

Mustafa knew that, for him, there were only two possible outcomes: victory or death. 'I won't come back from Syria unless as a martyr, or a carrier of the banner of victory.' This was his vow.

But determination would not be enough. The battle in Syria was not just costing Hezbollah thousands of casualties; it was stretching its financial resources to breaking point. Winning was going to require guns, and money. And half-way around the world there were men and women working in the shadows to ensure weapons would keep flowing into Mustafa's war effort.

More than three decades earlier, Mustafa, a teenager with a long thin nose and a shock of black, curly hair, walked into his parents' house in the southern Beirut district of Ghobeiry. He had come home that day with a guest, his cousin and best friend Imad Mughniyeh.

Saada, Mustafa's younger sister, was always excited when Imad came to visit. He was a serious, brooding boy a year younger than Mustafa who lived a short walk from the Badreddines in a cinder block house with no running water.

Saada knew that Mustafa and Imad had been spending long hours together debating politics and religion at the mosques close to their homes. Both lived near to the Green Line – a sniper-infested divide that sliced the city between warring factions. Their teenage years, since the outbreak of Lebanon's civil war in 1975, had been punctuated with the sounds of gunfire and artillery blasts, with stray bullets and shrapnel hitting Imad's parents' house.

The poverty-stricken Shia slums of southern Beirut, battered by conflict, were fertile grounds for the radical theocratic ideas that had inspired the 1979 Iranian revolution. As she listened to her brother and cousin's conversations, Saada felt something important was stirring in their neighbourhood. Young, disenfranchised Shias were openly challenging the older generation at the mosques. And the teenage girl could see that Mustafa and Imad wanted to do more than just talk. They were ambitious and were now busily training for the future.

At the time, Lebanon was awash with opportunities for young militants seeking to learn their craft. At first the two boys had been tempted by communism, reading texts by Leon Trotsky translated into Arabic. Then, as teenagers patrolling their neighbourhood during the fighting in Beirut, they ran into groups of Palestinian militants. Soon after, they were drawn into the orbit of Yasser Arafat's Fatah, attending training camps in the south of the country.

It was clear to the older militants at the camps that the two boys had talent. Mustafa began to learn how to make bombs. Imad was taken under the wing of Ali Salameh, the chief of operations for Black September, the terror organisation responsible for the massacre at the 1972 Olympic Games in Munich, and was recruited into Force 17, Arafat's personal security retinue. The cousins were fresh faced and inexperienced but they were disciplined, carefully studying military tactics and taking notes, whereas other young fighters merely wanted to fire guns. They began to gain a following among the new generation of Shia militants emerging round them.

During Imad's regular visits, Saada began to get to know him more. Captivated by his seriousness, she had secretly fallen in love with her cousin. She knew Imad, the son of a sweet seller, was poor. He had no means of supporting a wife or children. And she was not particularly religious. It didn't matter. Soon they were engaged.

In 1982, Israel invaded Lebanon and Mustafa and Imad took up arms alongside the Fatah fighters they had been training with. Both cousins suffered severe injuries in a gunfight, Mustafa almost losing the use of one of his legs. Saada begged her father to be allowed to stay with Imad to care for him, even though they were not yet married. Eventually, he relented.

Mustafa and Imad were now not only brothers in arms – they were brothers-in-law. Saada married her cousin in a simple ceremony conducted by the famous Shia cleric Mohammad Hussein Fadlallah, who employed Imad as his bodyguard. The young couple didn't have enough money for a party, or to buy Saada a dress for the occasion. Nor could they afford a place of their own, instead living in a makeshift room on the balcony of Imad's parents' home.

Imad tried to shelter Saada from his work. But she could see that every shred of his and Mustafa's energy was consumed by planning their next operation. After the 1982 war with Israel, Fatah left Lebanon and the cousins were left without sponsors. But a new, more dangerous force had taken Arafat's place. During the chaos of the war, the Iranian Revolutionary Guard had quietly established a training camp in an abandoned military base in the Bekaa Valley, and was eager to recruit the two ambitious young militants. Mustafa and Imad now had the might and resources of a nation state behind them – one that was willing to unleash spectacular violence to get its way. At the same time cadres of young Shias, backed by revolutionary Iran, were coalescing into a new organisation that would come to be known as Hezbollah – the party of God.

Saada knew she was never going to have a normal marriage. But in 1983, following the attacks that slaughtered hundreds of US marines plotted by her brother and her husband, the consequences of their life choices had become clear. They would now have to disappear into the shadows for ever. Mustafa and Imad were no longer boys talking in a mosque. They were terrorists in the crosshairs of some of the world's most powerful governments.

The wreckage of the marine barracks in Beirut had barely stopped smoking when, six weeks later, Mustafa set off on a new mission. Using a fake passport under the name of 'Elias Saab', he slipped into Kuwait.

Building on the skills he learned in the training camps, Mustafa had honed a sophisticated technique of hugely increasing the power of plastic explosives by surrounding them with gas canisters. One ordnance expert investigating the barracks attack noted that it would have required 'a masters degree in explosives, if not a scientist' to construct a bomb so deadly. Now, as part of an undercover team of over twenty operatives dispatched to the tiny emirate, Mustafa was about to again demonstrate his lethal talents.

On 12 December 1983, a devastating chain of explosions erupted across Kuwait in the space of ninety minutes. The opening blast went off at the US embassy, when a truck stacked with gas cylinders smashed through the building's front gates and detonated. As shaken onlookers surveyed the damage, which had crumpled the building's front annexe and blown out the windows of the nearby Hilton hotel, another car bomb went off outside the French embassy. Inside, the impact detached a crystal chandelier hanging above the ambassador's desk, sending it crashing down and missing his head by inches. One by one, the dizzying barrage continued, with blasts ringing out at the country's airport, its electric company and other strategic targets. A bomb made up of over two hundred gas cylinders hidden inside a truck failed to go off close enough to the country's largest oil refinery, saving it from exploding into an unending inferno.

A frantic manhunt began. As Mustafa and his accomplices raced to escape, Kuwait declared a state of emergency, throwing up roadblocks and temporarily forbidding women from wearing the veil while driving to ensure the culprits couldn't hide themselves. The Kuwaitis had little doubt who was behind the attacks. The bombs, the government said, were 'the first concentrated Iranian operation to export the revolution beyond its borders'. A fingerprint from a severed thumb found at the site of the US embassy blast was confirmed to belong to a known member of a terror group headquartered in Tehran. Police then discovered that guns and grenades had been secretly smuggled into Kuwait from Iran and hidden in oil barrels in the weeks leading up to the attack.

Two months after the blasts, twenty-one young men were led into a metal cage inside a courtroom in Kuwait City, surrounded by armed guards. Sitting among them as they laughed and joked was a man with black, curly hair called Elias Saab. After a short trial seventeen of them, including Saab – in reality Mustafa Badreddine – were found guilty of orchestrating the attacks and sentenced to death.

Imad Mughinyeh was not going to sit idly by as Saada's beloved brother rotted in a Kuwaiti jail, waiting to be taken outside and shot. He was going to use any means necessary to set his cousin free.

3

A Loaded Gun

Calabria, 2014

Far away from the battlefields of Syria, in a small town in the southern Italian region of Calabria, Salvatore Pititto stood in his vegetable garden as his wife pointed a pistol at his head.

But even as Antonella gripped the gun, she knew that blowing her husband's brains out couldn't change the thing that hurt her most: Salvatore's heart belonged to another woman. 'Even if I shoot her in the kneecaps you will still want her,' she told him. 'Because you are in love with her.'

It was true. For Salvatore it had been love at first sight. Over a decade before his wife threatened to kill him, a young girl from Ukraine stepped out of a train station in Calabria ready to start a new life. Oksana, twenty-one years old, with bottle-blond hair and horn-rimmed glasses, had no residence papers, no house and no job. She had come to Italy on the advice of a friend from back home, who had made the journey several years before and managed to find work.

Oksana's friend had come to pick her up. She had been driven there by an Italian man she knew through work. His name was Salvatore. He was thickset with a large head, buzz-cut hair and darting eyes that were slightly too small for his broad face. Salvatore wasn't tall, dark and handsome – but he was powerful, authoritative. And perhaps, as they stood outside the station, in her first moments in Calabria, he made her feel safe.

Salvatore was instantly attracted to Oksana and offered to help her. At first, he got her a job in the same place her friend worked: the local farming cooperative that produced cheese and milk. But Salvatore wanted Oksana closer. He found her another job, this time as a carer for the elderly couple who lived next door to him and his family.

The house of the elderly couple had windows that looked onto Salvatore's home. Sometimes Oksana spotted him, gazing at her as she worked. Soon afterwards they began an affair.

It wouldn't have been clear to Oksana exactly what Salvatore did for a living. But he had money, and knew a lot of important people in the area who could make life easier for her as she adjusted to a strange new country.

When the couple she cared for both died in quick succession, Oksana needed another job. Salvatore arranged for his new girlfriend to become an off-the-books checkout girl in a grocery, and for her to live in a small apartment above the shop.

The grocery was owned by an old woman who had three sons. One of them, a kind, sweet boy, began to take an interest in the pretty Ukrainian. The two of them started to take his elderly mother out for walks together. The family treated her like their own. Oksana then learned that the son had told his uncle he had fallen for her. Yes, there was Salvatore. But Salvatore and Antonella had been married for over a decade. They had three children. Perhaps it was sensible for Oksana to start thinking about other options.

Then, one day, the boy from the grocery abruptly broke things off. Oksana later learned that Salvatore had warned the boy's uncle: 'If I can't have her,' he said, 'nobody can.' People in the neighbourhood seemed to take what Salvatore said very seriously.

By then Salvatore had helped put Oksana up in her own apartment, registered in her name. She now had her own place, could speak the language and had a stable job. He started to bring strange men to her house, telling Oksana to leave the room so they could talk in private. She noticed that Salvatore was terrified of being recorded. Sometimes, he and his friends would drop their voices low and start speaking about strange things. Her boyfriend wasn't a farmer, but he would often say to someone on the phone 'I need to come and see the sheep today', or 'I'm coming to bring you the cheese'.

Little by little, Salvatore became less cautious around Oksana. Sometimes she was allowed to stay in the room while he and his friends had their discussions. He started to share little secrets with her.

One evening they were snuggled on the sofa in her living room, watching a TV drama about an undercover policeman who infiltrates a powerful Calabrian Mafia family. The hero was firing a machine gun.

'I have two of those,' Salvatore said with pride as he pointed at the television. 'What?' Oksana said. 'Kalashnikovs?'

'Yup,' he said. 'It's true, it's true.'

Oksana and Antonella had never met, but they knew about each other. Even if Antonella, a stocky woman with dyed black hair cut in a bob who wore blue Converse trainers, wasn't happy, what could she do? Men like Salvatore did not get divorced. He and his wife lived with their three sons in a cheaply built house in a dusty corner of Mileto, the small town of eight thousand people they had both been born in and had never left. To the side of the house was a small garden with several large orange trees. Antonella would tend the plot, where she grew vegetables.

Antonella knew Salvatore thought she was stupid. Sometimes he would ask her to perform small tasks for him, taking money here or picking up someone from there. But she knew he never trusted her, and always believed she would mess things up. Sometimes Antonella would ask her sons why their father treated her with such lovelessness. Did he speak to his friends like he spoke to her? But they didn't offer much sympathy. Growing up under the tutelage of their father, they were starting to toughen up.

Salvatore told Oksana that he and Antonella no longer shared a bed, his wife instead sleeping on the sofa. Oksana's existence gradually became an open secret. Sometimes Salvatore would take her out to have dinner with his friends, or to watch him play bowls with his sons. She was completely his. But Oksana would have known that he could never be completely hers.

Men like Salvatore were bound by a vow of secrecy. But, as time went on, the secrets got bigger. He trusted Oksana. He told her about his drug trafficking, and the caches of weapons his friends had hidden in fields. And he told her about his family, a family that struck terror into the people who lived in their small, poor town.

Oksana learned that Salvatore had a cousin called Pasquale who nobody ever saw. Pasquale and Salvatore had been born in the same year, one month apart. Pasquale was in a wheel-chair, having suffered a gunshot wound in an ambush years earlier. He had later been given a twenty-five-year sentence for murder and lived under house arrest in Mileto, having successfully appealed against being put in prison because of his disability.

Pasquale kept a large collection of weaponry, including M12 submachine guns, automatic rifles and a .38 revolver. Salvatore told Oksana in their late-night conversations about how close he was to his cousin, and how similar they were. Over time she discovered that Pasquale, despite being imprisoned in his house, seemed to know everything about everyone in town – even her. She decided it was wise to pay her respects. After returning from a trip back to Ukraine, she gave Salvatore a gift for Pasquale – a bottle of cognac and an ornamental boat covered in seashells. Salvatore told Oksana his cousin had given the little boat pride of place on his windowsill. Perhaps it was Pasquale's way of telling Oksana that, even though they had never met, he was keeping an eye on her.

It was Pasquale who had made Salvatore's family the kings of their town. Back in the 1980s, the cousins had started out as young hoodlums, hijacking trucks and extorting payments from local businesses under the protection of more powerful crime bosses. The teenage Pasquale quickly proved highly adept, even innovative, at coercing the businessmen of Mileto. Early in their criminal careers, an older boss had asked the boys to drop off a sealed envelope outside the house of a policeman. While they were on their way, Pasquale couldn't resist opening the envelope. Inside was a letter written in block capitals containing a chilling threat. From then on, he adopted a similar strategy for his own burgeoning extortion racket: why shake down someone in person, when you could simply drop them a note? Soon he developed a system of sending handwritten messages to his victims demanding payment, along with an intimidating flourish: a bottle filled with petrol, or a crudely built homemade explosive device. Once, Pasquale dumped a dog's severed head outside a businessman's house.

The Pititos began to rise up the ranks. The top Calabrian criminal families had for over a hundred years operated on a secret ranking system of membership, known as *doti*, or 'gifts'. For a young thug to be promoted to a higher gift, known as 'receiving a flower', he had to undergo a masonic-like initiation ritual performed by more senior members. And it was in 1988, in cell number 18 of Vibo Valentia prison during a brief arrest for robbery, that Pasquale became a made man. The boys weren't *picciotti*, or petty street thugs, any more. The Pititto gang had now been recognised by their elders as a fully fledged crew.

Over the years they had survived various wars against rival crime families, including the one that had put Pasquale in a wheelchair. Their command over Mileto was unchallenged. Still, the Pititto family were a provincial outfit, a small satellite with dominion over their little grey town only at the behest of far more powerful regional bosses. Salvatore would have known that the real money, and the real power, came from far away. And Salvatore was an ambitious man, ambitious for his family. He wanted the best for them.

Salvatore and Antonella's three sons, Giuseppe, Gianluca and Alex, were their future. Salvatore talked to Oksana about his boys all the time, beaming with pride. They were, he told her, growing up to be just like him.

Giuseppe and Gianluca, now in their twenties, had begun selling drugs in the town, and helping their father out with his business. Giuseppe, the oldest son, was engaged to the daughter of a partner of Salvatore's. The father of the bride had been saving money from drug deals to marry her off in a luxury ceremony with horse-drawn carriages. One Easter, Salvatore told Oksana he was particularly happy because Giuseppe had spent the day alone with Pasquale in his cousin's house, drinking grappa. It was a sign he was being groomed for succession. Everything was set for Salvatore's boys to have a wonderful future.

Alex, at twelve, was too young to be working for his father. It wasn't clear how much attention his parents and elder brothers were paying to Alex, a pudgy child who had shaved his hair at the sides and often wore a baseball cap. He did the things that boys his age do, going to school and spending the early evenings in the town square eating pizza with his friends and posting pictures on Facebook. But he could seem distant and depressed.

Back in Oksana's flat, the day after Antonella had pointed a gun at his head, Salvatore was telling her the story about his upset wife. As always, she was sympathetic.

'How is she not going to break up your family if she doesn't want you in it any more?' she said. It was his family, not Antonella's, and certainly not hers. Oksana knew she would only ever be an appendage, a possession. But Salvatore didn't appear bothered that his wife had threatened to kill him. He was instead angry at his eldest son. Giuseppe had clumsily left his gun hidden in the garden. That was where his mother had found it as she was out tending the vegetables.

'As soon as I saw her tilling the vegetables outside I knew that she would find it. "You are a fucking idiot," I told him.' Keeping guns in the house was fine. The mistake his son had made, in Salvatore's mind, was letting his mother find one of them. Still, he knew his wife, sad and ground down, would never dare pull the trigger.

*

Ever since Salvatore had taken over running his cousin's criminal affairs, he would regularly report back to Pasquale. But Oksana began to notice that Salvatore was going to meetings at his cousin's house more and more frequently.

And she could see that Salvatore was ambitious. On some evenings, he would tell her stories of the men he knew who had become rich beyond their wildest dreams through drug trafficking. Some, he would tell her, had ended up losing everything. But Salvatore was wilier, and more ruthless than the others; he was just waiting for his chance.

For years, he had been studying the more established crime families. He knew that the biggest profits went to those who could find a way to source large quantities of wholesale cocaine at a lower price than in Europe. And the only way to do that was to establish a supply route direct from Latin America. They had been trying for months to work with different brokers in Calabria, men who had experience importing hundreds of millions of euros' worth of narcotics for some of the most powerful Mafia families in Italy. Salvatore had tried contacts in Spain, but they had come to nothing.

Then, one day in 2014, the news that Salvatore had been waiting for finally arrived. One of the fixers he was working with received an excited call from his man on the ground in Colombia.

'Today, I had the deadliest stroke of luck,' the fixer reported breathlessly down the phone line. 'I got right to the top, the one who runs everything here. As soon as I get back, I am going to talk to the very highest boss, protected by three hundred people, you know. Here we are dealing with God himself.'

Salvatore might not have known it but there was a new god in Colombia, and he went by the name of Otoniel. Otoniel was the *nom de guerre* of Dario Antonio Úsuga, commander of the Úsuga clan, also known as the Clan del Golfo. The Clan del Golfo had emerged out of the ashes of Colombia's anti-communist paramilitary organisations after the turn of the millennium to become one of the country's dominant cocaine cartels.

When Colombia's paramilitaries had disbanded in 2006, they had left a gap in the market. Otoniel, starting out with just a few hundred men, began taking over their former cocaine trafficking operations from a base in the tropical region of Antioquia in the north of Colombia. In just a few years, the Clan del Golfo had grown from a fledgling start-up cartel to one of the world's top cocaine empires, shipping billions of dollars of drugs around the world. Otoniel's success had started to attract attention. This short, tubby guerrilla with a thick black moustache and dressed in military fatigues was now one of the world's most wanted men. The American government had put a $5 million bounty on his head.

He was exactly the sort of person Salvatore Pititto was looking to do business with. But he wasn't going to be able to do it alone. For the size of shipment he was thinking of, worth tens or even hundreds of millions of euros, he was going to have to find financial backers. He had to speak with his cousin.

Pasquale's house was a ten-minute drive from Salvatore's, down a narrow tarmac road lined with farms and olive groves. Salvatore and his friends, the same people who some-times came to talk business at Oksana's flat, were extremely paranoid when going to see Pasquale, constantly checking his house for listening devices or signs of police surveillance. They knew the police had in the past put hidden cameras in the woods nearby.

To avoid detection, they would enter Pasquale's house

through a concealed door inside a connected building. Salvatore would arrange his meetings with his cousin using coded text messages, pretending to anyone who could be intercepting them that he was visiting a lover, calling his cousin 'my love', and Pasquale responding by calling him 'my treasure'.

That evening, whispering inside Pasquale's house, they began to plot. Salvatore's personal life may have been becoming increasingly volatile, but there wasn't time to worry about the furious Antonella. He needed to focus on Colombia, and the opportunity that promised to transform his family's fortunes.

4

The Prague Sting

Prague, March 2014

Jack Kelly and his DEA colleagues were outside the Sheraton Hotel in central Prague, waiting. They were a long way from northern Virginia: Prague was a gothic maze of twisting, cobbled streets and tram lines. Jack's head was fuzzy with jet lag. The disorientation of unrelenting long-haul travel had by now become routine; packing a bag, leaving for Dulles airport, paying his neighbour to feed his two cats.

Word came from the Czech police: the man they were waiting for had landed. It was Ali Fayad, the Lebanese-born arms dealer based in Ukraine who the DEA believed had been involved in selling weapons now being used by Hezbollah in Syria. The DEA's undercover informants, posing as Colombian paramilitaries, had spent months trying to convince Fayad to fly to Prague to discuss a deal for twenty Russian-made Igla surface-to-air missiles, eight Igla launchers, four hundred RPG rockets and one hundred RPG launchers. The price was just over $8 million.

But exactly who Fayad was working for was unclear. To the DEA team in Prague, he appeared a sophisticated and well-connected arms merchant who had brokered weapons sales in Libya and Iraq. He had high-level contacts across various countries and acted as an advisor to the deposed Moscow-aligned president of Ukraine, Viktor Yanukovych. Fayad had told friends that he had met Vladimir Putin.

It had taken the DEA team hours of preparation, false starts and dead ends to get this far. Just getting Fayad to a country which had an extradition agreement with the United States was no trivial detail. The DEA's liaison officer had prepared the US embassy and notified the national police, who had agreed to execute the operation. It was critical to keep the time between the target flying in and the meeting as short as possible. The hotel room where the meeting was going to take place had been prepped with hidden recording devices and cameras. The room next door would be the control centre, where the Czech police and a DEA representative would observe everything. And the moment Fayad tried to walk out of the meeting at the hotel, they would swoop.

It was a classic Maltz-era overseas DEA sting. The plan was to arrange a weapons deal between Fayad and undercover informants posing as representatives of the FARC, the Colombian paramilitary and drug-trafficking organisation considered a foreign terrorist group by the State Department. This involved carefully selecting the right people from its stable of criminal impersonators. Like casting directors, the DEA had to judge if they looked the part, if they could act convincingly, and if they possessed the temperament to improvise should things take an unexpected turn. And they had to be skilled enough to extract the right information to present a compelling case to a US court. Arranging all of this – the flights, the hotels, the payments and the security – was enormously expensive. If a drug dealer doesn't show up to a street-corner sting, you can come back another day. If you fly a group of DEA agents and informants halfway across the world for a meeting in Central Europe and the target doesn't show up, you have burned tens of thousands of dollars – which is hard to explain to your superiors.

Getting undercover informants to pose as FARC operatives was by now a bedrock strategy for the DEA to make overseas arrests. Because FARC was a designated terrorist organisation, anyone who was found to have conspired to sell weapons to its operatives, real or acting, could be indicted under sweeping US narco-terror laws. Using fake Colombian militants was controversial but effective. The DEA's cadre of accomplished undercover actors had already taken down Monzer al-Kassar and Viktor Bout. They were now hours away from potentially claiming their latest scalp.

Jack was waiting outside the hotel with his colleague Jimmy Grace, who was in charge of the field operation. Jack had known Jimmy since their days drinking together as cub agents in New York. Jimmy was vastly experienced, having worked hundreds of investigations into some of the world's most dangerous international criminals. But as they waited for Fayad to arrive both men were nervous. It was a hard-learned lesson born of countless undercover operations and wiretap cases: no matter how carefully you planned, there were always going to be unpleasant surprises. And Jack could tell something was bothering Jimmy. Jimmy didn't know exactly what it was going to be, but he had become convinced that something was going to go wrong.

It was almost impossible to keep an operation like this a secret. Too many people, from the informants to the embassy to the numerous officials in the host country, had to be briefed in advance. DEA agents also knew that curious things sometimes happened to their targets – especially those working in the murky world of international weapons trafficking. Some simply fell off the face of the earth. With other targets, there were lingering suspicions that some of them had been approached by spies who found them more valuable as a source of intelligence than as prison inmates.

The first scare had come even before Fayad had got on the plane to the Czech Republic. Word had come through to the DEA via its informants that Fayad had been held up at the airport. They had immediately feared that he had been put on an international no-fly list and wasn't going to make it. But he was eventually let through. Then, once Fayad was in the air, a strange call had come through from the DEA's liaison officer at Interpol in Washington DC. Someone inside Interpol – they didn't know who – had asked if the DEA had an important operation underway in Prague. How did they know? Who had told them? Jack was paranoid. The Interpol system was sometimes abused by corrupt actors, and he immediately suspected a leak. He was trying to stay calm, trying not to worry that people working with Fayad could have been sent in advance to put the hotel under surveillance, who would spot the suspicious-looking Americans. It wasn't far-fetched to imagine a sensitive target would have friends in high places, people who had an interest in making sure he stayed safe.

An update came in from the Czech police. Fayad was now on his way from the airport to the hotel. The DEA believed it had already amassed enough evidence during previous meetings between Fayad and its informants to make a compelling criminal case against him. In the run-up to his trip to Prague, Fayad had been secretly recorded explaining how he would provide false documentation for the weapons ship-ment to make it appear it was destined for Ecuador or Libya, rather than Colombia. After one of the informants voiced a technical concern about US helicopters attacking FARC being capable of evading heat-seeking missiles, Fayad reas-sured him that the Iglas he was selling would have no problem reaching their target. The recordings they were hoping to get inside the Prague hotel room were to be the final flourish to make their case. Besides, recordings were nothing without an actual arrest.

Fayad's car pulled up to the hotel. Jack wanted to get a look at him. Jimmy was telling him to hang back near the entrance, to avoid looking suspicious, but Jack couldn't resist. He caught a glimpse of his face: a smartly dressed, slim, clean-shaven man with darting eyes. Fayad, businesslike, went upstairs to begin the meeting. The DEA team waited downstairs, nerv-ously checking their phones for updates. Jimmy knew it was important to let the Czech police do things their own way. The Americans were guests in their country, operating only with their permission. Trying to micromanage the arrest would be like a French guy running around telling him how to do a Bronx drugs bust.

An update came from inside the control room. The meet-ing was going as planned. The next thing they expected to see was Fayad in police custody. Then, suddenly, they spotted Fayad walking calmly through the lobby and out of the hotel. Jack panicked. What was going on? Why had they let him walk out of the meeting and onto the streets of Prague? They both watched helplessly as he got into a taxi which started to drive away. Jack instinctively began to run after him. But within a moment, Fayad was gone.

Some time later, after Jack had been left baffled and panting in the middle of a Prague street, news came in that the Czech police had pulled over Fayad's car. They had wanted to wait until he was in a less central location to make the arrest.

Later that evening, the Czech police held a celebratory dinner in a monastery for the DEA agents. Jack didn't go. Instead, he sat alone on the terrace of a city-centre bar, drinking a beer, nursing his jet lag and thinking back over the case.

Everyone in the DEA knew the arrest was just the start. Now there would be a battle to get approval from the Czech government to extradite Fayad to the United States to face trial. It could take years. And American law enforcement agencies snatching politically connected weapons dealers in foreign countries had a habit of provoking unexpected consequences. If Fayad was as important as the DEA suspected, then there was sure to be a reaction. But what they didn't yet know was just how far someone out there was willing to go to ensure that Ali Fayad would never see the inside of an American courtroom.

5

'Time is of the Essence'

Paris, October 1985

After being caught during the bombing raid in Kuwait, Mustafa was now on death row. He was being held in the sweltering heat of the country's high security Central Prison, his black hair shaved off and his life in the hands of the Emir.

But Mustafa was not going to wait patiently for execution. The prisoner known to his guards as Elias had quickly developed a reputation as one of their most dangerous and devious inmates. He raged against his captors, startling the guards by reeling off the names of their family members. Rumours began to circulate that he had attempted to make explosives out of chicken bones and other waste items sourced from around the prison to blow his cell door off. Others said he had slashed a jailor's face with a razor.

Back in Beirut, his brother-in-law Imad was busy plotting

to force the Emir to release Mustafa and the rest of the bombing squad they now called the 'Kuwait 17'.

In March 1984, the same month that Mustafa was sentenced to death, the CIA's Beirut station chief, William Buckley, was smashed over the head as he was leaving his apartment and bundled into a car. The kidnapping of the CIA's top man in Lebanon was nothing short of a declaration of war on the spy agency. Any doubt the Americans in Beirut had was now gone: they weren't the ones watching Imad, he was the one watching them.

And as his enemies chased his shadow, Imad knew that if he was going to set Mustafa free, he would have to perpetrate ever more spectacular attacks.

In December 1984, four armed men slipped through the security gates at Dubai International Airport and boarded a flight to Karachi. Fifteen minutes after take-off, the pilot heard screams coming from the first-class section of the plane, and a single gunshot. Moments later he felt a hand grenade pressed against his neck.

The hijackers seized control of the aircraft, taking its 162 passengers hostage and diverting it to Tehran. They demanded the release of Mustafa and the rest of the 'Kuwait 17', threatening to blow up the plane if they didn't get what they wanted. After landing in Tehran, the hijackers shot an American passenger and threw him out of the plane door. Three days into the stand-off, the hijackers murdered another American, tossing his bloodied, unrecognisable body onto the runway. Finally, on the sixth day, the hijackers released the remaining hostages and were allowed to flee.

A few months later, the White House was stunned to discover that Imad wasn't, as they had thought, hiding in a slum in southern Beirut. He was in Paris, staying in a suite at the five-star Hôtel de Crillon. One of the world's most wanted terrorists was sleeping just across the road from the US embassy near the foot of the Champs-Élysées.

Admiral John Poindexter, Ronald Reagan's Deputy National Security Advisor, dispatched an urgent message from Washington to the French government. 'We have learned from very reliable sources in three different countries that the senior Hezbollah terrorist leader Imad Mugniyah has recently arrived in France from Lebanon,' he wrote. 'We do not know what he has in mind, how long he might stay, or where he might go next, but we have every reason to believe that he is presently staying in the Paris area.'

Poindexter informed the French that Washington now possessed 'ample evidence' that Imad had been directly involved in the explosion at the barracks in Beirut two years earlier, and had masterminded other murders, hijackings and kidnappings. 'The enormity of Mugniyah's criminal actions,' he wrote, 'makes us determined to see that he is brought to justice.'

For one of the world's most wanted terrorists to be staying in a luxury Parisian hotel, enjoying rooms once frequented by Theodore Roosevelt and Winston Churchill, was bold to say the least. But even more brazen was the timing of his trip. Five months before Imad had travelled to the French capital, the Emir of Kuwait, the man who had the power of life and death over Mustafa, had a narrow escape when a suicide bomber drove into the royal motorcade. Within hours an anonymous caller to a Beirut press agency claimed the attack had been carried out by the Islamic Jihad Organization – the same group that had claimed responsibility for kidnapping William Buckley, as well as several other bombings connected to Imad. 'We hope the Emir has received our message: we ask one more time for the release of those held or all the thrones of the Gulf will be shaken.' Some even believed that Mustafa had played a part in organising the assassination attempt against the Emir from inside his cell.

A month later, Imad orchestrated the hijacking of Trans World Airlines Flight 847 from Cairo to San Diego, seizing control of the aircraft shortly after it had stopped off in Athens and flying it to Beirut. The hijackers issued another demand for the Emir to release Mustafa and the other members of the 'Kuwait 17', and for all Israeli forces to withdraw from southern Lebanon. The hijackers then tossed the corpse of a twenty-three-year-old US navy diver onto the tarmac. After a gruelling fortnight of negotiations, the remaining hostages were released, and the hijackers allowed to slip away.

Then, in October 1985, the same month the Americans learned Imad was staying in Paris, the Islamic Jihad Organization announced they had murdered Buckley, and released a picture of his corpse wrapped in a white shroud.

By coming to Paris, Imad was laughing in the face of the world's most powerful government. But perhaps he had become cocky. The spies tracking him knew he had recently travelled to Europe on a passport in his own name, suggesting that he believed that his identity was still a secret. It was possible that by choosing to come to Paris 'the Fox', as he was known, had made the first and final mistake of his career as an international terrorist.

Inside the White House, a fierce debate broke out. President Reagan had already personally approved a request from the CIA to kidnap Imad off the streets of Paris. But others were more cautious. Snatching Imad without informing the French would be a diplomatic provocation. The men around the table eventually agreed it would be best to ask the French to get him themselves.

'Time,' Poindexter warned his French counterpart, 'is of the essence.' The agents tailing Imad had already lost track of him once. At one point they were unable to establish if he had actually ever been in the French capital at all. Then, two weeks later, the CIA sent the White House an update: Imad was back in their sights. They now had to pray that the French would get to him before he slipped away.

Armed with American intelligence, the French security services raced to the Hôtel de Crillon. A team of commandos abseiled down the side of the building. But when they crashed through the windows there was no twenty-two-year-old terrorist mastermind. Instead, they found a startled fifty-year-old Spanish tourist.

Back in Beirut, the CIA prowled the streets hunting for Imad, stuffing dollar bills into the pockets of anyone who might have information about his whereabouts. But Imad had become a flicker, a silhouette. He had removed any trace he could have left behind: his high school records, his passport application papers, any civil record with a hint of his face or biographical details. Mossad were searching for Imad, too, but the Israeli spy agency also had almost nothing on him – just a faded photograph, many years out of date, and no clue about his location.

The spies had some scraps to go on. Imad, US intelligence analysts wrote in a secret assessment, was 'a fierce-looking, bearded young man of below average height'. They were dealing with 'a cunning, resourceful, coldly calculating adversary for whom virtually any act of violence or revenge performed in the name of Shiism is permissible'.

But Imad was careful. He never slept in the same house twice. He never left a building the same way he had entered it. He never gave public statements, or appeared on television or radio, and his name had never appeared in the press. Some sources said he was fluent in Arabic, English, French, German and Farsi, but it wasn't clear where he could have mastered some of these languages. As his legend grew, rumours began to circulate that he had undergone plastic surgery to alter his appearance.

This didn't mean Imad's enemies didn't sometimes get close. Every so often he would be glimpsed before he some-how managed to get away. In March 1985, a car bomb detonated outside the home of Mohammad Fadlallah, the cleric for whom Imad had worked as a bodyguard – and who had married him and Saada. Imad, however, wasn't there. Fadlallah survived but the blast killed Imad's brother and seventy-nine others, including women and children. No group ever claimed responsibility for the attack, but many suspected it had been carried out by Lebanese operatives funded by the CIA. Later, the American spy agency got a tip that Imad had been sleeping at a religious school in the south of Beirut. For a price of $12,000 the informant offered to put car bombs on each side of the building, detonating them simultaneously when Imad was inside, guaranteeing that it would instantly collapse and kill him. Fearing huge civilian casualties, the Americans declined the offer.

Imad had unleashed a tidal wave of violence across the Middle East and yet Mustafa was still languishing in a prison cell in Kuwait. But at least he was alive. The Emir had still not given the order to carry out the death sentence, perhaps fearing the bloody consequences if he did so. And the Americans had little doubt about the importance of the prisoner in Kuwait Central Prison known as Elias. Despite his murderous reputation, his welfare had become a priority for the US Secretary of State, who wrote a memo quizzing one of his ambassadors about Mustafa's condition and whether his family had been able to visit him.

Meanwhile Saada, now living safely in Tehran, gave birth to her and Imad's first son. They named him Mustafa. Her husband's campaign of hijackings, murders and kidnappings to free his cousin went on. In February 1988, militants in south Lebanon snatched an American Marine Corps colonel named William Higgins, who was serving on a United Nations peacekeeping mission. Two months later a Kuwait Airways flight from Bangkok was hijacked and diverted to Cyprus. Again the hostage-takers demanded the Emir release the prisoners; they murdered two passengers but still he refused.

In August 1990, an unexpected event stunned the Middle East. Saddam Hussein invaded Kuwait and his Iraqi troops emptied the country's prisons. Elias rushed to the Iranian embassy. From there he was spirited back to Beirut. After six years behind bars, Mustafa was finally reunited with his brother-in-law Imad. On 23 December 1991, the corpse of

William Higgins was left at the side of a road near Beirut airport. Four days later the remains of William Buckley, the American spy kidnapped in 1985, were dumped in a rubbish bag near a mosque.

6

Prayers in the Night

Calabria, 2014

Close to Salvatore's town of Mileto lived a woman named Natuzza, who had been born into a large family of peasants in the 1920s. When she was a baby, Natuzza's father ran away to Argentina, leaving her mother to raise her children alone and unable to afford to send the young girl to school, meaning she never learned to read or write.

As a child, Natuzza began to suffer from strange, painful and inexplicable marks on her body. She started to have seizures, during which she would speak in tongues. Her mother called on the local Catholic priest, who performed an exorcism. When it didn't work, Natuzza was locked away in an asylum for several years.

After returning home, she started to notice shapes being formed from the red blotches on her hands, feet and sides. During her confirmation, aged sixteen, Natuzza felt a wet patch on her shoulder. It appeared to be the image of a crucifix formed out of blood. The startled priest sent her stained undershirt to a Catholic university in north Italy for analysis. The results were inconclusive. But news soon began to spread about this strange young woman. Some claimed they had seen blood on her skin form into human faces, or words in Aramaic or Greek. Natuzza, other villagers said, had spoken to them in their dreams, or they had seen her in two places at the same time. One man was terrified when she appeared inside his house in the middle of the night, rushing through the hallways and switching on the lights. Another witness reported that when he removed a bloodied bandage from her wrist, he saw the words 'I am the immaculate conception' written in French.

As Natuzza grew older, the reports of her apparent miracles grew more frequent. The marks of Christ's stigmata, she said, had started to appear on her wrists. Sometimes, her family claimed, she would be performing everyday tasks, or eating lunch, when she would begin 'travelling'. In these trances she could hear the voices of angels and speak with the spirits of the dead.

People from around the region started to make pilgrimages to her hamlet and asked her to communicate with their dead relatives. Soon hundreds were arriving every week for an audience with the mystic, with widows in black headscarves forming long queues outside her home each morning. Natuzza also began to attract the attention of sceptical university professors and scientists eager to investigate the wild claims made about her. For some, the reports of her miracles were simply a mass delusion fuelled by superstitious folk Catholicism. Others concluded that Natuzza suffered from Gardner-Diamond syndrome, a rare skin condition that caused bleeding lesions and hysterical emotional episodes. But for her devotees Natuzza was a modern-day saint – a poor, humble and bloodied embodiment of the sufferings of Christ on the cross, atoning for the sins of those around her.

Oksana, Salvatore's mistress, believed in such salvation. Some evenings, when she was alone in her apartment, she would fall asleep in bed praying for Salvatore. Perhaps she was praying for his safety, knowing when she awoke the next morning he could have been arrested, or shot. Or perhaps, as she learned more about his business dealings, she was praying for his soul.

Sometimes, when Salvatore returned at night, she would tell him about her prayers. They made him angry. And when he got angry, he often became violent. When Oksana objected to one of Salvatore's strange visitors staying in her flat, he hit her so hard that blood streamed from her face. She told the doctors she had fallen down the stairs. The next day she started to have fainting spells. Maybe hearing about Oksana's prayers made Salvatore angry because he knew he was already beyond salvation.

And maybe the poverty-stricken corner of Italy Oksana had found herself living in was too. In Mileto people would disappear overnight, never to be seen again. Everyone knew their fate. Some gangsters in Calabria would bury bodies in shallow graves, others dissolved their victims in acid. Relatives knew it was wise not to ask too many questions. One evening in 2014, a seventy-eight-year-old woman in Mileto was abducted in the middle of the night, taken to a field and shot in both legs. Nine years before, her son had vanished.

Salvatore's town was a place where you did what you were told. If not, your house could burn down. Men would drive round the streets firing Kalashnikovs. Sometimes they tossed homemade bombs into local businesses who refused to pay protection money. During Holy Week the processions carrying statues of the Virgin Mary through nearby villages would pause outside the houses of the most powerful crime bosses, dipping the icon as a sign of respect.

Salvatore, Pasquale and their gang had for years ruled Mileto through extortion, robbery, murder and terror. Yet they saw themselves as men of honour – noble criminals bound by a secret code. Salvatore told Oksana those he dealt with from other villages were 'clean people' – people like him, and his cousin and their friends. She was praying for the soul of a man who seemed to believe he didn't need to be saved.

Yet there was one crime such remorseless killers could not justify: an act for which there could be no forgiveness, a sin that not even Natuzza's bleeding stigmata could wash away.

On Thursday 29 September 1994, at around 10.30 p.m., a family of American tourists were driving down the Salerno–Reggio Calabria motorway in their rented Lancia Y10. Reginald and Margaret Green, from Bodega Bay in California, had come on holiday to Italy for a road trip with their seven-year-old son, Nicholas, and four-year-old daughter, Eleanor.

After picking up their car in Rome they had driven south to visit the Ancient Greek temples of Paestum. They were now driving down the toe of the boot of the Italian peninsula, on their way to Palermo. Margaret was exhausted and had wanted to find a place to stop and rest, but the service area they had pulled into had been too bright and loud. They decided to push on.

Reginald drove down the motorway while his wife and children slept. Suddenly, he spotted a car in his rear-view mirror. It was dark, but Reginald could sense something wasn't right. The car behind had started speeding towards them. Margaret, now awake, saw the car move into the fast lane and come up alongside them. Reginald asked his wife to look out of her window and tell him what was happening.

She could see there were men inside the car wearing black ski masks. They screamed at them in Italian. The Americans couldn't understand, but it was clear they were trying to force them off the motorway. This was a robbery. Reginald slammed his foot on the accelerator.

Then he heard a loud crack. Their back window shattered. The men were firing shots at the car. Reginald didn't have time to process what was happening. All he could do was drive, drive as fast as he could. There was another loud bang. Reginald's side window burst. Shards of glass sprayed over him, cutting his arm as he gripped the steering wheel. He kept speeding down the empty motorway, trying desperately to find a public place or police officer.

Then, in an instant, the chasing car dropped back into the darkness. Terrified, Reginald kept driving. The wind was now rushing through the blown-out car windows. Eleanor was crying, but Nicholas didn't stir. Margaret shielded them from the cold with clothes. After around ten kilometres of road they finally came across some traffic police and pulled over. In shock, they began to explain as best they could that they had been the victims of an attempted armed robbery. It was only then they realised that Nicholas was unconscious in the back of the car. He had been shot in the head.

An ambulance rushed the boy to the local hospital, but it couldn't deal with his injuries. So he was taken across the straits of Messina, to a hospital in Sicily. But the doctors told his parents that his injuries were too grave for them to operate.

Seven-year-old Nicholas Green had been murdered.

After a thirty-four-day manhunt, police eventually caught the two men who had shot at the car. They denied being there that night, but eventually were convicted for the murder. It had been a terrible case of mistaken identity: the shooters had been waiting to rob a jewellery dealer driving a Lancia car identical to the Greens' rental vehicle. Even for a country accustomed to terrible acts committed by savage organised criminals, the awfulness of the crime shocked the nation. It was clear that something truly terrifying had started to metastasise in the villages of Calabria. 'Our shame,' was the headline in one Italian national newspaper. 'Italy cannot absolve itself,' said an article in *La Repubblica*. 'An absurd death has slapped us in the face with something no one wants to acknowledge – there is a no man's land run by bandits who decide the life and death of whoever passes through.' The killers, it transpired, were from Pasquale Pititto's crew in Mileto. One of them was his brother-in-law.

Perhaps, late at night when she prayed, Oksana would beg a higher power that her boyfriend might become someone else. But by then she had been in Mileto long enough to know that men like Salvatore Pititto didn't change.

In the winter of 2014, Salvatore drove to a small square facing a pinkish terracotta church with blue stained-glass windows in the centre of San Gregorio d'Ippona, a small town near Mileto. Sitting alone on a bench underneath an orange tree was a short, silver-haired man in his late fifties, about ten years older than Salvatore.

It was from this bench that Filippo Fiarè managed a multimillion-euro criminal empire. Over decades, the Fiarè family had built their operation into a massive enterprise that spanned bribing politicians, controlling businesses across Italy as silent partners, owning real estate in the centre of Rome and using complex networks of shell companies to launder money. But Fiarè didn't wear expensive clothes or have an expensive car. Anyone who saw him sitting outside the church dressed in a fluffy blue fleece might have thought he was a farmer, or perhaps an electrician. He didn't need protection, and that was the true sign of his power. He could sit alone, reading a newspaper on a park bench as visitors came and went, passing him handwritten notes, or pulling over in a car to exchange a nod or a single word.

By late 2014, Salvatore's gang had established contact with the Colombian cartel. Five thousand miles away from Calabria, near the mouth of the Currulao River by the border with Panama, an area controlled by paramilitaries with black balaclavas and automatic weapons, sat eight tonnes of cocaine, hidden in a banana plantation.

Salvatore now needed support to pull off a drug shipment far larger than anything he had attempted before. He had begun to gather various local crime bosses and businessmen to form a joint venture to finance the operation.

Salvatore needed money, and the man he was going to see had a lot of it. Arranging a private meeting with Filippo Fiarè took careful preparation. Fiarè never spoke about business on the phone. He never spoke a word about business inside his house, or in any enclosed space.

After Salvatore arrived in the square, the boss got into his car. The two men then drove to an olive grove about five minutes outside town. Standing under the Calabrian sun, Salvatore outlined the details of the deal that was going to change his life.

He would have known that taking risk capital from a man like Fiarè was a dangerous proposition. The Fiarè family were far more important than Salvatore's, and stood nearly equal with the most feared crime families in Italy. In the ranking system of Calabria's crime bosses, Rosario, Filippo Fiarè's brother, held the 'Medallion', a rare criminal status that made you and your family untouchable. The Fiarès paid attention to the smallest details of their operation – it was how they had stayed in business for decades. It was even said they kept track of the names of the children of all the men they had ever murdered, just in case they were foolish enough to think of revenge as adults.

Rosario had been in prison since 2005, leaving Filippo as the most senior member of the family still free. Smaller outfits, like Salvatore's, would operate under the authority of more powerful families like the Fiarès. Kickbacks and tributes from below made these families rich. But the real money – what transformed men like Filippo Fiarè from rural bandits into millionaires – was cocaine.

Salvatore's new connection promised to establish direct contact with one of Colombia's most powerful cartels: the very top of the global narcotics food chain. No more middlemen. No more disruptions to supply. It was risky business, and would involve sending their men to the furthest corners of the Colombian jungle. But if you controlled the supply of cocaine, you controlled the market. And controlling the market made you invincible. The Colombian connection promised to let them go directly to the source, open a geyser of drugs they would be able to sell across Europe.

They got back into Salvatore's car and drove back to the bench outside the church – Filippo Fiarè's throne. With Fiarè's investment agreed, Salvatore now needed to send his men to Medellín to inspect the drugs with their own eyes.

7

A Funeral

Florida, May 2014

The arrest of Ali Fayad in Prague had been a success. But Jack Kelly now faced a task that made him far more nervous.

The DEA had been invited to present its work to a group of top United States defence and national security officials at the MacDill Air Force Base in Tampa, Florida. It was going to take place at the United States Special Operations Command, or SOCOM, centre inside the airbase, and had been organised by its commander, William McRaven – the veteran four-star admiral who had overseen the mission to kill Osama bin Laden. McRaven had asked the DEA, the FBI and other agencies to pool their intelligence and evidence on the use of international criminal networks by Iran and Hezbollah, and to present their findings to an audience of 'distinguished visitors'. And the man tasked with taking the stage in front of some of the most important people in US national security was Jack.

For DEA bosses, the meeting was a golden opportunity to discuss their work on Hezbollah and Iran with other agencies. For Jack, it promised the vindication he had been seeking for years. During Project Cassandra, he had frequently bumped up against intelligence analysts who were suspicious of a guy from the DEA messing around in Middle Eastern matters. This was a chance for him to settle the argument. All it required was for Jack to deliver the presentation of his life.

The Tampa air in May was humid. After Jack and his colleagues arrived at the city-like airbase they locked away their phones in secure boxes and stepped inside the facility where they were to be cocooned for the next two weeks. Jack looked around. This wasn't going to be a simple PowerPoint presentation. The SOCOM auditorium was like something out of a Las Vegas light show, with stadium seating overlooking banks of screens, and an interactive floor that could light up with maps, videos and animations that would flash past as speakers expertly pirouetted through their material.

But before any of that, Jack, his colleagues and the guests from the FBI, Homeland Security and analysts from the intelligence agencies had to agree what they were going to include in the presentation. Jack delivered the DEA's assessment. For decades, it had been widely accepted that the majority of Hezbollah's funding came from Iran, its long-standing patron and sponsor. However, as a result of stringent US sanctions against Tehran, the cost of rebuilding its forces following the 2006 war with Israel, and now Hezbollah's incredibly expensive involvement in Syria, the group needed to find alternative ways of raising cash. The Project Cassandra investigations, Jack told them, had amassed substantial evidence that showed Hezbollah's armed wing, known as the External Security Organisation, had increasingly turned to shadow international finance and procurement networks to illicitly source US dollars, weapons and military technologies. These networks were not only being used to evade sanctions, they were also connected to large-scale drug money laundering schemes coordinated by a network of criminal businessmen the DEA had dubbed super facilitators.

Jack knew before he arrived in Tampa it was never going to be an easy sell. He and his DEA colleagues didn't always see eye to eye with other US agencies during these sorts of meetings. Jack was determined and direct, and that could rub people up the wrong way. Some couldn't stand him. But they all had to accept that he brought in cases.

Several years earlier, working with officials from the US Treasury, the DEA discovered that drug money was being laundered via a complex scheme involving trading second-hand cars through West Africa, and was then being sent to a bank in Beirut. Based on the DEA's investigation, the US government brought a civil forfeiture case against the Lebanese bank, fining it $102 million for moving money to 'Hezbollah-controlled money laundering channels'. After the Lebanese bank case, Maltz took Jack into his office and pointed at the cartoon screensaver of him surrounded by sharks. 'Welcome to the island,' he said. Still, that case had given them what some agents called street cred. Jack was even invited by the CIA to deliver a lecture about the bank case at its headquarters at Langley.

Jack was convinced these schemes went far beyond that one bank. While some of those operating in these shadow networks were simply criminal opportunists who provided illicit services to the highest bidder, the DEA possessed evidence that others were in direct contact with senior Hezbollah officials and were seemingly acting under their protection. The DEA called this Hezbollah's Business Affairs Component, or BAC, and Jack believed it was possible to prove the various criminal nodes connected directly to the very top of the organisation. The DEA's assessment could be diplomatically explosive. Hezbollah had always staunchly denied any involvement in crime or drugs, both of which were anathema to its religious beliefs. But not only had the DEA found evidence connecting criminal super facilitators to the top of the organisation, it also believed it had credible evidence that showed the BAC dated to the 1990s, when Imad Mughniyeh had set up such a network to raise covert funds for his operations. Jack sometimes felt that DEA guys like him weren't meant to speak the names of terrorist masterminds like Imad Mughniyeh.

Why was he telling them all this? Because the DEA's main objective in Florida was to convince the assembled officials to allow it to pursue a criminal prosecution against top officials from Hezbollah and Iran. They strongly believed the evidence they were picking up through informants, wiretaps and investigations showed this was more than just a random group of criminal businessmen laundering drug money and shipping weapons. If they could prove that the activity they were seeing was in fact a centrally orchestrated conspiracy then they could make use of the US's so-called RICO laws, used to prosecute complex criminal groups, to indict the entire organisation.

RICO laws allowed indictments of what were sometimes called hub and spoke conspiracies: a criminal network in which one person or group – the hub – has many different conspiratorial agreements – that is, dozens or even hundreds of spokes. The spokes didn't need to know each other, or work with each other. But if they were all serving a single organisation, in this case Hezbollah, then that organisation could be prosecuted.

For Jack, it was brilliant in its simplicity. An indictment like that would be the greatest case of his career, the crescendo of years of painstaking street-level investigations around the world. But the idea of a US law enforcement agency launching a RICO case against Hezbollah or Iran was enough to send some people at the State Department into meltdown.

It was immediately clear, in the Tampa conference room, that the intelligence analysts were more than just sceptical – they were hostile. Some strongly disagreed with the DEA's assessment, doubting the entire basis for its intelligence. What did drug suspects and informants know about terror organisations? For others, it made no sense that a militarily disciplined and religiously devout organisation like Hezbollah would be involved in illicit activities. Hassan Nasrallah, its Secretary-General, was on the record denying any involvement in contraband or trafficking, blasting the allegations as black propaganda invented by his enemies. An exasperated Jack pointed out to the intelligence analysts that the Obama administration's National Security Council 2011 'strategy to combat transnational organised crime' report had declared that the US government was 'concerned about Hezbollah's drug and criminal activities', and had directly connected the Lebanese bank Jack had helped investigate to international narcotics trafficking and 'the terrorist organisation Hezbollah'. His intervention seemed to make little difference.

The conference was becoming heated. The man from the FBI, an agency the DEA had often butted heads with, appeared to be on the same side as Jack, and had brought a large amount of material to sift through. But the intelligence analysts, Jack believed, had intentionally brought nothing. It seemed to him that they hadn't come there to collaborate. Instead, they pushed back on every point and fiercely protected their turf. The intelligence agencies often looked suspiciously at the DEA's attempts to jump into anything connected with terrorism. Of course the DEA wanted to go after Hezbollah, they thought. It needed to cook up some adventure to justify more funding, to stay relevant after the failure of the drug war. But the Middle East was their territory, not the DEA's.

The other problem was one of philosophy. Law enforcement agencies like the DEA gathered evidence for criminal cases, which would eventually be put before a court of law. Success for them was measured through convictions: without them, nothing they did had any purpose. Intelligence analysts saw the world very differently. They didn't have to build evidence for criminal cases. They gathered information to inform policymakers. None of the intelligence they assembled, or the reports they wrote, would end up in front of a judge.

All the people in the room had been flown down to Florida to bring together the strengths of US intelligence and law enforcement – to 'connect the dots', as Maltz would say. And yet everyone was getting defensive, angry. A mood of mutual suspicion had taken hold. The representatives from the different agencies were under explicit instructions not to send anything they learned inside the room back to their headquarters. But some had started to suspect that others were leaking their talking points to their colleagues.

Jack was getting frustrated. One side would make a point, the other would pick it apart. They were getting nowhere. One of the guys from the FBI had had enough. 'You are a fucking zero!' he yelled at one of the intelligence analysts. 'We came here to do a job, and you came here with nothing at all!' The analyst looked like he was about to cry. It was turning into a disaster. What had promised to be one of the most important moments of Jack's career was starting to feel like one of the worst weeks of his life.

By Friday the atmosphere was close to toxic. Jack was

scheduled to take what they had written so far and perform a dress rehearsal. That morning he had woken up feeling awful. His ears were blocked, which sometimes happened when it was hot and humid; he felt sick with vertigo. He stood up in the auditorium and began to speak. Everyone from inside the conference room was watching him intently. Dizzy, he started to stumble over his lines.

The presentation was a slick, tightly choreographed multimedia stage act, in which he had to perfectly time his delivery as the images flashed automatically across the screens. If he missed a cue, he lost his place. Jack had done what felt like hundreds of presentations, and had never messed one up. But this felt like he was being asked to perform a one-man show on Broadway without having seen the script. 'He can't do it,' said one of the FBI men, shaking his head. 'He can't do it.'

They all returned to the conference room. It had been a complete mess. They had just days left to fix things, and everyone was tired and angry. Jack needed to get off the airbase. He needed some space to recharge, to go home and clear his head. If he flew out that evening, he could return in time for the next round of rehearsals on Monday, before the main event later that week.

He gathered his things, picked up his phone and got in a car heading to the airport. In the car, Jack's phone rang. What could it be now? What else could go wrong?

'It was my sister,' Jack told his colleague who was also in the car. 'My dad is in hospital. He is on a ventilator. She said he isn't going to make it.'

Jack raced back to his parents' home in New Jersey. He arrived at the hospital where his mother, brothers and sisters had gathered around his father. The doctors said only the ventilator was keeping him alive. Shortly after Jack got there the doctors switched it off. His family began to prepare for the Catholic wake, and the funeral.

Jack rarely went back to East Brunswick. He had spent most of his childhood dreaming about the day he would leave. It was a place of endless rows of generic houses, streets that led nowhere, a town centre that was crowned with the deadened concrete of the East Brunswick Mall.

Jack's father had been a history teacher at a public high school in Brownsville, Brooklyn, and had moved the family to East Brunswick in the late 1960s, not long after the New York teachers' strike. It was a time when the town's population surged after the construction of the New Jersey Turnpike. The large Kelly family had moved from cramped housing in Staten Island to a newly built middle-class home with a yard and woods nearby. His brothers and sisters were old enough to remember New York. Jack was only three when they left. One of his earliest memories was the faint, crackling echoes of a radio broadcaster excitedly reporting the 'miracle' Mets' journey to winning the 1969 World Series.

The youngest of six children by five years, Jack had always been the baby of his large Irish-Polish family. His dad had been strict, keeping him to an 8 p.m. curfew until he left for college and rarely letting him hang out with other kids unsupervised. By the time Jack arrived at Rutgers, he had never even sipped a beer.

Both sides of Jack's family had been built on blue-collar, unionised jobs. They were policemen, firefighters, teachers and soldiers. And Jack's father, a life-long Democrat, made sure his kids understood what unionised labour had done for them. As an adult, Jack would sometimes have debates about it with colleagues in law enforcement who were politically suspicious of unions. Many of these guys came from similar backgrounds. Jack would say, if it wasn't for union jobs we wouldn't even be here. We wouldn't have made it to college. It was as if his father had been talking instead of him.

Being back home made Jack think back to his childhood. As a kid, he always had a temper. He had wanted to box, but his parents refused. Instead, they enrolled him in numerous organised sports from the age of six. During the summer holidays he would be packed off to football practice, leaving his friends behind to bask in the warm evenings while he was screamed at by his coaches. Jack took sport unbelievably seriously. This would sometimes boil over into fights with local kids over games or punching one of his older brothers in the stomach because he lost to him at basketball. He remembered the crushing pressure he put on himself each time he stepped up to pitch in baseball, so nervous he felt physically sick. If a bad ball got hit into the horizon, Jack would stand there, tears welling up. His dad would come over and console him: It wasn't a big deal, it was OK. When Jack reached fifteen, his father bought him an early computer, and he began to experiment with trying to code programmes to predict basketball games, and the weather.

On Jack's mother's side (the Polish one) they lived long into old age, but the men on the Irish side never seemed to get very far. His childhood had been punctuated by the wakes and funerals of Irish Americans who had died before their time.

His grandfather had been a lieutenant in the NYPD's antisabotage squad during the Second World War. Each morning he would take the ferry from Staten Island to his office in Manhattan. One day he investigated a ship fire and, his family believed, inhaled a lot of smoke. The next day he was on his regular train to the ferry terminal when the conductor, thinking he was asleep, tried to wake him. But he had died of a heart attack. He was just thirty-nine years old.

The next year, Jack's father lost his only brother to rheumatic fever. At fifteen, he was the only male left in his immediate family. Jack knew his dad as an optimist. But he could also feel the weight of that sadness on him. After his dad suffered these childhood tragedies he was sent to Catholic school. His father had always told Jack that the Catholic Church had saved his life. The family would attend church in East Brunswick every Sunday, and the children would go to Bible classes where they were taught that if a sinful thought crossed your mind, then you had committed a sin.

Jack's father fused his Catholicism with a strong belief in social justice. Decades teaching history in a Brooklyn public school had put him in daily contact with the social and racial inequalities of one of the poorest neighbourhoods in New York. He had always encouraged his children to think about politics and the wider world, and to question accepted wisdom. He worked hard to educate them about civil rights, Martin Luther King and the history of slavery. He encouraged his children to read Ralph Ellison's *Invisible Man*.

For Jack and his siblings, the dinner table became a debate stage. Around their kitchen table their father would explain his views on issues such as abortion. As a Catholic he was against abortion. But at the same time, he strongly believed women should have the right to choose. His thinking, he told his children, was that throughout history wealthy people had always been able to pay enough to get one. It was the poor and the marginalised who would suffer simply because of their social position and lack of money. To ban abortion would force poor women into dangerous operations that could kill them. To some in East Brunswick in the early 1970s, this sort of talk was heretical. But Jack's father possessed the spirit to think for himself.

Typical of a large Irish-Polish family from Staten Island, they would explode into arguments, talking over each other, everyone getting louder and louder trying to make their point so they could be heard over everyone else. Some of Jack's siblings would take a contrarian position just to rile up the others, and they would all cut each other off mid-sentence. If you already knew what someone was going to say, what was the point of letting them finish? Why give them the head start? It was a conversational style that had helped Jack fit in during his early years in the DEA. Everyone in New York talked that way – yelling at each other. Derek Maltz did it, as did many of his friends at the SOD. It was loud and direct, but mostly playful and good-natured. They all understood each other. Later, when Jack was out of New York and working with people from other parts of the country, he could tell it could infuriate them. He had tried to keep it in check, but sometimes he offended people.

In 1991, when Jack was twenty-four, his dad dropped him off in New York for his first day at the DEA. It was now time to say a final goodbye to the old man. During the wake and funeral, Jack had done everything he could to block out what was happening back in Florida. But he knew he would have to go back to Tampa: the presentation was on Wednesday. After the funeral he drove to the airport.

Because of Jack's bereavement, the responsibility for giving the speech had passed to one of his younger colleagues. Part of Jack was disappointed, but he couldn't deny it was also a relief.

The next morning the assembled top generals, government officials and prosecutors took their seats in the auditorium and watched the presentation on Hezbollah's ties to international drug trafficking and crime. It had taken days of arguments, but the DEA had managed to keep the bulk of their material, fighting off the attempts by the intelligence analysts to remove it. The presentation brought up the case of Ali Fayad – the man the DEA had arrested in Prague – claiming

he had collaborated with the Russian and Iranian governments and had ties to Hezbollah and the Syrian regime.

Jack was pleased. It was a good presentation. But he had
a nagging suspicion that their arrest of Fayad had unnerved
some people inside government. The audience were invited
to make comments. The first came from a senior official. Was
the DEA not concerned about the potential consequences
of launching big criminal cases against Iran and Hezbollah?
Surely there was a risk they could retaliate with attacks
against US national interests.

Another official jumped in. 'So are you saying that you fear
a terrorist attack because of action by US law enforcement?'

'Yes. That is exactly what I am saying,' was the response.

A general weighed in: 'Even on the battlefield sometimes
we have to measure our attacks as we don't know what the
counter-attack might be.' Jack couldn't tell if he was siding
with the official who'd asked the question, or with the DEA.
But the official nodded in agreement, seemingly taking the
general's comment as supporting her concerns about retaliation against American targets.

Jack knew that there were people in the room who believed
there was no benefit in the United States antagonising
Hezbollah or Iran with inconvenient criminal cases. He also
knew the US government and Western allies were setting
in motion diplomatic negotiations with Iran over its nuclear
weapons programme. What the DEA was suggesting would
only make those negotiations more complicated.

After Jack and his colleagues returned from Tampa, it had
become clear to the DEA that the presentation had failed.
They had walked away with nothing. Before the meeting,
they had all known that getting support for their plan was
going to be a long shot. But the hope had been there. Now
the chance of pursuing a single big conspiracy case against

top Iranian or Hezbollah officials felt like it had melted away in the Florida sun.

Jack, still grieving the loss of his father, was distraught. A RICO case was always the knockout blow that would have been his greatest achievement as an investigator. Perhaps it had always been a fantasy. Sending in the DEA to conduct a sting operation on an arms dealer in Europe was one thing. The US arresting a top Hezbollah official on criminal conspiracy charges was completely different. As some of the senior officials in Florida had feared, an operation like that could easily provoke a huge terrorist attack – or even start a war. Could a DEA criminal case ever be worth that?

Back at his desk in Virginia, Jack was tempted to swallow his disappointment and move on. Word at the SOD was that Maltz, after eight years as Special Agent in Charge, was preparing to retire. It was almost unheard of to have lasted in a job like his for that long, but somehow Maltz had done it. He had built the SOD into what it was, and opened the door for agents like Jack to pursue new kinds of cases. But he couldn't run it for ever.

Perhaps Maltz calling it a day was a sign that it was best for Jack to let it all go. He didn't need more stress. He was a mid-ranking DEA agent who had enjoyed a good career and had completed twenty-three years of service – just two years away from being eligible for retirement. Jack was only in his late forties, but he was shattered by the relentless work and travel, and constant worrying. He had put a chart up on his condo wall, counting down the days until he hit twenty-five years. He couldn't imagine himself retiring. But just the knowledge that one day he could helped to keep him calm. Winding things down would be good for him. Better for his health, better for his mind.

Jack drafted an email to his bosses at the DEA. 'The United

States Government's lack of action on this issue has allowed Hezbollah to become one of the biggest transnational organised crime groups in the world,' he wrote. 'As we have shown in our investigations the super facilitator network uses this criminal activity to provide massive support to the Iranian Hezbollah Threat Network and other terror groups helping fuel conflict in some of the most sensitive regions in the world.' Jack was calling out the lack of assistance from other agencies, and from the Department of Justice.

It wasn't a wise thing for a man looking for a quiet life to do. But Jack wasn't going to retire just yet. He pressed send.

BOOK TWO

BOOK TWO

8

'Sami Issa'

Beirut, February 2005

One day a mature student wrote an application to be accepted into the Lebanese American University in Beirut to major in political science. 'I would like, at the end of my training,' the student explained, 'to grasp and deeply understand the dynamics and the rules that control the political world, and to be able to plan for changes.'

He was accepted for a place even though he had forgotten to attach a photograph to his application. He introduced himself to his new classmates as 'Safi'. Safi was in his late thirties and seemed to the other students to be a businessman who had chosen to return to university after making some money. He was short and bearded, and would often hide his cropped, receding hair under a baseball cap. On some days he would wear a suit; on others he would wear jeans. He also walked with a noticeable limp – his leg appeared to be clamped in a brace under his trousers.

Safi disappeared from classes for months at a time. These unexplained absences meant he had to frequently apologise to his professors for missing essay deadlines and exams. On one form, which asked the absentee student to 'briefly, explain your reasons for leaving the university, and what you have been doing since then', he appealed that he had been living 'with my family in Dubai, and for family and business reasons I stopped studying in LAU for about one year, hoping to continue my study in this university'. In another, he said his long disappearance had been 'due to a medical case', which meant 'I couldn't make my finals which led to my incomplete grades'.

In spite of his patchy attendance record, Safi was hungry to learn, and when he did turn up he scored respectable marks. He lobbied hard to be accepted into the popular Politics 301 class, which focused on American government and politics. He also signed up to other subjects including 'the political power of international organisation', and the politics of Germany.

As time went on the small number of students who got to know the mysterious Safi a little better learned that outside university he wasn't called Safi at all. To his friends outside the university, many of them female, he went by the name Sami Issa, and owned a chain of jewellers in Beirut called Samino.

Sami clearly enjoyed the finer things in life. He would be driven around the city in luxury cars, often with a squad of bodyguards. On some days he would ride in a silver Range Rover with tinted windows, on others he would be seen in a Porsche Cayenne, an Audi A8 or a BMW convertible.

While the sun was up he would often be at the marina spending time on his yacht, also called *Samino*, and in the evenings he would head out to Beirut's shisha bars, luxury hotels and restaurants. On some evenings he would hold court in the Phoenicia Hotel, on others he would be at the Grand Café, eating sushi, or relaxing at Holiday Beach Resort, near where his yacht was moored.

But Sami Issa's real passion, more than American politics or luxury foreign cars, was women. Wherever he was, it was normally with one of his girlfriends. So numerous were his lovers that his bodyguards would lose track. Maybe Sami had fifteen close female friends, maybe it was twenty. One day they would see him with one woman, the next day he would be with another. But while his security team struggled to keep up with his busy romantic life, Sami was clearly skilled at juggling the attentions of dozens of companions, firing off texts to his flames calling them 'my life, my soulmate, my darling'.

But whether they met him at university, at his jewellery stores, or smoking shisha late into the evening, no one really knew much about Sami Issa. Though charming, he was strangely reluctant to share personal information. His accent suggested he was from southern Lebanon. He also fasted on certain holy days, leading some to presume he was Shia, but Sami never talked about his faith or his background.

On some nights he would invite a group of male friends back to one of his apartments to smoke shisha and play cards. They would joke about girls or discuss where they were planning to go out. But they would never talk about their personal lives. Nor would they discuss politics, something that might have been considered strange for a man passionate enough about the subject to return to university to study it. His friends noticed that the apartment was bare, with little furniture and no family photos.

Sami Issa's employees also didn't know much about the life of 'the boss'. He was clearly a busy and important man, who could disappear for months at a time. Sami's jewellery business appeared to be doing well, but he was a hands-off owner. He didn't seem to know much about precious stones, or be particularly interested in the details of its daily operations.

Perhaps there were understandable reasons for Sami's behaviour. As a wealthy jeweller, Sami was a possible target for robbery or kidnapping. His bodyguards quickly learned they had to follow a set of strict rules if they were going to work for Sami Issa, rules that suggested he had reason to be far more cautious than the average playboy.

For one, they were not to ask him personal questions, such as anything to do with his family. They were also to be constantly looking out for unknown people following him or them. 'Whenever you're going home or going back,' he instructed one of his bodyguards, 'never take the same route. Always try to take a circuitous road.' Sami would often ask his bodyguards to pick him up and drop him off on highways or main roads. When he was being escorted by them, Sami would be in a car up front, his other bodyguards following in a four-by-four with their boss relaying instructions using a walkie-talkie.

All this was not unheard of in a city like Beirut, where kidnappings were common. What was harder to explain was that the weapons licences that Sami Issa procured for his security team, allowing them to have Glocks and machine guns in their cars, were issued by Lebanese military intelligence. But Sami was rich, perhaps with friends in high places willing to do him favours.

As time went on, his security team began to gain more insight into Sami's quirks. They may have known almost nothing about his history or family background, but they could tell they were working for an extremely paranoid individual. No one was permitted to take photos of him; if he was in a place where someone was taking pictures he would tell his bodyguards to try to stop them, or he would leave. He would often go out wearing a baseball cap and sunglasses, and would occasionally change his facial hair from a beard to a goatee or a moustache in an attempt to alter his appearance. He appeared at pains to hide his face from security cameras, putting his baseball cap on and dipping his head when he entered luxury hotels, or lowering his cap when he came close to CCTV cameras inside shops or near cash machines on the street. So reluctant was he to be recorded or photographed that he didn't attend a beauty contest filled with young women that he had arranged to promote Samino jewellery.

Sami wasn't just worried about photos. Once, two bodyguards accompanied him to buy a mobile phone. Issa picked up the phone and, after examining it, requested that one of the guards give him a cloth so he could wipe away his fingerprints. On another occasion, he went shopping for clothes and asked his bodyguard to unzip a jacket for him, then place it on his body to minimise touching the garment. After eating at a restaurant, Sami would dip a tissue in water and wipe down his knife and fork. When he went on his frequent outings to smoke shisha he would bring his own pipe and tobacco, never using the café's. Sami rarely touched money. Instead, he would get his bodyguards to pay for items in cash for him.

The boss's constantly ringing mobile phones was another sensitive issue for the bodyguards. Sami often carried a Samsonite briefcase in which were stored sometimes as many as four or five phones, which on occasion would all go off at the same time. Maybe the playboy jeweller was managing his girlfriends. Or maybe he was working on secret business deals.

Under no circumstances would a member of his security team be allowed to look at his phone screen. Instead, they would have to flip it face down, and hand it over to him. One time a bodyguard showed some initiative, opened Sami's briefcase and handed the boss a ringing phone. Sami wasn't pleased. 'Did you see what it was?' he asked him. The bodyguard responded that he hadn't. 'You just closed the briefcase as it was?' Sami continued. The bodyguard said yes. Sami began to shake his head. The man never dared touch the briefcase again.

If one of his guards' own phones rang, Sami would demand to know who was calling before they answered it. And he would almost always call them from a private number. On the rare occasions Sami called from a visible number the instructions were clear: 'Don't give my number to anyone.'

It was probably by the time of the car crash that Sami Issa's bodyguards had started to realise that their boss might have been involved in more than just selling jewellery and seducing women. Sami had begun asking them to follow a complex counter-surveillance routine to ensure no one was following him. This involved rotating between his various luxury vehicles throughout the day, and secretly switching the cars' licence plates. The bodyguards would park one of Sami's cars in an isolated part of a street, in an underground car park or hidden behind another vehicle, before making a rapid change. Anyone who had been attempting to track Sami's movements by logging his licence plate would be left scratching their head.

Some of Issa's cars would have piles of spare licence plates hidden under newspapers in the boot. And some of the numbers were distinctive. His Mercedes SLK would sometimes have the plate number 100000. Another plate Sami used had been issued by Lebanese military intelligence. Like most things about Sami Issa, exactly how he had come into possession of this special licence plate was something none of them knew. But by then they had learned not to ask too many questions.

Then one day Sami had a car accident on a Beirut street while driving in his Range Rover with his bodyguards. The accident was not severe and nobody was hurt. But shortly after it had taken place a lieutenant colonel from Syrian intelligence arrived to check if he was OK. Why, the bodyguards might have thought, would a Syrian spy rush to the scene of a car accident involving a jewellery dealer? It appeared they weren't the only ones tasked with keeping him safe. Sami evidently had powerful people from foreign countries watching over him.

And then, just like that, Sami vanished. His briefcase full of phones fell silent. He was no longer seen enjoying his nights in upmarket Beirut hotels. Some of his old shisha-smoking friends tried to contact him, but all they heard was a message telling them the line had been deactivated. Perhaps Sami had gone abroad again, or had suffered a family or health emergency. Still, it was very strange to just drop off the face of the earth without saying goodbye.

Not long before Sami Issa stopped being seen in the hotels and cafés of Beirut, a political crisis was mounting across the border in Syria. Bashar al-Assad was coming under growing pressure to withdraw the Syrian soldiers who had been occupying parts of Lebanon since they invaded in May 1976, during the country's civil war.

Over decades the Assad family had become accustomed to ruling over its smaller neighbour as if it were a province of their own, with feared Syrian intelligence officers in Beirut backed by tens of thousands of troops following diktats from

Damascus. Then, in May 2000, Israel announced it was with-drawing from south Lebanon, leaving Syria as the last foreign power occupying the country. A month later, Hafez al-Assad died. His seemingly mild-mannered son Bashar, who suc-ceeded his father only because his favoured elder brother had unexpectedly died in a car crash, took on the responsibility of protecting Hafez's brutal legacy at home and abroad.

Now Bashar's grip over Lebanon was under threat. Rafic Hariri, the Sunni billionaire property tycoon turned prime minister, had begun negotiating a Syrian withdrawal from his country. In September 2004, the UN Security Council passed a resolution calling for all foreign forces to withdraw from Lebanon and cease interfering in the country's politics. A month before the UN resolution, Hariri had been sum-moned to Damascus by Assad. He returned from the meeting sweating, telling allies that the Syrian dictator had issued a threat: either Damascus would have its way 'or I will break Lebanon over your head'.

On the evening before Valentine's Day 2005, Sami was up late, texting one of his girlfriends who had been complain-ing that he hadn't been showing her enough attention. At 2.31 a.m., he sent her a cheeky message: 'If you knew where I had been, you would be very upset.'

At around 12.50 the following afternoon, Rafic Hariri left the Place de l'Etoile café in downtown Beirut and got into a black armour-plated Mercedes S600 guarded by a six-vehicle convoy.

Hariri was under no illusions about the threats to his life. As a precaution, he always kept his travel plans secret up until the very last minute, even keeping senior members of his own staff in the dark. Earlier that morning his security team had performed multiple rounds of bomb sweeps, his body-guards using sniffer dogs and chemical detectors to search for explosives. Three of the vehicles in Hariri's convoy carried four-gigabyte jammers, the strongest available, to block electronic signals that could be used to remotely detonate a roadside bomb. None of this was going to be enough.

About five minutes after Hariri's convoy had left the café, it had reached the palm-tree-lined seafront promenade close to the St. Georges Hotel. Slightly ahead, a Mitsubishi Canter truck slowly moved into position. Suddenly, a huge explosion ripped through the air, leaving a vast hole in the ground surrounded by black smoke, human screams and fire. A suicide bomber had detonated military-grade explosives inside the van, the equivalent of two tonnes of TNT. Hariri was killed instantly, along with twenty-one others; 226 bystanders were injured.

The Hariri assassination sent shockwaves through the Middle East. Fingers immediately pointed towards Syria.

Mass protests erupted in Lebanon against the Syrian occupation. George W. Bush, the US president, ramped up pressure on Assad, saying 'get out – not only get out with your military forces, but get out with your intelligence services, too. Get completely out of Lebanon.' On 26 April, the last Syrian troops left the country, ending a twenty-nine-year military presence.

A preliminary United Nations investigation released shortly after the blast said the evidence pointed 'to the possibility that Syrian officials were involved in the assassination'. One witness, a Lebanese newspaper publisher who had spoken to Hariri before his death, said that the prime minister had told him that Assad had threatened to 'blow him up' and hunt down and murder his family wherever they were in the world. Two months later that witness was killed by a car bomb.

While the UN investigators strongly suspected Assad's regime of having a hand in the bombing, they still didn't know the identity of the operatives on the ground who had perfectly orchestrated the assassination. They uncovered what appeared to show repeated coordination between members of a bombing team in the run-up to the attack. A significant part of this phone activity was connected to numbers controlled by a mysterious playboy jeweller – a man called Sami Issa.

The phone data appeared to show that Sami had been running an intricate surveillance operation on Hariri for months before the assassination. There were some clues to his real identity. There was one number Sami had called thousands of times. It belonged to a woman called Saada: the sister of Mustafa Badreddine and wife of Imad Mughniyeh. Sami had been sent birthday greetings on 6 April 2000. And 6 April, as it happened, was Mustafa's birthday too. One of his phones had received calls from a number in Saudi Arabia in late May of that year, at the same time as Mustafa's wife had gone on a trip there. The jewellery dealer, the lothario, the mature student with a limp studying American politics who wanted to 'understand the dynamics and the rules that control the political world' had in fact been Mustafa Badreddine all along.

After the assassination, Sami Issa sent a friend to the university to quietly pick up his certificate in political science and was never seen again. Mustafa had pulled off what was perhaps his most audacious operation yet. And once again he had vanished into the air like smoke.

9

The Mafia Goes to Medellín

Calabria/Medellín, October 2014

Oksana knew Salvatore was a cruel man who had done terrible things. But inside her apartment he was gentle and affectionate. Oksana's home, it seemed, was Salvatore's place to escape to. He would spend hours with her at night, sitting on her sofa or watching her cook as they talked about his life, and his dreams for the future.

Her flat wasn't grand, but it was a place of her own. She lived about fifteen minutes' drive from Salvatore on a long, narrow street close to a piazza with a church framed by large concrete pillars. In the summer, cascades of pink bougainvillea would spill out from her neighbours' balconies and locals would gather outside in the sun on the café terraces.

Oksana had arrived in Italy with nothing and, in Salvatore's eyes, he had given her everything: a flat, a job, a life. Every so often, something would happen to remind Oksana that none of it was really hers. Once, Salvatore gave a friend the keys to the apartment so he could secretly meet a woman there while Oksana was out at work. And, after the friend's wife discovered his affair and threw him out, Salvatore demanded that Oksana let him hole up at her place for two weeks.

She hated these intrusions. But her boyfriend's mind was elsewhere. His gang had contacted the Colombian cartel and he had gathered the investment to fund the deal. Now he needed to assemble a team to travel to Colombia, inspect the quality of the merchandise and open negotiations to buy a shipment larger than anything he had ever attempted before.

The first and most important position Salvatore needed to fill was that of manager. This person would be the international drug trafficking equivalent of a construction foreman – in charge of managing communications with the Colombians, supervising the people the Italians sent over to Latin America and haggling over the price, quantity and eventual delivery of the cocaine to Europe.

The man Salvatore selected for the job was Pepe, a veteran Italian drug trafficker who had years of experience managing complex deals for some of the top crime families in Calabria. Pepe, who had a broad boxer's nose, was a fierce negotiator. He combined a ruthless logistical efficiency with a volcanic temper that would ensure no one stepped out of line.

The next job on Salvatore's squad was equally important. He needed to send someone to Colombia to inspect the quality of the drugs in person and demonstrate to the cartel that his side was serious. He picked Antonio, a young, energetic and ambitious member of his gang who had shown the potential to rise through the ranks of Calabrian organised crime. Antonio, who often wore shorts and flip-flops, whether he was committing serious felonies or collecting his wife from her job at the shopping mall, would act as Salvatore's eyes and ears on the ground in Colombia.

The final position was by far the least appealing. The opening stages of an international drug deal are always the most delicate. There was a tried and tested way of establishing trust between a buyer and seller so each could become confident enough to move ahead. Both sides would send a guest, known as a guarantee, to stay with the other for the duration of the transaction. This was to demonstrate that you were committed. But the person also served as collateral, a human promise that each side would stay honest. If something went wrong – one side stealing the other's money or refusing to pay – then the guest would be killed.

Salvatore and Pepe knew this was the way it had always worked. It meant you never sent one of your best men over first. The person they recruited to serve as the human guarantee was a Dominican-born man who lived in Calabria, called Osvaldo. The plan was that Osvaldo, who spoke both Italian and Spanish, would travel to Colombia with Antonio to inspect the quality of the cocaine and then stay on until the transaction was completed.

The team was now in place. But Salvatore knew that, to get the deal moving, the Colombians would first have to dispatch their own human guarantee to Italy.

'The important thing is that the people arrive here,' Pepe told the broker over the phone. 'As soon as the people arrive here, we have the money ready.' But to get the cartel to send one of their men to Europe, the Italians would first have to make a small down payment. 'They don't trust us to send people blindly,' the broker told him.

Within weeks the Colombians had sent over their guarantee, a tubby man who called himself El Colonel. In spite of his impressive-sounding nickname, the Colonel was in fact a low-ranking cartel operative in his fifties from Uruguay, who for years had been grinding out a living as a travelling transatlantic narcotics salesman. In a career slump and suffering from heart problems, the Colonel had got into various bungles and mishaps but had somehow managed to escape unscathed. While his competence was questionable, the Colonel's main attraction for his employers appeared to be his ownership of a Swedish passport, allowing him to slip in and out of Europe without a visa.

The Colonel, Salvatore and Pepe were told, would communicate with a top Clan del Golfo manager in Colombia known as Jota Jota, who was in charge of coordinating parts of the cartel's trafficking activities in Europe. Jota had men stationed in the Netherlands and Spain, the cartel's two main cocaine importation hubs across the Atlantic, and reported directly to a man known only to the Italians as the General, who appeared to sit at the very highest level of the cartel. It was Jota, taking orders from the General, who would ultimately decide how and when any shipment would be sent to Salvatore and Pepe. If the deal progressed, Jota himself would travel to Europe to oversee the final stages, but until then the Italians were going to have to deal with the Colonel.

By sending the Colonel to Mileto, the men from the cartel had shown they were serious. The next step was for Salvatore to send Antonio and Osvaldo to Colombia to meet with representatives of the cartel and to see the merchandise with their own eyes.

On 17 October 2014, Antonio and Osvaldo landed at Rionegro airport in Medellín at just after 5.30 p.m. The Colonel, in Calabria, had messaged his colleagues in advance with their pictures and flight details, and instructions to pick them up, take them to a warehouse and be friendly. 'I hope they treat them well,' he wrote to his colleagues in a WhatsApp message, 'because I am fine here.' The Colonel wasn't merely being hospitable. He knew that if anything unexpected happened to either of them then he would never make it back from Italy.

Salvatore and Pepe had given Antonio and Osvaldo €20,000 in cash for expenses and established the operational security protocols for their communications while they were in Colombia. If they needed to reach the bosses back in Italy, they were to call a burner phone that had been given to the Colonel and relay messages through him. This would reduce the chance of any incriminating conversations being intercepted by law enforcement. To be extra safe they were to speak only in general terms, avoiding mentioning real names or places.

Antonio and Osvaldo were taken to the warehouse in Medellín but quickly realised they were going to have a problem. They had handed over a large amount of money to the cartel to cover administrative expenses but now needed to travel hundreds of kilometres into the Colombian jungle to reach the remote location where the cartel was actually storing the cocaine it was planning to ship to Europe. The trip was going to cost many thousands of euros more – and they didn't have it.

Osvaldo called the burner phone to relay the message to Pepe. It quickly became apparent that the Colonel was struggling to stick with their agreed telephone protocol. 'Listen to me! Listen to me!' Osvaldo chastised him down the line. 'Don't call me by my name. Call me Pedro, or Juan. We need money for tickets. We need money because we are going to go "upstairs". Tell the gentleman, the one you live with, to give me a call because we need to talk to him. Tell him to call us as soon as possible.' The Colonel anxiously enquired about how they were being treated. Osvaldo reassured him that they were fine, and again stressed the need for Pepe to get in touch as soon as possible.

Back in Italy, Pepe was running a tight ship. When he got the message from the Colonel that the money he had sent with Antonio and Osvaldo had already run out, he was far from pleased. Still, he called Antonio, who explained their predicament: 'We have to go for four days to another place and it's 2,500 kilometres from here,' he told him. But wiring more money to Colombia was a risk. It created a clear evidence trail for police and so Pepe wanted to know how every euro was being spent.

'What do you need the money for?'

'We have to go to the other side of the country. We have run out of money. I am paying for everything, eating, sleeping ... petrol.'

It was critical, he told him, that they were sent the cash as soon as possible because he was due to meet with Jota Jota and leave for the hidden drug storage facility within days.

'So if we don't send the money on time then everything will be delayed by three weeks?' Pepe said.

'Yes, by three weeks.'

Antonio would have known that Pepe was not a man to be trifled with, especially not about money. Pepe had already drilled into him the importance of being parsimonious, issuing orders to abstain from late-night drinking sessions, prostitutes or lavish meals. They were on Salvatore's dime now. Finally, after some additional pleading, Pepe agreed to wire over the additional cash on the strict condition that it was to be spent for work purposes only. They were on a business trip, Pepe reminded Antonio, not a holiday.

'Tighten up!' he commanded. 'Screw less, eat less and try to eat at home.'

*

To see the drugs, Antonio and Osvaldo would have to go deep inside Clan del Golfo territory, a lawless zone ruled by armed enforcers dressed in military fatigues and hiding their faces. One of the cartel's main storage points was the Finca Aurora, a remote banana plantation hidden near the mouth of the Currulao River, about thirty kilometres from the Colombia–Panama border and around eight hours' drive from Medellín. Working there were hundreds of peasants, living out of around fifty wooden huts with zinc roofs as the stench of cocaine hydrochloride wafted through the air. Around three times a week a truck would arrive bringing food. Concealed inside the trucks were small batches of white powder which, slowly, had been amassed into a treasure ready to be shipped from the nearby port of Turbo around the world.

The rumour on the plantation was that the Finca Aurora was under the direct control of Gavilán, the second-in-command of the entire Clan del Golfo and one of the most wanted men in Colombia. The Italians' broker on the ground had been right: they had made contact with the gods.

Hidden in an underground bunker beneath the plantation were hundreds and hundreds of large grey tarpaulin bags filled with pure cocaine – over eight tonnes. So much cocaine that it could fill a swimming pool. So much cocaine that, perhaps, it was impossible to look at it without feeling insignificant.

In any case, having seen the drugs with his own eyes, Antonio's job was now done. He just needed to say goodbye to Osvaldo, the guarantee, and return alone to Italy. Antonio left Colombia on a flight to Madrid. From there he had booked a connecting flight to Rome, then would head south to Calabria.

Back in Italy the Colonel was getting nervous. It had

been two days since he'd heard anything from Antonio. No phone call, no message. What if something had happened to him? The Colonel's mind raced. Contact between the cartel and the Italians was still in its infancy, and both sides were twitchy. All it would take was one mistake, one stupid argument, one perceived slight – and blood could be spilled.

This was the grim formula of being a human guarantee: the potential for a sudden and brutal daisy chain of murders. The Colonel knew that if Antonio had been killed then he would be killed, too. And if the Colonel was murdered in Italy, then the men from the cartel would make Osvaldo disappear. He needed to know that Antonio had returned safely.

The Colonel called up Osvaldo on the burner phone to get his fellow guarantee's opinion on their predicament. 'It's OK, nothing has happened to him,' Osvaldo reassured. 'He has left. If something had happened to him, we would have already heard about it.'

Osvaldo suggested that the Colonel ask Pepe to call Antonio's wife.

'He is crazy for her,' he said. 'Wherever he ends up, he will connect to WiFi and send a WhatsApp to his wife, or get on Skype.'

It wasn't necessary. To their collective relief, Antonio reappeared in Italy to report back to Salvatore and Pepe. He had been unreachable because he had turned off his phone during his flight, and then kept it off because he wanted to avoid being tracked by the police. The Colonel could relax.

With Antonio back things were looking up for the two guarantees. The cocaine deal could now start to move ahead, bringing forward the moment when the Colonel could return to Colombia and Osvaldo could come back to Italy. 'Everything is being organised to get you back,' the Colonel reassured Osvaldo. The important thing now, the Colonel said, was that Antonio gave a positive report to Salvatore about the quality of the drugs and the trustworthiness of the Colombians. 'That is the only problem I have.'

The Colonel didn't know it yet, but this was going to be far from his only problem.

10

Babyface

Virginia, Fall 2014

Jack Kelly was back at his desk at the Special Operations Division surrounded by stacks of papers, intelligence reports, wiretap transcripts and organisational charts. He had begun to work late into the evenings. It felt like he just needed one small breakthrough, one spark to ignite the case.

But the further he stood back from it all, the more infinite in scale it would have appeared. Outside, far away from his desk in a bland office block in a small corner of Virginia, was an ocean of crime. Every second of every day someone was moving money, drugs or weapons across borders. Latching on to just one conspiracy, trying to make sense of one tiny piece of flotsam crossing that ocean, was almost audacious. 'Connecting the dots' or 'putting the puzzle together', as Derek Maltz always told his agents at the SOD to do, meant believing you could make sense of things that were, perhaps, too complex for anyone to comprehend.

After the Tampa meeting, Jack knew that if he was going to build a case around what Hezbollah affiliates were doing in Europe, he was going to need intelligence. And not long afterwards, he learned from colleagues in Colombia that one of the DEA's undercover informants had infiltrated a money-laundering operation run by a man known as Alex. Alex was a young Lebanese man who had moved to Medellín and had begun offering his services to two of the main Colombian cartels – the Clan del Golfo and La Oficina de Envigado. Both had been selling ever larger amounts of cocaine to organised criminals based in Europe, taking advantage of the higher price they could realise across the Atlantic. This booming trade meant that the Colombian suppliers needed to take large payments of cash in Europe and somehow move them back to Latin America. Alex's business was to facilitate these transactions, taking a percentage of the drug money in return for arranging for the cash to be picked up in Europe, transferred to the Middle East, and laundered safely back to Colombia.

The DEA's information suggested that Alex had family ties to important figures in Lebanon, some of whom appeared to be connected to people within Hezbollah. Jack knew that if the DEA agents on the ground could somehow track the money Alex was laundering for the cartels, then it could lead them to whoever it was in the Middle East that was working with him. It would also allow the DEA to gather information on the organised criminals in Europe, in countries like Italy and Holland, who were buying cocaine from the Colombian cartels. It was a slim lead, but it was something.

It helped that the DEA was better positioned than most to work with foreign law enforcement agencies. While many countries viewed attempts by the FBI to run cases on their territory with some caution due to the sensitivity around intelligence work, the DEA tended to be seen as less of a threat. Jack could use the DEA's source network to bring a European police force valuable leads. And those officers would give the DEA the information they uncovered. Jack hoped that the intelligence they were getting from the investigation into Alex would form the seed of a new case.

But he also knew how much had to go right to get operations like this off the ground. Over his career, he had seen countless leads melt away. Bringing in an international case took a mix of hard work, buy-in from your superiors and pure good luck. Sometimes, during his hours of poring over reports and phone records, Jack would think back to a case he had worked on many years before. It had promised to be one of the greatest of his career, but it had ended in disappointment. And, in those late nights at his desk, it gnawed at him.

It had all begun in 2007, when Jack, who had by then been at the Special Operations Division for a couple of years, received a call from the DEA's Miami office telling him they had discovered something interesting. The Miami division had been running a complex undercover investigation into a Colombian drugs boss known as Don Pacho. Don Pacho, whose real name was Francisco Antonio Florez Upegui, was a leading figure in La Oficina, the murderous Colombian criminal organisation with roots in the enforcement wing of Pablo Escobar's Medellín Cartel.

During their investigation into Don Pacho, the DEA Miami office had thrown up multiple wiretaps targeting him and his associates. One of these had picked up Don Pacho speaking to a man with a very strong foreign accent when he talked in Spanish. The agents put a wiretap on the man's phone, and discovered that many of his other conversations involved him speaking in a language that none of them understood.

By chance, a young DEA agent called Michael happened to be walking through the Miami office that morning. His boss, who knew Michael was an Arabic speaker, asked him to come and listen to the recordings. It turned out that the man they had recorded talking to Don Pacho was speaking in Lebanese Arabic. Michael was flown down to Colombia to sit in a wire room, translating hours and hours of calls. In them, the man connected to Don Pacho discussed, in extensive detail, cocaine shipments, percentage profit shares and weapons. When the DEA asked the Colombian authorities what they knew of this man's identity they said they didn't know much, but that their sources had told them he was a man from Lebanon living in Colombia, nicknamed Taliban.

Taliban, the calls appeared to show, was working with La Oficina to ship large quantities of cocaine via Jordan and then into Syria. The DEA's Miami office called up Jack Kelly. He was intrigued. Anyone moving cocaine through Syria, he suspected, would not be working alone. It was almost inconceivable that they would be able to operate without the protection of a powerful local partner.

It smelt like the start of a major case. Jack wanted to find out more. The DEA already had several Spanish-speaking informants who had infiltrated Don Pacho's organisation. To get close to Taliban they were going to need an agent who spoke Arabic. Michael was desperate to be chosen. But he had always been told by his superiors that he would make a problematic undercover agent. Michael looked and talked like a cop. He had served in the US Marines, and walked with what his colleagues called 'a military gait'. Eventually, however, Michael's enthusiasm convinced his bosses to pick him. What they now needed was to devise a way to get him close to Taliban without arousing suspicion.

Then one morning, the solution to their problem walked through the doors of the US embassy in Panama City. A local businessman called Abdul, who ran an import-export company, was being extorted by a top lieutenant and assassin working for Don Pacho, known as Babyface. Babyface was demanding that the businessman launder money for his organisation. This had put Abdul in a terrible position. Either he agreed and became a criminal, or he declined and risked being killed. So he picked a third option: he drove over to the US embassy and asked to see the FBI. The FBI agent instructed him to walk down the hall and speak with the country representative of the DEA. The DEA representative in Panama called up the Special Operations Division in Virginia to tell them that a promising confidential source offering information about Don Pacho had just come in off the street. Soon they came up with a plan. Abdul was to tell Babyface he would work for him, and that he knew some criminal contacts in the United States who could help them.

Several weeks later, Babyface and Abdul caught a flight to Miami, where they were met at the airport by a party of flamboyantly dressed undercover informants and agents working for the DEA. It was night-time in downtown Miami, and Michael was sitting alongside Abdul in a convoy of cars taking Babyface from the airport to a high-end restaurant. It was important to find a place so gaudy and expensive that a hardened criminal would be convinced no police could ever afford to eat there. Part of the DEA's plan was for Michael to be part of the wider entourage, posing as a US-based Middle Eastern contact of Abdul's who had come to greet his friend at the airport. This would allow Abdul to make a brief and unthreatening introduction between Babyface and Michael, opening up the chance for Michael to be put in touch with Taliban at a later date. Michael, however, was not meant to attend the dinner that evening, only to drop off his 'friend' outside.

The convoy pulled up at the restaurant. Babyface walked over to Abdul, who immediately introduced Michael. Babyface, it transpired, had unexpectedly good manners for an assassin, and insisted that Abdul's friend join them for dinner. Michael had little choice but to say yes.

Everyone present knew the secret of winning Babyface's trust was to avoid speaking directly about business, and instead to try to appear as relaxed as possible. But during the meal Babyface turned to Michael and said in Spanish, 'I understand you speak Arabic. What is your connection to Abdul?' Michael, still unfamiliar with being an undercover agent, tried his best to appear calm. 'I launder money through the Middle East,' he replied. Babyface was intrigued. He said: 'I may have a favour to ask. We have a guy called Taliban who we fronted 450 kilos that he took to Jordan. He hasn't been able to sell them. If you have connections over there and could help, we would be very interested.'

And with that, Michael had won his introduction to Taliban, the man who Jack now believed could lead the DEA into places in the Middle East it had never been able to reach.

With Babyface vouching for him, Michael travelled to Bogotá. The DEA had learned from Colombian law enforcement that Taliban was a Lebanese Sunni Muslim called Chekry Harb, who had found himself in a sticky situation.

Harb had at first been reluctant to meet with Michael, worrying that he had been sent by the cartel to collect on a debt or even kill him. It took several weeks of reassuring phone calls and false starts, but finally Harb agreed to see him in Bogotá. Harb explained his dilemma. He had been busy shipping two containers of cocaine a week from Colombia to Port Aqaba in Jordan, but several of his recent shipments had run into problems. One had got wet and was now impossible to sell. But Harb had pre-sold part of that shipment, meaning he owed both Don Pacho and his buyer in the Middle East a lot of money. If Michael could somehow help him sell the rest of the load and settle his debts, he told him, then it would solve a painful headache. Harb invited Michael to travel to Amman to inspect the drugs in a warehouse.

Back in the Special Operations Division, Jack was getting increasingly excited. If he could get the DEA and other US agencies to authorise Michael to travel undercover to the Middle East and meet with Harb, then he might be able to discover who Harb was reporting to there. That would open up an entirely new phase of the investigation and potentially reveal a top-level target.

Jack and others at the DEA began to discuss the case with the Jordanian police, who had also picked up information about Harb's activities. It appeared that the shipments he was sending from Colombia to Port Aqaba were being collected and driven overland to Jordan's border with Syria. There, the Jordanians said, the drugs were received by officers from Syria's Air Force Intelligence Directorate, the most feared and powerful spy agency of the Assad regime, responsible for everything from counter-surveillance to torturing political opponents. The Jordanians suspected that the cocaine was then moved to a warehouse in Damascus, and on to Lebanon, from where it was smuggled through Turkey and into Europe. The local police set up wiretaps to monitor the phones Harb was using on his trips to the Middle East, passing their findings to the DEA. They learned that he would use a Syrian cell number and, whenever a shipment arrived from Colombia, stay in Damascus for several days.

The DEA had historically been given broad authority to send agents to Latin America and the Caribbean. But crossing the Atlantic, especially to work in the Middle East, was a very different proposition. For Michael to be allowed to meet with Harb in Amman, the DEA would have to get CIA permission. This was critical to avoid Michael unwittingly stumbling into the middle of an investigation being run by an allied intelligence or law enforcement agency.

The situation had been made even more complicated by the fact that Babyface, having taken an unexpected liking to Michael, had now started to enquire whether he could help Don Pacho's organisation launder drug money. The first job the cartel gave Michael was to move a small test amount. Michael and a colleague picked up several million dollars in cash from the cartel and within days it was sitting in a bank account in Miami. Babyface was extremely impressed by their speed and efficiency. It was almost unheard of to be able to move cash into the legitimate banking system so quickly. Michael appeared to be a gangster of the very highest calibre. Soon he was being asked if he was able to launder far larger amounts. He went to collect an armoured truck stacked with suitcases and wheelie bags filled with $20 million in bank notes from outside a hotel in Guatemala City.

Meanwhile, the DEA had learned that Chekry Harb was now staying in a safehouse under the watch of Syrian intelligence in Damascus. Back at the Special Operations Division, Jack knew the window for getting Michael to Jordan to meet with Harb, and potentially his handlers, could slam shut at any minute.

After picking up the $20 million, Michael had smuggled it into the US embassy to be seized. This meant the clock was now ticking on Michael's time as a criminal super-fixer. It might have been plausible to Don Pacho and Babyface that laundering such a large amount of money would take more time than before. Soon, though, they would start to ask difficult questions. And the moment Don Pacho realised that Michael had stolen his money he would have to be pulled out for his own safety, and the operation would be over.

But the sign-off the DEA needed for Michael's meeting with Harb in Amman still hadn't come through. The CIA, for reasons unknown to the DEA, had been stalling. Jack was furious. Michael called up Harb in a last-ditch attempt to gather information, but he had suddenly gone cold. 'I don't know who you are,' he said. 'I don't know anything about drugs.'

It was too late anyway. The DEA leadership decided the time had come to bring down the curtain on the operation. Michael and his fellow undercover agents were exfiltrated and 130 people were arrested in raids across Colombia and Central America, including Don Pacho and his top lieutenants. The cash Michael had picked up in Guatemala was flown back to Miami in two US government planes. Chekry Harb, who had returned to Colombia, was arrested a day before he was due to fly back out to Damascus on an Air France flight.

The operation had been a great success, and the DEA leadership were delighted. Based on evidence from 370 wiretaps, which had recorded over seven hundred thousand conversations, they had seized over $42 million in assets, 3.7 tonnes of cocaine, and arrested four people on the US Attorney General's list of international drug kingpins, including Don Pacho. But for Jack it was a crushing disappointment. He would now never know who Chekry Harb was speaking to in the Middle East.

What Jack had no idea about at the time was that Israeli

intelligence had also been watching Harb. And the Israelis possessed classified information that the DEA didn't. The year before Harb was arrested, the Israelis had learned that he had met with an extremely sensitive person who was staying in Damascus under the highest level of protection from the Syrian government. It was a person the Israelis had been hunting for decades. It was Imad Mughniyeh.

11

Midnight in Damascus

Damascus, February 2008

In the early evening of 12 February 2008, Imad Mughniyeh walked out of a building in an upmarket suburb of southwestern Damascus and towards his parked Mitsubishi Pajero SUV.

For a man like Imad, the Syrian capital was a rare place where he could feel safe. He was forty-five years old now and had been living a life of violence and secrecy for more than two decades. His once slim face was larger, and his hair had turned grey. Thirty years after he and Mustafa had first signed up as teenagers to the Fatah training camps in Lebanon, Imad was on the wanted lists of forty-two countries. The FBI had put a $25 million reward on his head. Mossad, which referred to him by the codename Maurice, had been trying to kill Imad for years. But every time anyone got close, he had managed to get away.

Over the years many had denied he even existed. 'No,

there's no one of that name among us,' said Hezbollah leader Hassan Nasrallah when asked about an operative named Imad Mughniyeh in a 1990s television interview. His own comrades often didn't know what he looked like. One senior Hamas commander in Lebanon thought a man who had asked to meet him one day was a local salesman. In fact it was Imad in disguise.

And people were out there hunting for Mustafa, too. Several weeks before that evening in Damascus, in January 2008, a thirty-one-year-old Lebanese police captain called Wissam Eid met with investigators from the United Nations in Beirut to give them evidence he had uncovered relating to the assassination of Rafic Hariri three years earlier.

Eid, a policeman with a computer science degree, had made what appeared to be a significant breakthrough. He had analysed the call records of every mobile phone that had been used close to the site of the explosion opposite the St. Georges Hotel. This data revealed a network of 'red' phones that had been used by what appeared to be a hit squad tracking Hariri's convoy. As the investigators began to follow the trail of evidence uncovered by Eid, they would discover that many of the calls connected to a man known as Sami Issa. But Eid was unable to help them further. Eight days after they met him, he was murdered by a car bomb.

Imad continued to walk towards his car. Earlier that evening he had been in a meeting with two very important men: Qasem Soleimani, head of Iran's elite special forces unit the Quds Force, and General Muhammad Suleiman, a top Syrian security official many suspected was in charge of Assad's chemical weapons programme.

Over the years, Imad had developed a close, almost brotherly relationship with Soleimani. One day, during the Israel-Hezbollah war in 2006, Imad had returned home to see Saada and pick up some food. He pulled up on a motorbike with another man on the back. Imad introduced his wife to his friend Haji Qasem, the grey-bearded Iranian commander.

Up until then, Imad and Saada's marriage had been spent moving around covertly from place to place, rarely being able to see their families. Saada was always fearful for her husband's security. After the 2006 war they settled in one place, finally giving them the sense of stability they had always lacked. But friends could sense that Imad was exhausted by the constant planning, organisation and hiding. Perhaps it was this weariness that, for the first time in his life, had made him sloppy.

In Damascus he had started to relax, dropping the extreme levels of caution and paranoia that had made him so invisible. Imad would travel around openly, without trying to conceal who he was meeting with. He would stay for months on end in the same operational apartment in the area of Kafr Sousa, and would receive high-level Iranian, Syrian and Palestinian guests at his home.

The Israelis believed that Imad had begun to see three good-looking local women, supplied to him by General

Suleiman, and that he would visit his female friends without bodyguards. If true, then such carelessness, even in a fortress city like the Syrian capital, was more evidence that Imad was taking far fewer precautions than was wise. That evening, as he walked towards his car, he was being observed by two undercover spotters. Covert operatives had been tracking him for weeks, waiting for the right time when no civilians were close by. On several other occasions he had been accompanied by friends or was in a busy place. But tonight, in a car park in a Damascus suburb, Imad was finally alone.

Hidden inside his Pajero was a remote-controlled bomb. An explosion tore through the vehicle, ripping his body into pieces.

*

Syrian police and intelligence officers raced towards the scene of the explosion. Soon, footage of the flaming vehicle, burning brightly in the Damascus evening, was broadcast on Iranian state television. News began to rush across the Middle East and beyond about what had happened.

For Bashar al-Assad it was an acute embarrassment. Not only did the world now know he had been harbouring an international terrorist, but he had also failed to protect his guest. Syria's spy agencies immediately started to point the finger at their rivals, blaming each other for the security lapses that had allowed the assassination to take place. Both Tehran and Hassan Nasrallah in Lebanon were furious, with some in Hezbollah believing that Syrian negligence was responsible for their loss.

In life Imad had been a flicker, a phantom. In death he burst into existence. The man who Hezbollah had once denied ever having heard of was immediately elevated into the pantheon of the movement's greatest martyrs. Two days after the bombing, thousands of mourners took to the streets in the pouring rain in the southern suburbs of Beirut, close to where Imad and Mustafa had grown up. Imad's refrigerated coffin lay on a stage, draped in a yellow Hezbollah flag and surrounded by black-uniformed and beret-wearing guards. A brass band played, and hundreds of politicians, clerics and other dignitaries filtered through metal detectors manned by black-suited security guards. Hassan Nasrallah addressed the event via a video broadcast from the safety of his secure bunker. He vowed revenge. 'Haji Imad's blood will mark the beginning of the downfall of the state of Israel.'

Imad's mother sat among the mourners holding previously top-secret pictures of her dead son in military uniform and with a thick grey beard. Imad was the third of her sons to die in a car bomb. She didn't have any childhood pictures of Imad left. For security reasons, he had taken them all away.

At a memorial service, Imad and Saada's teenage son Jihad gave a defiant speech. 'We are going to stay on this path, the way of resistance and the way of Nasrallah!' The crowd roared back at him in response. Tears poured down the faces of the mourners, including the stern-faced security guards.

Any intelligence officers watching the event would have been looking to see if Mustafa was hidden somewhere in the crowds, paying his respects to his dead cousin. For almost their entire lives it had been Mustafa and Imad. Now, Mustafa was on his own.

12

Human Guarantees

Calabria, Winter 2014

Antonio had returned safely from Colombia and Salvatore now wanted to move ahead with a shipment as quickly as possible. The job of the Colonel, the human guarantee sent by the cartel to Calabria, was to act as a communication channel between the two sides as they worked out the terms of the deal.

Salvatore had been careful to make sure his strange guest from Colombia never stayed in one place for too long, to avoid attracting unwanted attention. At the start of the Colonel's stay, Salvatore had put him up in a room in his own house in Mileto for a few nights, later moving him to Oksana's flat and then on to stay with Pepe. But it quickly became clear that the visitor had terrible manners: he was infuriating the women in Salvatore's life with his boorishness. Oksana loathed having to clean up after the Colonel, who had also managed to enrage Antonella with his constant eating and apparent lack of gratitude for her hospitality. Salvatore and Pepe decided it would be best for everyone if the Colonel was relocated to a remote farmhouse.

It was from there the guarantee was to wait by his burner phone for news from Colombia; he would pass any information on to Pepe, who would tell Salvatore. The Colonel, however, was getting confusing messages from his bosses about the progress of the deal. They would tell him a shipment was ready to be sent to Italy. But then he wouldn't hear anything from them for days. For the Colonel, it felt as if no one seemed to know exactly what was going on. And Pepe, a man with a dangerously short temper, was starting to lose his patience with the guarantee.

Sitting alone in the farmhouse for most of the day – with Pepe arriving every so often to breathe down his neck – the Colonel was becoming acutely aware of the danger he was now in. Each day that passed without the deal moving ahead increased the chance that the Italians would make him disappear. In Colombia, the Colonel knew that his organisation took people 'to the mountains', and they never came back. In Calabria, some Mafia killers had fed their victims alive to pigs. The only person the Colonel had to confide in was Osvaldo, who found himself in the same predicament thousands of kilometres away.

Osvaldo and the Colonel's duties meant they were talking regularly on their burner phones. And as time went on, they had started to strike up the sort of intimate relationship only two men who were human collateral in the middle of an international drug deal could develop. They were two junior, disposable employees stuck on different sides of the world doing the same menial job. Each needed the other to survive (and not screw up) if they were going to get home safely. They had developed a sort of understanding – a bond.

The Colonel, the focus of Pepe's mounting fury, was miserable. 'Every day a man comes to bring me lunch, the farmer's son,' the Colonel told Osvaldo one evening. 'He comes at 11.45 a.m., he leaves me lunch and dinner and then he goes. And I don't see anyone until the next day.' Under stress, the Colonel had begun to take twice as many heart pills as normal; he had run out of medicine. 'I would like you to be in my room, to see what I am enduring,' he said. His fellow guarantee offered his solidarity. He would speak to Pepe and try to calm things down.

Osvaldo, stuck in Medellín, with no news about what was happening with the deal, was also becoming desperate. He complained to the Colonel about his lack of money, and how Pepe had refused to send more cash after Antonio had returned to Italy.

'I can't stay here like this, I can't stay like this in a place,' he said. 'I can't move. I don't have a euro, I don't have a penny in my pocket, not even for a top-up. I can't stay here like this!'

But Osvaldo also knew from his own conversations with Pepe that the Italians were becoming convinced that the Colonel was the main impediment to the deal moving forward. The Colonel had first arrived in Calabria with the bombast of a travelling salesman, making great promises to Salvatore and Pepe about the quality and quantity of the drugs his organisation possessed and the speed with which they would be dispatched. This had been an error. Owing to the delays, Pepe was now convinced the Colonel had been lying to him.

Osvaldo decided to level with his friend. 'Listen to me,' he told the Colonel. 'I will be honest with you. There have been mistakes, and because of the mistakes people don't trust what you say as much any more.' Perhaps Osvaldo was trying to be helpful, or perhaps he just wanted to stop Pepe from losing patience and killing the Colonel – if that happened then the chances were he would be eliminated, too. But the Colonel was taken aback. He had only been telling the Italians what he was being told to convey by his bosses back in Colombia. Part of the confusion came from the language barrier. Pepe did not speak much Spanish. And the Colonel's Italian was poor. To communicate, they frequently typed words into Google translate on the Colonel's phone.

'I write what they tell me to write, I write the shit they tell me to,' the Colonel said, attempting to defend himself. 'When Antonio calls you tonight you tell him that my hands are clean. I am just doing what they tell me to do,' he said. 'They say "write this", and then we immediately translate it into Italian using Google ... Don't get angry with me because I have nothing to do with it.'

Osvaldo reassured his friend that his warning was for his own good. 'I tell it like it is because for me you are a person who has a lot of value, and a lot of respect,' he said.

The Colonel was stinging at the unfairness of the situation, but Osvaldo's warning had made him realise he was running out of time. He had attempted to placate Pepe by asking his bosses to send someone more senior from the organisation to smooth things over with the Italians. But several days had passed and there had still been no news. The Colonel urgently needed to reach his line manager in Medellín and explain to them how bad things had become.

He rang the number. But instead of the line manager picking up it was his assistant. The Colonel got straight to the point. 'When are the people arriving? They have to arrive

urgently, otherwise you know what will happen to me ...
Someone has to come and represent me, please, otherwise
they will kill me here!' The assistant was unmoved. He told
the Colonel he would have to wait for the line manager to
return to get an answer.

It must have felt to the Colonel that his employers did not
entirely appreciate the precariousness of his situation. This
shouldn't be happening to him, he thought. He was a citizen
of the European Union. They couldn't just murder him.
There must have been a misunderstanding. All he had to do
was to explain the situation. The Calabrians had the money
ready. Antonio had been to Colombia to inspect the drugs.
He just needed to speak to the line manager. That would fix
things. Everything was set. The deal would soon be completed, and he would be able to go home.

Finally, some hours later, the Colonel got a call back.

'They said they were sending people, and as long as I am
here, what have they sent me here to do?' the Colonel pleaded
with his line manager. 'To make a bad impression with the
Italian gentleman?' But his manager stopped him dead. The
cartel bosses, he told the Colonel, had requested that he come
back to Colombia before anyone else could be sent out to Italy
to move the deal ahead. The Colonel's heart sank. He was
now in an impossible situation. Pepe was refusing to release
him until he saw some progress with the deal. But now he
was being told that unless he went back to Colombia the deal
was on hold.

'And where do you expect me to find the money for a ticket
to come back?' the Colonel pleaded. 'How am I meant to get
there? By swimming?'

Pepe was in the room with the Colonel, listening to the
conversation unfold and getting increasingly enraged. 'The
Italian man who is with me here is very pissed off because

you have changed the plan,' the Colonel explained to his line manager. Suddenly, Pepe grabbed the phone. He had decided it was time to take matters into his own hands.

'The time has come to speak clearly,' he barked down the line. 'So where is the stuff? . . . We have the money; you have the stuff. If you want to sell it, that is. Because I am tired, I can't take it any more. In half a day you change your word fifty times. Nothing has arrived here, because if eight tonnes had arrived and I didn't know about it I would cut my own head off right away.'

The Colonel took back the phone. He would fix the situation, he promised.

'I will find a way to get back, and I will leave this gentleman in a good situation,' the Colonel told his boss. 'You have my word. I will not leave Pepe here with nothing. I will come back, and everything will be solved.'

Reluctantly, Pepe agreed to allow the Colonel to return to Colombia. But days later the Italian heard some news from Osvaldo that made him boil over with anger. The Colombians were now apparently saying the price they were willing to sell the cocaine for had increased.

'Osvaldo, my balls are swollen, too swollen!' Pepe raged. 'I am not interested in dealing with people who change their word from one minute to the next. That's it: I don't want to know anything any more. I won't give them a lira more, not even for my own funeral.'

Osvaldo attempted to calm his boss down, but Pepe was by now at breaking point. The request for more money had pushed him over the edge.

'I don't know why the price has changed . . . I am not interested in these people. They have balls as big as a lorry.'

Osvaldo was trying to stay positive. The deal was still possible. And he reminded his boss that he was the one who had been stuck in Colombia for months trying to get it over the line.

'I am here to do things well, to make it all go well,' he told Pepe. 'I don't do anything that isn't good for us, you understand?'

But Pepe was fed up. Fed up with the constant requests for money, both from the Colombians and from Osvaldo. Fed up with having to say no. 'Listen to me. Do you understand that it is not easy to chase money without seeing shit? Everyone here thinks I am Uncle Scrooge.'

And then there was the matter of whatever it was that the Colonel had said or done to infuriate Antonella. 'He said stuff to Salvatore's wife,' he later explained to Osvaldo. 'He said a lot of shit. We gave him whatever he wanted . . . and then you talk to a wife? There are other things that I'll tell you about later, because these are things that can't be said on the phone.'

'The Colonel has blocked everything,' Osvaldo agreed. 'Jota Jota is going to kick his ass.'

After the Colonel had raced back to Colombia, he told his superiors about Pepe's anger, threats and less than hospitable treatment of him. Based on the Colonel's report from Italy, the cartel leadership decided that working with a hothead like Pepe was not worth the risk. If the deal was to go ahead, then from now on they would work only with Antonio and Salvatore directly. It was looking increasingly likely that Pepe and Osvaldo were going to be cut out of the transaction altogether. This would mean they wouldn't receive any payment for the deal being completed. They were now facing having worked for months for nothing.

Pepe was incandescent with rage. He wasn't just going to kill the Colonel. He was going to decapitate him. 'If I get that pig in my hands, I will cut his head off!' he raged down the phone to Osvaldo. 'I promise you that if the Colonel comes back here I'll kill him just for the fun of it. I'll kill him under the cameras in the street!'

He may have been a hardened drug trafficker, but Pepe was a man who appreciated historical detail. No, cutting the Colonel's head off like a farm animal would not be enough. Pepe was going to string him up in the same Milanese square as Il Duce in 1945. 'I'll kill him in Piazzale Loreto, for fuck's sake, in Piazzale Loreto like they killed Mussolini! They haven't understood a fucking thing here, do you understand? If they think I'm taking the piss I'll take all Colombians here and I'll kill them right away, right now. All of them! They've broken my balls!'

As Osvaldo listened to Pepe ranting about the various ways in which he was planning to murder the Colonel it would have been clear that his boss was not especially bothered by the awkward position he was putting his junior employee in. Osvaldo wasn't stupid. He knew that if he and Pepe were being cut out of the deal, then he would no longer serve any purpose for the cartel. And he had also heard rumours that Jota Jota was angry at the Colonel for not having handled things smoothly in Italy.

Pepe was full of regrets. Regrets about the payment for a deal he was now never likely to see, and regrets that he had ever agreed to let the Colonel return to Colombia.

'If I knew what I know now he wouldn't have gone back there, I guarantee it,' he told Osvaldo.

Some days later the Colonel, now back in Colombia, called Antonio in Italy. Antonio confirmed that Pepe and Osvaldo were out. Salvatore had ordered that Antonio would now oversee all phone contact with the cartel. Both sides had decided that a high-level meeting was the only way to get things back on track. Jota Jota was going to travel to Italy to meet with Salvatore.

The Colonel began arranging his boss's travel itinerary and documents for the trip to Milan. 'Tomorrow Jota Jota will have his visa,' the Colonel told Antonio. The rest of the information, including a copy of Jota Jota's passport and flight details, would be sent to the Italians in an email.

The question now was what should happen to Osvaldo. He was stuck in Colombia as a guarantee without a purpose. Salvatore no longer needed him. The Colonel and Osvaldo had been through a lot together over the last few months. They had shared their fears, their hopes. They understood each other. They had become friends. But Osvaldo was no longer useful. The Colonel believed the time had come for Osvaldo to be murdered.

'What do you want to do about Osvaldo? Do you want to send him a return ticket, or is he finished? Give me an order – what do we do?' he asked Antonio.

Antonio had already made his feelings about Osvaldo clear to the cartel men: 'I don't give a shit about him. Throw him in the sea.' But Salvatore had ordered that nothing could be decided about the guarantee's fate until Jota Jota had come to Italy.

'Let's do everything after Jota Jota arrives here,' Antonio told the Colonel. 'Forget about Osvaldo and Pepe. They don't work with us any more.'

'If you want us to kill him here, no problem,' the Colonel said. 'If you write me an email telling me to kill him, I will kill him right away. This guy cannot go back to Italy. He knows everything, he knows too much.'

'Let's talk to Jota Jota when he comes here,' Antonio said. 'We will talk with Jota and then I'll let you know, OK?'

Back in Colombia, Osvaldo was getting increasingly

nervous. He needed to speak with Pepe. He had noticed a change in attitude from his hosts. Osvaldo had become convinced that both he and the Colonel were going to be taken to the mountains and killed together.

'They want to take the Colonel up to the mountains,' Osvaldo told Pepe down the phone line. 'The commander has told them to search for the Colonel so they can take him there, and me too!'

But Pepe did not seem particularly preoccupied by Osvaldo's concerns. The thing Pepe cared about was that all his stressful work with the Colonel would now be for nothing. He was not going to see a euro in commission, even if Salvatore's big shipment went through.

Osvaldo had to shut up and calm down. The way they would solve this problem, Pepe told him, was to reiterate to Jota Jota that Pepe still had the ability to move shipments of cocaine in Europe for the cartel. Jota was a businessman. And killing Osvaldo would deprive them of a useful customer.

'You tell Jota Jota to come here with stuff, with however much stuff he wants, and to call me,' Pepe told Osvaldo. 'In one week I will move all the stuff and he will leave with the money. Then I will show him if I am a shit or a serious person, understood?'

What Pepe was suggesting was a serious risk. Their bosses had cut them out of the negotiations. Pepe had failed. And now he was asking Osvaldo to go behind their backs and try to start moving cocaine into Europe.

'Salvatore and Antonio must not know about this. Do you understand? They must not know that you talked to me about these things.'

No one got to cut Pepe out of a deal like this. Not even Salvatore Pititto. He was going to get his revenge.

'When our operation ends, then I'll play a nice trick on

both of them. I'll take them to the mountains and that'll be
the end of the story. We'll take them to the mountains and
we'll explain to them who the shits are. I'll cut their heads
off and hang them on a pole!'

13

Murder in the Blue Moon Café

Calabria, 2014

Salvatore had by now shared many secrets with Oksana. She had hosted the Colonel at her flat, and knew about the cocaine shipment her boyfriend was working on. But perhaps the day Oksana knew that Salvatore truly loved her was the day he told her about the murder.

It began a year earlier, when Salvatore told Oksana one morning there had been a big problem during the night. He and the others in the gang had been called to an urgent summit at Pasquale's house. In the rush, Oksana couldn't make out exactly what was happening to cause the commotion but from what Salvatore had said it seemed to have something to do with a fire that had broken out in the countryside.

Whatever the problem was, it must have been serious

for Salvatore to race over to his cousin's house. Pasquale, sitting in his wheelchair, was still the king of Mileto, the man who ruled over every inch of that grey, crumbling empire of dirt.

Almost twenty years had passed since the murder of the American boy Nicholas Green, and his killers had been released from prison. One had become a state witness and gone into hiding in the north of Italy. The other, Francesco Mesiano, had returned to Mileto. He had been twenty-two when he went inside, and had served almost two decades behind bars. Back in the village some now called him 'the madman'. And almost as soon as Francesco returned from jail the trouble began.

The Mesiano family were tight with the Pititto family, and some of them had been in the gang since their early days of robbing trucks and shaking down local businesses. Outside the village, the Mesianos had a plot of land that bordered the fields owned by another family, the Coriglianos. For decades the two families – the Mesianos and the Coriglianos – had coexisted in peace. At points they had been close, almost like cousins or brothers. But since Francesco, called Franco by his family, had been back in Mileto, a series of grievances had started to fester between the two clans.

Franco, according to the complaints the Coriglianos made to the local police, had started to graze his animals on their land, ruining their crops. The Mesianos owned a bakery in Mileto, and the Coriglianos owned a mini market. When Marianna, the matriarch of the Corigliano family, went to the bakery to complain to Franco about him destroying their fields with his livestock, he became enraged. He was backed by Pasquale Pititto, and he wasn't going to apologise to anyone. 'Tell your husband he needs to leave that land, or else I will kill him,' he warned her. 'There are many of us. You don't want to go against us.'

Marianna left the bakery in disgust. In retaliation, the Corigliano family decided their supermarket would no longer buy bread from the Mesiano bakery. It was a seemingly trivial act of defiance. But in Mileto even tiny arguments could end in blood being spilled.

Soon after the Coriglianos began their boycott, someone crept up to their farmhouse in the middle of the night, poured petrol over their front door and set it alight. They also set fire to the blue Piaggio Ape parked outside. The police came and took statements from the Coriglianos. Did they see anything? It had been too dark. Who had a motive to burn down their house? Marianna said she didn't know: 'Our family hasn't had grievances with anyone.' She told the officers that they did not want to file an official complaint for the damage caused by the fire. There was nothing more to do.

The next evening, rumours raced around the village that Giuseppe Mesiano, Franco's seventy-five-year-old father, had died of a heart attack. When the police went to Giuseppe's house, they found the old man lying on his back on the concrete veranda. His arms were outstretched, his legs slightly apart. He wore blue suede shoes, and a thin gold medallion engraved with a picture of a saint spilled out over the top of his T-shirt.

The police forensics team found an ashtray on a garden table with three recently smoked cigarette butts, and two empty bottles of German beer. The old man had been sipping them in the setting summer sun. He'd also been running some errands. Near his corpse was his car, with the boot open and a crate of water bottles close by. It appeared that Giuseppe had been ambushed while he was unloading the vehicle: he'd been shot multiple times, and beneath his cold body was a pool of blood.

A few days later a funeral was held for the old man. The police came down to watch the event, concerned that the murder of a Mesiano risked sparking a violent and unpredictable response. They noticed that there was a significant absence among the mourners. No one from the Corigliano family had been invited. They were not welcome.

Two months later, on a sweltering summer afternoon, the Coriglianos' eldest son, Antonio, drove his red Fiat Punto into the centre of Mileto and parked outside the Blue Moon Café. It was part of his daily routine to stop there at around 3 p.m. for an iced coffee. He entered the Blue Moon, where the smell of fresh dough was wafting through the air. The café's owner served him his drink and returned to the kitchen at the back to carry on preparing the pizzas he was making. As the owner began to knead the dough, several gunshots rang out. He rushed to the front of the café, and through the window saw Antonio Corigliano slumped over the wheel of his car.

Outside, the streets of Mileto were silent, aside from the running engine of Corigliano's red Fiat. The keys were in the ignition, and the front windows were down. The inside of the car was covered in blood, and a spattered pack of Marlboro cigarettes was on the front passenger seat next to the murdered man. Whoever had come for Antonio that afternoon had known exactly where and when to strike. It was also clear that Antonio had been expecting trouble. When the police arrived, they found a 7.65-calibre Beretta semi-automatic pistol in the glove compartment with the serial number punched out.

And that's when Salvatore told Oksana what had happened: after the murder of Giuseppe Mesiano, the Pititto gang, allied with the Mesianos, had held a crisis meeting chaired by Pasquale at his house. Gunning down a Mesiano was an outrageous challenge to Pasquale's authority in Mileto. Yes, they wanted revenge. But this was also about control. A message had to be sent to anyone who dared to think they could kill one of their people without suffering the consequences.

As Salvatore recounted for Oksana, at the meeting they had decided the only possible culprits for the murder were the Corigliano family. They had been the ones who had got into an argument with Franco over his animals grazing on their land and had stopped buying bread from his family's bakery. So, in retaliation, one of the Pititto gang had sneaked out in the middle of the night and set fire to their farmhouse. The Coriglianos were the only ones with a motive to shoot Franco's father, and so, after Giuseppe's death, Salvatore, Pasquale and others decided to ambush Antonio Corigliano.

Sitting inside Oksana's flat, Salvatore went into great detail as he told her what he had done that day. Salvatore drove a stolen scooter; another man rode pillion. As Corigliano left his house and drove towards the Blue Moon Café, they followed him. When he had finished his iced coffee and returned to his car, Salvatore had driven the scooter up to the driver's side and the other man unloaded seven 9x21 pistol rounds through the open window. They then sped off into the side streets of Mileto. No one had seen a thing. Antonio Corigliano had to die, Salvatore told Oksana, because their gang 'owed it' to the Mesianos to get revenge.

In the early years of their affair, Salvatore would hide his business from Oksana. Now he was trusting her with his darkest secrets. Perhaps Salvatore was confessing his crimes to her to unburden himself. Or perhaps he was trying to justify what he had done. Whatever the reason, they were now irreversibly bound to one another.

14

Cookies in Paris

Paris, Early 2015

Inside Jack Kelly's cubicle at the Special Operations Division, his wall charts were becoming increasingly sprawling. The information coming back from the DEA's undercover informants in Colombia about Alex, the twenty-six-year-old Lebanese money launderer living in Medellín, had opened up a new phase of the investigation.

Based on those reports, the DEA had obtained judge-authorised warrants to throw up wiretaps on Alex's phones, and to intercept his messages and emails. Jack had then run the numbers Alex was contacting in Europe and the Middle East through the SOD's data systems. This almost immediately showed that the young money launderer was communicating with phone numbers that were known to be linked to drug trafficking in various European countries. By tracking the activity of these numbers, Jack and his colleagues were able to gather further evidence that Alex was helping to facilitate pick-ups of large amounts of cash from drug traffickers looking to send payment for cocaine shipments back to the cartels in Colombia.

One of the organisations Alex was laundering money for was the Clan del Golfo, the cartel that – unbeknownst to Jack – was attempting to move eight tonnes of cocaine across the Atlantic to Italy with the help of an Italian gangster by the name of Salvatore Pititto.

The DEA had known for years that Colombia's cartels had shifted the focus of their trafficking activities towards Europe. There were several good strategic reasons for this pivot. Firstly, the Colombian cartels could sell their cocaine for a far higher price than they could get sending their drugs north to the Mexican cartels, making Europe a more profitable market. Secondly, by circumventing the Mexican groups they could keep a far larger chunk of the profit for themselves, rather than having terms dictated by the kingpins who controlled border access between Mexico and the United States. And thirdly, Europe tended to be a far less aggressively policed market to operate in than the United States or Central America.

Shipping large quantities of cocaine from Colombia to Europe was relatively simple. Ports like Rotterdam or Genoa were vast: thousands of container ships arrived each week, holding tens of thousands of individual containers. The sheer volume meant it was impossible to check each container, and very easy for contraband to slip through.

The Colombian cartels would establish contact with organised criminals in Europe and arrange to send them shipments of cocaine to be picked up from the ports. The criminals would then sell the drugs, and large amounts of cash would pile up in Europe, some of which would need to be sent to Colombia to pay for the shipments.

These growing piles of dirty money presented a far more complex logistical challenge than the drugs. Laundering millions of euros back to Colombia required a great deal of skill and organisation. It could not be done via a regular bank transfer, as depositing large quantities of cash would immediately be a red flag. Instead, the cartels and their customers needed the services of specialists who possessed the international networks to quietly ship tens of millions of euros in bank notes across borders.

This was where the Middle East came in. European criminals who were becoming top customers for the Colombian cartels were increasingly sending drug money through Middle Eastern banks to be laundered and sent to Latin America.

The leads the DEA had generated by monitoring Alex's phone had already started to produce results. They had given the SOD precise information about the exact times and locations of large drug money pick-ups that they had passed on to European police, resulting in several large cash seizures in Holland. They had now noticed a new pattern of pick-ups happening in France. Yet Jack knew they were seeing only half the story. Confiscating drug money on the ground in Europe wasn't enough to build the case.

It seemed obvious to him that Alex was a small part of something much larger. The DEA's informants in Colombia painted a picture of him as a loose-lipped braggart who repeatedly boasted to the undercover informant of his powerful family connections in Lebanon. 'My grandfather is the prime minister!' he wrote in one text message. 'And trust me, my father and uncle, *jeje*, better I don't say who.' But Alex appeared to be a facilitator, not a boss. He would regularly receive older guests from the Middle East in his apartment in Medellín, and he would communicate with numbers registered in Beirut.

Jack's examination of the phone data had led him to suspect that the bags and briefcases of cash that Alex was arranging to be picked up by couriers in Europe were being transported to banks and exchange houses in Beirut. On Islamic holidays, Alex would tell the cartel that 'his people' were not able to work that day.

As the DEA continued to monitor Alex's phone activity, the SOD's databases showed that some of the numbers he was communicating with outside of Colombia were already known to the US government. Jack felt like he was inching closer. But he still needed solid evidence to make a prosecutable case. And because most of the activity they were watching was passing through Europe, he knew it was going to be crucial to win the backing of European police.

He was going to have to go to France. He loved France, especially its cafés and red wine. But working there also made him nervous. Perhaps Jack was paranoid, but he often had the sensation that he was being watched.

A few years earlier, Jack and a colleague had been sent to Paris to meet a man who had worked at a Lebanese bank, which the DEA and US Department of the Treasury had investigated for facilitating money transfers for Hezbollah. The bank needed to pay a fine to the US government, but no one in the Treasury Department could figure out exactly where it was hiding its money. Jack hoped the man he and his colleague were meeting in Paris would provide the answer.

Before the meeting, Jack had known it was highly likely that if the source had agreed to talk then he would have told his handlers. And given the bank's connections with Hezbollah and Iran, there was a reasonable chance that somebody out there would surveil the meeting.

Given their concerns about being followed Jack and his

colleague had decided not to tell the source which hotel they were going to take him to. Instead they told him to meet them at a restaurant on the Place Victor Hugo – a large circular junction with ten roads leading into it and a fountain in the middle – while a third agent watched from a distance to see if anyone was tailing them.

After strolling around in the Parisian sunshine for long enough to feel confident that no one was spying on them, the two Americans walked with the source to the Renaissance Trocadero, a Marriott hotel a few minutes from the Trocadéro Gardens, opposite the Eiffel Tower on the other bank of the Seine. Once inside, they put a 'Do not disturb' sign on the hotel room door and began the interview.

BOOM. BOOM. BOOM. Someone was banging on their hotel-room door. Jack jumped out of his seat. BOOM. BOOM. BOOM. He shot a nervous look at his colleague.

'What do you want?' Jack yelled in the direction of the door. 'Who is it?' They had put the 'Do not disturb' sign up. Why was someone banging on their door right now?

'You must open the door,' the voice on the other side responded in broken English. 'I have goodness for you. You must open the door.'

Jack squinted through the peephole. Outside stood a man in a bellboy uniform. Jack's colleague was scrambling to get the source to hide under the bed. The source was angrily refusing to hide.

'Get the hell out of here,' Jack yelled. 'We don't need anything.' His mind was racing. Was it an Iranian agent? Or could it be someone from the French security services?

Jack opened the door and saw the man hurrying down the hall and into a stairway. He went to follow him, but then thought better of it. He took the lift to the lobby. At the reception desk, he asked if the hotel had sent anyone to his room. They said they had not. Then Jack saw the man in the bellboy uniform in the courtyard.

'Why did you try and get inside my room?' Jack snapped at him.

'I had goodness for you,' he said. 'Cookies!'

The Americans had booked a premier room. Premier rooms always came with cookies.

The bellboy bearing cookies might have been innocent but shortly before Jack was due to head back to Europe, he and his colleagues discovered that there had been a leak. During a routine email search warrant, which gave the DEA access to a target's entire inbox, agents were shocked to see what looked like a grainy mobile phone photo of one of Project Cassandra's organisational charts. They couldn't be sure, but it looked to have come from a briefing note Jack had shared with police across Europe several years before. The photo appeared to have been hastily taken from inside a prosecutor's office.

Jack's paranoia suddenly seemed justified. The email data showed that the image had been forwarded multiple times, including to a high-ranking criminal facilitator in Lebanon. It was now clear that some of their targets were fully aware they were being watched by the DEA. And they appeared to have moles somewhere inside European law enforcement.

It was a reminder to Jack to be careful. Still, his investigation was finally taking shape. The DEA had now mapped out a complex network of phone contacts between money launderers in Colombia and the Middle East, and money couriers working on the ground in France, Holland, Germany, Spain and Italy. The next step was to follow that money – to find out who was on the other side. They needed to set up a surveillance operation in one of these countries to see who was picking up the money, and where exactly they were sending it to.

15

The Translator

Syria–Lebanon Border, July 2015

While Jack Kelly continued to investigate the leads in Europe, he and his colleagues at the Special Operations Division were still nervously awaiting news about the fate of Ali Fayad. It had now been almost a year since Jack had gone to Prague to help arrest the Lebanese arms dealer in the sting operation at the Sheraton Hotel. Fayad, meanwhile, was in legal limbo, trapped in a cell in Pankrác Prison, notorious for its violence and overcrowding.

The DEA was confident the case was solid and that the Czech government would ultimately agree to extradite Fayad. Based on the DEA's evidence, the US Department of Justice had charged him with conspiracy to kill officers and employees of the US government, conspiracy to acquire and transfer anti-aircraft missiles and conspiracy to provide material support to a foreign terrorist organisation. If convicted he would be facing the possibility of a life sentence.

But Jack also knew extradition requests were unpredict-able. One Czech judge had already ruled that Fayad could be handed over to the US government. Then a higher court reversed the decision. Fayad's file was now in the hands of the Czech foreign minister, who would have the final say. The US embassy in Prague could lobby the Czechs, but ultimately the decision would be theirs alone.

Thousands of miles away from Fayad's prison cell, a silver Kia minivan was speeding down a dusty road in Lebanon's Bekaa Valley. Inside the van were five Czech citizens and a Lebanese man, heading for a prearranged location outside the town of Kefraya. It was a dangerous place for foreigners. It was a Friday evening and the sun would soon start to set, and they were just thirty minutes away from the Syrian border, the invisible line between them and the brutal war raging between the Assad regime and anti-government fighters, including the Islamic State.

The first of the five Czechs in the van was a portly man in his fifties called Jan. He was Ali Fayad's main defence lawyer, and had come to Lebanon on what he said was a fact-finding mission in support of his client's fight against extradition. Sitting alongside him was a young translator called Adam, the only one of the travellers who spoke Arabic.

Also with Jan and Adam were two Czech television journalists. They had come along at Jan's request, to film a video about Fayad to raise awareness about his case back home. Their plan had been to combine this work with other reporting. Earlier that day, they had managed to record sev-eral interviews with refugees from the Syrian conflict. Jan had dangled the prospect of an enticing scoop to justify the trip: if the journalists stayed in Lebanon long enough, there was a chance that one of his new contacts could arrange an exclusive interview with Syria's besieged president.

The fifth Czech man didn't talk much. There was an unsettling air of mystery about him. Jan had told the others only that he was his legal assistant. And then there was the Lebanese driver, Ali Fayad's brother, who was paying the lawyer on behalf of his sibling and had arranged interviews with people in his home village for the camera crew.

That day, Fayad's brother had helped Jan set up a meeting between the two journalists and a man known only as Malem, who they had been told was a representative of the Syrian opposition. The group had brought $5,000 in cash as part of the agreement. It wasn't obvious to Adam, the translator, why a member of the Sunni opposition would want to meet in an area that Shia militants controlled. But no one seemed particularly concerned.

The van pulled up at the location, where Malem was waiting for them. Suddenly, a group of men wearing masks and carrying weapons surrounded the vehicle and demanded that everybody get out. The armed men told the Czechs to hand over their mobile phones, strip naked and change into different clothes. Just before they were all handcuffed, Adam managed to text his girlfriend that he was in trouble. The next thing they saw was darkness. Their captors had put hoods over their heads, then split them into two groups and bundled each into different vehicles before speeding off into the night. Somewhere along the way they stopped, and they were transferred into new vehicles before being driven away again.

When the armed men finally pulled Adam's hood from his head, he didn't know if they were still in Lebanon or not. He found himself in a small, freshly cemented room that was divided by a set of prison bars. One of the masked men walked into the room. Smiling, he said, 'Welcome to Daesh.'

*

Hours later the silver minivan was discovered by Lebanese police abandoned by the side of a road. Inside were the Czechs' passports, wallets and mobile phones, as well as the journalists' camera equipment. The Lebanese authorities alerted the Czech embassy in Beirut. It was too early to tell exactly what had happened, but a kidnapping seemed highly probable. In 2011, a group of Estonian cyclists had been snatched off the road at gunpoint by kidnappers in the Bekaa Valley. (They were eventually released.)

'At this moment we can confirm we are missing five Czech citizens together with one Lebanese citizen,' a Czech Foreign Ministry spokeswoman confirmed shortly after the news broke. 'A huge security operation is going on now in Lebanon. We are of course in close contact with Lebanese security forces and also with the government.' No one had contacted the embassy to claim responsibility, and it wasn't clear if the missing men were even still in Lebanon. Their identities were being kept secret for their own protection.

Almost a week after the kidnapping, an email appeared in the inbox of the Czech embassy, addressed to the President of the Czech Republic. The anonymous message claimed to be from those holding the five Czech citizens. The hostages would be set free, the email said, if the Czech Republic agreed to drop the extradition case against Ali Fayad and release him at once. It didn't appear to matter to the kidnappers that they had snatched the lawyer who was in fact trying to get Fayad released. Fayad was apparently valuable enough for them to take matters into their own hands. And by taking the arms dealer's brother hostage they didn't just have leverage over Prague, but over Fayad too.

Sitting in his cell, Adam hadn't seen sunlight since the day of the kidnapping and still had no idea which country he was in. They had been hooded and moved to new locations several times. The windows in every new cell were sealed shut and blacked out. In some of the places there was a toilet in the room, in others they had to ask to be escorted across the hall and were watched by a man holding a gun as they relieved themselves.

Adam had learned, to his immense relief, that their kidnappers were not actually members of ISIS, Al Nusra or any other militant Jihadist group. The men had simply told the Czechs they were ISIS to terrify them into cooperating. Now Adam could see they were concerned enough about keeping their hostages healthy to give them food, water and clean clothes. The kidnappers had certainly shown they could use violence: one of them fired a gun near one of the captives, and another slapped Adam across the face. But they appeared disciplined – and to be following orders from someone else.

'We want to sort out a problem between your country and ours,' one of them told Adam.

The translator couldn't tell who the kidnappers were working for, but it seemed to him that they were trained military operatives. It also appeared from their accents that they were Lebanese Shias. Some of them would use words like 'we' and 'us' when talking about events in the region that suggested they were connected in some way to Hezbollah.

Malem, the man who had lured them into the trap, asked the other masked men to take the prisoners into a separate room to be interrogated. As the only Arabic speaker among the prisoners, Adam became the translator for every interaction between the Czechs and their captors. At the start, the kidnappers repeatedly asked each of them about what they were doing in Lebanon. But it became apparent that they already knew almost everything about the five men, including the dates they had flown into Beirut, what they did for a living and the names of their wives and girlfriends.

The armed men took the fifth Czech, the quiet man who had come along as the lawyer's legal assistant, in for interrogation. Was he really a lawyer, Malem asked? That was the job the man had written down on his immigration form, filled out in English, at Beirut airport. Malem said he had seen the form. Was the Czech man, he continued, in fact a spy working for Czech intelligence?

Earlier, one of the kidnappers had asked Adam which Czech was 'the spy' – one of the two journalists or the quiet man working for the lawyer? Adam had said he had no idea what they were talking about. Then, during one of the interrogations, the quiet man confessed. Yes, he was an agent with Czech military intelligence, working under cover.

Adam was as stunned as he was confused. He had taken a simple job working as a translator for a lawyer and two journalists. Now he was not only being held captive by masked men in an unknown location, but he had also been pulled into an affair far beyond his comprehension. Why was a member of Czech military intelligence travelling with their party in Lebanon? Had the lawyer known all along that his 'assistant' wasn't who he claimed to be?

It immediately struck Adam that the men in masks were no random bandits. If they already knew about the fifth Czech's true identity, then they had to be connected to a state intelligence agency, or government of some type.

But Malem didn't appear angry about the presence of the Czech spy. Instead, he mocked him for his poor tradecraft for having flown into Lebanon on his own passport. Malem had evidently known this secret long before the kidnapping had taken place. In the email the armed men had sent to the Czech embassy in Beirut addressed to the Czech President, they had not only demanded the release of Ali Fayad. They had also revealed that they knew the fifth Czech's true identity and his exact job title.

When the prisoners were given food and water, one of the masked men began to talk with Adam. A couple of years earlier, two Turkish pilots had been kidnapped by gunmen in Beirut as part of a plot to pressure Ankara into negotiating the release of nine Lebanese Shia pilgrims who had been abducted by rebels in Syria. Hannibal Gaddafi, one of the sons of the deposed Libyan dictator Colonel Muammar Gaddafi, had also been kidnapped in Lebanon by armed men, who demanded information about the mysterious disappearance of a famous Shia cleric in Libya in the late 1970s. One of the captors hinted to Adam that his team had been behind those operations, but the translator couldn't discern if he was telling the truth. Thinking he had built up a good rapport with his captor, Adam asked if he could be taken to the roof to look outside for a moment. The man said no.

As the days went on, Malem's interrogations increasingly turned to the issue that clearly mattered to him the most: Ali Fayad never setting foot in an American courtroom.

The hostages were surprised by how well informed their kidnappers were about events in the Czech Republic. They asked the captives about different court decisions relating to Fayad, and seemed to know all of the dates for his extradition hearings. The kidnappers had made it perfectly clear to the Czech government what they, or whoever they were working for, really wanted. They didn't want money. They wanted Ali Fayad. He was to be released immediately, and the US extradition had to be dropped. Otherwise none of the five prisoners would see sunlight again.

*

Back in the Czech Republic, Ali Fayad had started to open up to the police about how he had come to be caught by Jack Kelly in a Prague hotel room offering to sell surface-to-air missiles to men posing as Colombian paramilitaries.

Previously, Fayad's legal team had argued that their client had been a victim of an unlawful sting and should be released. In response, the US Department of Justice told the court that the DEA operation to arrest Fayad had not involved entrapment, which was illegal under Czech law, because the Lebanese arms dealer and his accomplices had been planning their crimes long before the sting took place.

Fayad now had a different explanation. He said that he had agreed to meet the DEA's undercover informants not because he wanted to commit a crime, but because he had been trying to solve one. He had come to Prague, he claimed, to gather intelligence on the suspicious activities of the men who wanted to buy weapons from him. This was because, in addition to his work as an international arms dealer and advisor to the deposed president of Ukraine, he had an entirely different job – one that until then had been a closely guarded secret. Fayad told them he was an undercover agent working for Lebanese military intelligence.

16

To Do the Impossible

Milan, Early 2015

Salvatore paused in front of the palm trees facing the arched steel entrance of Calabria's main airport, Lamezia Terme. He was dressed entirely in black: a black zip-up jacket, black jeans and black trainers, and a black cap pulled so far over his face that the rough, greying stubble on his chin looked like snow on a mountain peak.

It was first thing on a Monday morning. All around him were commuters dragging wheelie bags, catching the early flight back to the north of Italy after a weekend with their families. Salvatore also had a black wheelie bag, and a black carry-on case.

He got in line to board the Ryanair flight to Bergamo. Once there, he would be picked up by Antonio and driven to Milan, where they would collect Jota Jota, who was arriving from Colombia that evening. Everything now depended on that meeting going to plan.

Too much time had already been wasted with the Colonel. Unfortunately, Salvatore knew that he and Antonio, for now at least, had to continue to do business with him. In the days running up to Jota's arrival, the Colonel, now back in Colombia, had been organising the logistics of his boss's visit to Europe. But, as with seemingly everything involving the Colonel, there was a problem.

The Italians, as agreed, had purchased Jota Jota's plane ticket and Antonio had emailed the flight itinerary to the Colonel. Jota would catch an Avianca flight leaving Medellín at 10 a.m. on Saturday, arriving in Bogotá an hour later. His next flight would depart from the Colombian capital for Madrid on the same afternoon. He would arrive at Madrid Barajas the following morning and then catch his connecting flight to Milan, where Antonio would be waiting at the airport to collect him with Salvatore.

Then came the bad news. On the day of Jota's flight to Europe the Colonel called Antonio: 'Jota Jota is still in Bogotá.' The airline, the Colonel told him, would not let Jota leave without a return flight booked. These were the standard rules for his visa. The Colonel told Antonio that he would need him to book a new ticket. Antonio was furious. Jota had to be in Milan by Tuesday at the very latest to meet with Salvatore. If he was late, then the deal was dead.

'No, Colonel, you listen to me,' Antonio shouted down the phone. 'Don't put me in this situation! If I have to go and tell them to buy another ticket, then they will tell me to drop the whole thing. Don't put me in this situation!'

The Colonel, Antonio reminded him, had already almost destroyed the whole deal because of his behaviour in Italy.

'They did not want anything more to do with you, and you know it. But I insisted because I know you . . . I insisted . . .

Don't make me look like shit now. Make sure that Jota Jota is here on Monday!'

The Colonel, realising the gravity of the situation, informed Antonio that he would attempt to fix the problem. Shortly afterwards he called back.

'Don't worry!' he said. 'I already have the lady from the travel agency solving the ticket problem. Tomorrow, I will put Jota on the plane in Bogotá, then he will get to Madrid and by Tuesday he will be in Milan.'

Antonio reminded him of their terms. If Jota Jota did not get there in time, then the whole thing was over. 'If he doesn't come by Tuesday, they will have smashed everything, and that would be a pity. Because I'm working hard here, you understand? Colonel, get him here by Tuesday, Tuesday max. Salvatore is arriving today, you understand?'

The Colonel tried to reassure him again. 'You are working hard, I am working hard.' But reassurances from the Colonel were never particularly reassuring. And there was a last detail the Colonel needed to double check.

'Listen, Antonio. Only Salvatore will be there, right? No Pepe—'

'Yes, that will be it. No Pepe. But you understand that Salvatore is arriving in Milan because he knows that tomorrow Jota Jota will be there to organise everything? You understand, Colonel? We have to do the impossible to get him here.'

That evening, Jota Jota boarded his flight to Madrid. He was on his way.

Antonio knew something was wrong as he drove his wife's silver Volkswagen Golf down the motorway from Milan to Bergamo's Orio al Serio airport to pick up Salvatore. It had been gnawing at him for the whole journey. There was a small light inside the dashboard, a dull red glow that he had never noticed before.

Antonio already knew that at any moment they could be being watched. And he was sufficiently paranoid to know that, if the police were not trying to record them on his phone, then they could easily have put a listening device inside the car. As soon as Salvatore got into the passenger seat at the airport, Antonio explained his concern.

'Look, look at this,' he said, pointing at the dashboard. 'It has been here since this morning. God damn it, it's connected!'

Salvatore began to rage. If Antonio was correct, then everything they said could be being recorded. If they removed the device, then whoever had put it there would know they had discovered the surveillance. If they left it, they could be tracked.

It was hard to tell. The police were certainly capable of putting a bug in the car. But it was Antonio's wife's car. Maybe it was nothing. And even if there was a tracker, it might not be active. Antonio tried to calm Salvatore, telling him the light could simply be an inactive device from an old investigation.

'We have to take the entire dashboard apart, to see where the wires are connected,' Salvatore said. 'Otherwise, what are we doing? What are we doing? Do you understand, asshole?'

They bombed down the motorway searching for a place to stop. Eventually they pulled off into a shopping centre. There, in an empty car park, the two men got to work ripping apart the dashboard panel. As soon as it came away they could see there was some kind of electronic device inside. They tore it out, and the dim light Antonio had spotted inside the grille of the dashboard went dead.

'What the fuck is this?' Salvatore said as they inspected the mess of cables. 'A microphone? ... Is it a power supply?'

Antonio didn't know. 'An antenna? A recorder?'

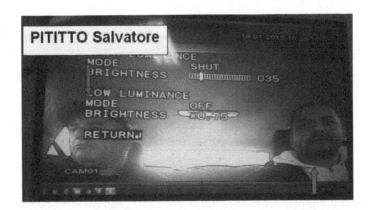

They weren't taking any chances. They dumped the device in a bin and drove on. In other circumstances the sensible decision would have been to abandon the car and abort the meeting with Jota Jota. But they had spent weeks arranging for him to travel thousands of miles to see them. If they failed to pick him up, everything they had been working towards would be destroyed. It was too late to go back now.

They pulled up in the car park at Milan Linate airport. Antonio took out some pieces of paper, copies of Jota Jota's travel itinerary and identity documents that had been emailed over by the Colonel. Salvatore inspected them.

'This is him,' Antonio explained. 'He doesn't speak any Italian.'

Salvatore could see the passport Jota Jota was travelling on was in the name of Jaime Eduardo Cano Sucerquia. The passport photo was of a dark, handsome Colombian, forty-eight years old. Maybe it was his real identity document, maybe it wasn't.

An hour later, Jota Jota emerged from the arrivals gate. He was dressed in a cream zip-up sports coat, white trousers and brown loafers; he was pulling a large black suitcase on wheels. Antonio took him to the car park, where Salvatore was waiting. Salvatore politely helped the Colombian put his luggage in the back of the car, and Antonio walked away for a moment. Unable to communicate, Salvatore and Jota Jota briefly stood together in silence, their hands in their coat pockets. Then Antonio returned, pulled out two burner phones and gave one each to Jota and Salvatore. The three men got into the car and drove away.

It was a long drive back to Calabria. Salvatore rang Antonella and Oksana to let them know he was on his way home. He had a multi-million-euro drug shipment to negotiate, and Jota Jota was only going to be in Italy for a few days. Salvatore knew it was critical that they cover as much ground as possible.

The discussions were to take place at a small hotel not far from Mileto, owned by a family of small-time crooks whose youngest son spoke Spanish and could translate for Salvatore's Colombian guest. Salvatore would also spend the next few days meeting with representatives of Filippo Fiarè and his other investors to update them on the deal.

The discussions went more smoothly than anyone could have expected: it was the first episode in months that gave confidence to both sides that the deal might actually come together. Jota Jota explained the logistics of the transaction. His organisation, Jota reminded the Italians, had eight tonnes of cocaine stored in the banana plantation near Turbo. Out of that, 1.5 tonnes were available to ship into Europe in the near future.

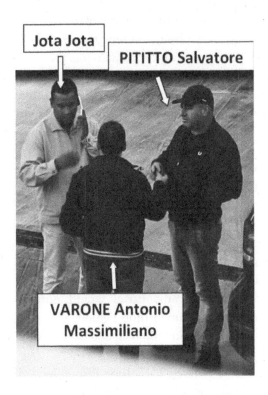

Jota Jota

PITITTO Salvatore

VARONE Antonio Massimiliano

To move forward, both sides would have to agree on certain unbendable terms. Jota told the Italians that he worked only with bananas. If they were going to send the drugs from Turbo to Italy, then they would have to be hidden inside a banana shipment. Secondly, both sides agreed that the first shipment from Turbo to Italy would be a smaller quantity – four hundred kilograms – to confirm the route was secure. If that worked, then the rest of the drugs would be shipped out over the next few months.

The Calabrians would put up a down payment for 25 per cent of the initial shipment, with the rest of the drugs staying in possession of the cartel, to be sold directly by their people in Europe.

Also, the Colonel was to be cut out of the deal. The Italians were still angry with him, and now that they had opened a direct channel of communication with Jota they didn't want – or need – to deal with him ever again. Jota Jota returned to Colombia. Over the next few weeks, he and Antonio continued to work out the finer details of the transaction over email.

'The Colonel has nothing to do with this any more,' Jota wrote to Antonio.

'Jota, don't worry, it's just you and us,' Antonio replied. 'All the other people who were there before I won't talk with them any more. I won't answer the phone to them. I don't want to deal with anyone else, just you.' There was still a significant amount of work to do, such as arranging for payment and choosing which Italian port the drugs would be delivered to. But, finally, they had a deal.

Jota explained that the cartel would now dispatch a new representative, named Jhon Peludo, to work with the Calabrians to oversee the shipment and liaise with Colombia.

A month later, in March 2015, Jhon Peludo landed at Milan Malpensa airport on a flight via Frankfurt, wearing a white baseball cap, blue jeans and black gloves. Antonio picked him up and handed a burner phone to the Colombian to call Jota.

Jhon was a tubby man with a round, soft-featured face that gave him the appearance of an overgrown teddy bear. His cuddly exterior was, however, deceptive. He was one of Jota's top trouble-shooters and had been dispatched to Europe to help soothe the ill will lingering from the episode with the Colonel. 'I am not a child, I am a person of experience,' Jhon told a colleague back in Colombia over the phone some days after he had arrived in Italy.

To Jhon, the Italians did indeed appear finally ready to move. But it was important for the cartel bosses to stay calm.

'I cannot rush these people,' he reported. 'I have to let them organise their things, I can't be on their backs.'

The Colonel, he said, had caused an even bigger mess than the cartel had first realised. Whatever the Colonel had said to Antonella had clearly not been forgotten by the Italians. 'I don't know what happened to him here, but he said things he shouldn't have been talking about and now I am having to reorganise things . . . I don't know why he made promises he can't keep. It makes people angry.'

Some days later, Jota checked in with Jhon again, to see how the Italians were treating him. Jota also wanted to know if Salvatore had finally told him what to do about Osvaldo. Was the ex-guarantee to be set free, or taken to the mountains to be murdered?

Osvaldo, still stuck in Colombia, wouldn't have known it but by now the Italians had decided that getting rid of him wasn't worth the hassle. 'I asked Antonio, "Do you want us to take care of him?" and he said, "No, no. I don't want anything like that. It is best to leave that man,"' Jhon told Jota. Osvaldo would be allowed to live.

Meanwhile the stress from his run-in with the Colonel had taken its toll on Pepe, the spurned broker. He had been rushed to hospital with heart problems, ending his hopes of getting revenge on Salvatore for cutting him and Osvaldo out of the deal.

Now, with Jhon in Italy, Salvatore knew almost everything was in place for the Colombians to send the first batch of cocaine to Europe. All that remained was for him to deliver the cash.

17

A Home Run

Paris, Spring 2015

Jack Kelly and his colleagues were working around the clock to analyse the phone data that had been coming in from the infiltration operation the DEA was running against Alex, the money launderer working out of Medellín.

Jack now knew that to move the investigation forward the DEA needed to pass the intelligence they had to the French police. But he also knew that the first tip had to be rock solid. If it turned out to be a dud, the DEA would lose credibility and the investigation risked grinding to a halt. It was like the opening move in a game of chess. If they made a mistake, it would hinder every further move they made.

Building on the information coming in from Colombia, Jack knew that a man, known only as Samir, had been dispatched to collect several million euros in cash from a contact he would meet in a small Algerian restaurant called the Oasis in Montreuil, an eastern suburb of Paris. The cash belonged to Colombian drug traffickers who had been shipping containers of cocaine to Mexico and Europe.

Jack called the DEA's country attaché in the US embassy in Paris and passed over the information. The attaché contacted France's specialist anti-money laundering unit, the Office central pour la répression de la grande délinquance financière, or OCRGDF. The attaché had a good relationship with a police captain at the OCRGDF called Quentin Mugg, whom Jack had first met during a briefing he had given to European police. Jack had been impressed by Mugg, a sharp young chain-smoking investigator who had previously worked in domestic intelligence before focusing on complex money-laundering cases.

Armed with the tip, Captain Mugg and the OCRGDF team set up a surveillance group to watch Samir pick up the money. The French police quietly waited, and at 5.20 p.m. he walked into the restaurant. Mugg now faced a difficult decision: should they arrest Samir right after he had collected the cash, or should they instead let him leave and covertly monitor him to gather more evidence?

Mugg decided it was better to wait – a choice that immediately paid off. After Samir made the pick-up, Mugg and the French police were able to listen in as he called a number in Lebanon. Samir told his contact in Beirut that he had successfully received the '110' in Paris, but that '80' of what he had collected was 'garbage' – meaning it was made up of smaller-denomination bank notes. The next day Samir drove the cash he had collected to Monaco.

As they gathered more information about Samir, they discovered that he was a Lebanese luxury car dealer in his late thirties, born in Beirut but living in Düsseldorf, and called Hassan Tarabolsi. Tarabolsi's phone geolocation data showed he frequently drove around Europe, stopping in locations for only a short amount of time – the clear implication was that he was making regular money pick-ups across the continent.

Mugg's team began to trace the numbers that Tarabolsi had called in the Middle East following the collection at the Oasis restaurant. They noticed that one of these numbers matched with a phone line belonging to a Lebanese businessman called Mohamad Nourredine. Nourredine, they learned, worked out of an office in Beirut. As Mugg continued the preliminary investigation, he discovered that one of Nourredine's Lebanese phone numbers had appeared in the records of a man who had been stopped by Dutch police several months earlier with half a million euros of suspected drug money in a black Adidas sports bag hidden behind the driver's seat of his Toyota. Geolocation data from Nourredine's phones showed that he had recently travelled to France, flying into Charles de Gaulle airport and staying near the Champs-Élysées for a few days before leaving for Rome.

The French police now had the evidence they needed to open a formal investigation. Mugg rushed to the Ministry of Justice to open the case. He needed a codename, and the only one he could think of was Cedar, a reference to the tree on the national flag of Lebanon.

A few days later, Jack got a call from the DEA attaché at the American embassy in Paris. 'Jack,' he said, 'I think this is going to be a home run.'

With the French wiretaps fully up and running, Mugg's team quickly uncovered more members of the network of drug money couriers being coordinated by Mohamad Nourredine in Beirut. Couriers were being dispatched across Europe to meet with organised criminals who had purchased cocaine shipments from Colombia, picking up large amounts of cash owed to the cartels. After the couriers collected the money, they delivered it to other people in their network, who would then transport it to Beirut, where it was laundered back to Latin America. The operation appeared to be moving tens of millions of euros a month from Europe, via the Middle East, back to Colombia.

As they continued to listen to the network's calls, the French police learned that the group was careful to speak in codes, and to change numbers frequently. Nourredine, when talking to Tarabolsi, would rarely mention specific amounts. Instead, he would discuss the cars that he needed picked up or delivered. A 'Mercedes 250' would mean €250,000, an 'Audi 200' was €200,000 and a 'BMW 430' meant a collection worth €430,000. If the couriers were going to pick up a million euros, they would simply refer to 'a truck'. And if the denominations of the bank notes involved in a pick-up were small, then they would mention that the car had 'small seats', or 'a 50 shoe size', meaning fifty-euro notes. If the couriers needed to travel to the Netherlands, they were visiting 'the oven'. For Belgium, it was 'the mill'.

The investigators learned that Tarabolsi, the top money courier, was Nourredine's cousin, and had received funding from him to set up a transportation company in Germany. Tarabolsi himself would relay instructions coming from Beirut to other couriers, who would drive to locations in Italy and Spain to make pick-ups and return with the money hidden in secret compartments in their vehicles. One collector, known as Jimmy, lived in Italy and would pick up money from Naples, before driving it over fifteen hundred kilometres to the car garage Tarabolsi ran in Düsseldorf.

Jimmy would be given specific instructions to avoid being caught. Tarabolsi would tell him to remove the screwdriver from his car, so he didn't give an easy tip-off that he'd hidden money in one of the panels. He also reminded him to change his mobile phone number regularly to avoid being intercepted. 'This is what you are going to do,' the French police listened to Tarabolsi telling his junior colleague. 'First thing tomorrow ... you are going to get a new one.'

The network employed various techniques to transport the cash to Beirut. One of these was purchasing luxury cars with the money, including Porsches and Range Rovers, which were shipped from Europe to Lebanon or Africa, where they were sold for cash. Another was to buy expensive watches, such as Rolexes or Patek Philippes. The group had bought €14 million of watches from a single store in Münster in little over a year. Some of the watches were taken by boat to Lebanon, and some were brought into Beirut airport by couriers, who were waved through by customs and airport intelligence.

It had taken only a few weeks for the investigation in France to start building an intricate picture of the money-laundering network operating across Europe. But Jack Kelly sensed that it went further. The DEA had been busy finding out as much as they could about Mohamad Nourredine.

Wiretaps showed that he was in almost daily phone contact with another Lebanese businessman called Adham Hussein Tabaja. Jack was stunned when he learned this. Tabaja was one of the top targets on the DEA's list of Hezbollah super facilitators. US intelligence agencies had identified Tabaja as one of the organisation's most important financiers, reporting to the highest level of its leadership and its Islamic Jihad covert operations unit. Tabaja, they knew, was working alongside operatives under the control of the Iranian commander Qasem Soleimani, to smuggle large sums of money through the Middle East to fund Hezbollah's involvement in the Syrian civil war.

The DEA could now connect Nourredine, a money launderer moving cocaine proceeds around the world for European mafias and Latin American cartels, with the weapons flooding into Syria. But there was more. Nourredine wasn't only in regular contact with Tabaja. He was also communicating with Mohamed Badreddine – the brother of Mustafa Badreddine, the man leading Hezbollah's fight to protect Assad.

The web that Jack Kelly was revealing appeared to connect some of the planet's most nefarious individuals – ruthless, dedicated criminals working in South America and Europe – and a conflict in the Middle East that was rippling out around the world. Alone, these were men pursuing disparate criminal enterprises. Together, Jack could now see, they had combined into a force far too powerful for any of them to control.

18

The Eternal City

Rome, April 2015

Surely the last thing on Salvatore Pititto's mind, as he hurtled towards Rome with the cash to pay for his drug deal hidden in the boot of his car, was the civil war in Syria.

As he joined the motorway, he took out his phone and killed it. Power off. Battery removed. He knew the police could be watching. He didn't know exactly how, but he knew. Not long ago, he and Antonio had discovered the dull red glow under the grille of the dashboard of their car in Milan. Maybe they had installed spyware on his phone. He was paranoid, but people in Salvatore's line of work could never be too paranoid.

Perhaps in that moment, switching off his phone as he barrelled ever closer to the Italian capital, he felt a sense of control. If the police were tracking him – his phone a blinking dot moving across a map on some operations room screen – the signal had just gone dead.

Salvatore didn't know the name of the man he was meeting at five o'clock. He didn't even know where he was meant to meet him. But he knew exactly what he was going to Rome to do. It had taken months to get to this point. Hundreds of hours of planning and stress.

At exactly the same moment, Jhon Peludo, the man the cartel had sent to Italy to oversee the money drop, was on a train heading for Rome Termini station. Somewhere around Salerno, as Jhon's train pulled out of a tunnel, his burner phone buzzed with a message from an unknown number.

'Ciao. This is Castro. This is my number.' Jhon Peludo punched in a two-letter response – 'OK' – and pressed send.

The plan had always been for Jhon to travel to Rome by train, and Salvatore by car. It was one thing to be caught with a case of unexplained cash. It was another to be caught with the money and a drug trafficker working for the Clan del Golfo.

Both would have known the risks. Salvatore had spent months putting this deal together, raising investment from the ruthless Fiarès. If the money never arrived, he knew there would be consequences. It didn't matter who he was meeting that afternoon; all that mattered was that the money was delivered safely to Latin America. The instructions from Medellín were clear. Be in Rome for five o'clock. Wait for the message with the address. Drop the cash. Leave.

Jhon had been in constant contact with his bosses back in Colombia, feeling out the Italians, making sure they were still trustworthy. That was why the cartel had sent him to Europe, he had explained to Salvatore's gang some days before they set off for Rome. Because he had the ability to 'look inside people'.

Just before the Colombian's train pulled in to the station, Castro sent him another text message: 'Via Castro Pretorio, number 28.'

Salvatore parked near Termini station. He met Jhon and they walked with the bag towards the address. Rome was crumbling. The streets around the station were lined with run-down hotels and money transfer shops. This wasn't Salvatore's Italy. The city had money, political power, history. Yet it was sunken. Trashed like a squat.

They arrived at an apartment building caked with pollution and graffiti, and stepped through the arched oak doors at the front. Upstairs, behind one of the doors to dozens of flats, Castro was waiting.

Far away there was a civil war raging in Syria. Hundreds of thousands were fleeing the country to try to find safety in Europe. That same week more than six hundred people, many of them Syrians, drowned off the Italian coast when a boat coming from Libya capsized. It was estimated to be the largest number of refugees ever to die in the Mediterranean in a single incident.

Salvatore and Jhon almost certainly weren't following what was happening in Syria. But Castro was. The man who accepted Salvatore's money in Rome was a Lebanese used-car dealer living in the north of Italy. On his Facebook page he had posted images of Hezbollah fighters who had died in what he called the 'holy defence' of Syria – men under the command of Mustafa Badreddine. 'We will not forget you,' Castro wrote of the men he hailed as martyrs.

Two days after collecting the money, he left Italy on a flight to Beirut.

19

'Mustafa Badreddine is Present'

Syria, Mid-2015

Mustafa was somewhere in Syria, surveying the smoking battlefields of a civil war that appeared to be moving against him. In the Qalamoun Mountains, close to the Lebanese border, Hezbollah fighters manned heavy machine gun positions, yellow flags emblazoned with the face of their commander's dead cousin flying above them.

Mustafa was an old man now, a survivor who had somehow managed to stay alive and evade capture for over three decades. The task that lay ahead of him in Syria was going to be the most difficult and important mission of his career. By the middle of 2015, Assad's control over the country had fallen to a fifth of its territory; rebels were rapidly advancing to the coast, the heartland of the dictator's Alawite sect.

In March, the Syrian regime had suffered one of its biggest defeats since the conflict began: it was humiliatingly routed from the north-western Idlib Province. By July a coalition of jihadist groups including al-Nusra Front, al-Qaeda's affiliate in Syria, launched an assault on the government-controlled parts of Aleppo, the second city.

The fighting had rapidly morphed from a popular uprising into a full-scale proxy war, one that threatened to turn the regional balance of power against Iran and Hezbollah. Mustafa's fighters, alongside Iranian troops under the control of Imad's old friend Qasem Soleimani, had won several important battles. But they had also lost many men. And if the regime continued to lose territory at this rate, then it was at risk of losing the entire war.

Four years earlier, the Arab Spring, the wave of anti-authoritarian protests that had broken out across the Middle East and North Africa, had arrived in Syria. It took little time for the regime to crack down: Assad's soldiers fired on crowds that included women and children, and arrested thousands. Syria's notorious security agencies committed unspeakable atrocities against those they rounded up. In May 2011, the mutilated body of Hamza Ali Al-Khateeb, a thirteen-year-old boy who had joined protests against the regime, was returned to his parents. He had been burned, shot and castrated. A video released by his family of their murdered son's remains triggered more protests.

As images of the horrific violence circulated around the world, the United States and European leaders called for Assad to resign. 'For the sake of the Syrian people,' President Barack Obama said in August 2011, 'the time has come for President Assad to step aside.' Turkey and Qatar, once allies of Syria, were disgusted enough to demand the Syrian dictator went.

Assad did not listen; instead he unleashed more indiscriminate violence. A group of defectors from the armed forces formed the Free Syrian Army, its leaders based out of a camp across the border in Turkey. In November 2011, rebels fired shoulder-mounted rockets and machine guns at a Syrian Air Force Intelligence base in Damascus, striking at the heart of the regime's security apparatus for the first time since the protests began. Soon the army defectors were fighting forces loyal to the regime in several large cities across the country.

Back in Lebanon, Hassan Nasrallah watched the events unfolding across the border with unease. The crisis enveloping the Assad regime presented a grave threat to the long-standing 'Axis of Resistance' alliance between Hezbollah, Iran and Damascus. Syria had long been a vital ally for Hezbollah, allowing a critical supply route for weapons and other aid from its main patron, Iran, to run through the country. Should the regime fall, Nasrallah knew his group risked being isolated.

US intelligence learned that by late 2011, Nasrallah had begun to hold weekly strategic coordination meetings with Bashar al-Assad. The man who accompanied him to Damascus for these meetings was his top military commander, Mustafa Badreddine. By the start of 2012, Mustafa had been put in charge of commanding and coordinating a Hezbollah military operation in Syria.

His work began in secret. While Nasrallah had voiced support for the Assad regime, Hezbollah had kept quiet about whether its forces were fighting on the regime's behalf. Rumours began to circulate that members of Hezbollah's elite Unit 910, previously led and shaped by Imad, had been dispatched to assist the Syrian regime in putting down protests. Soon obituaries of Hezbollah fighters under Mustafa's command appeared in Lebanese newspapers, with no explanation of the circumstances or location of their deaths. Over the summer of 2012, fresh graves for 'martyrs' began to be dug in Lebanon. Hezbollah finally acknowledged in October of that year that one of its senior commanders had died, but said only that he had been killed 'performing his jihadist duty', without saying where he had fallen.

By May 2013 the secret was out. The Syrian opposition announced that they had discovered Mustafa Badreddine was in Syria. He was preparing an offensive by Hezbollah elite fighters, trained by Iran in urban warfare tactics, to clear the border town of al Qusayr of anti-Assad rebels. The Free Syrian Army issued a statement: 'It has been confirmed that Mustafa Badreddine is present on Qusayr's front where he is leading Hezbollah's operations.' Five days later, Hassan Nasrallah gave a speech marking the anniversary of Israel's withdrawal from southern Lebanon. For the first time, he openly acknowledged that Hezbollah was fighting in Syria. 'Syria is the resistance's main supporter,' he said. 'We believe our actions to be a defence of Lebanon, Palestine and Syria.'

Nasrallah would later say he never wanted Mustafa to go to Syria, judging him too important an operative to risk on the ground – but Mustafa insisted on crossing the border, telling him, 'I can't run a field [of] such importance and [that can have] such a critical impact and challenge to Lebanon from here.'

Al Qusayr was a town of thirty thousand people in a country of more than twenty million, but its fate had the potential to alter the direction of the civil war. Located in Syria's Homs District, it was a traditional transit point for goods travelling across the border into Lebanon, making it an important logistical hub for rebels to smuggle weapons and fighters. It also formed a critical part of the front in the battle for Homs, Syria's third-largest city, through which runs the highway that connects Damascus to the north of the country, and which provides access to the country's Mediterranean ports.

Syrian government forces had entered al Qusayr in August 2011 to crush early protests, and began to cut telephone lines, electricity and water supplies. As refugees from the town fled across the border into Lebanon, Assad's troops employed counterinsurgency tactics, throwing up military checkpoints, cutting off the town from access to the Homs–Damascus highway to stop rebel fighters and arms coming in, and using snipers and indiscriminate fire against civilians. But still the protests continued.

In early 2012, the United Nations had attempted to negotiate a ceasefire and proposed a six-point peace plan. But neither side halted the fighting across much of the country, including in al Qusayr. Regime troops continued to defect to the rebels. Former members of the elite Syrian 77th Brigade fought fiercely, using small arms, hit-and-run tactics and raids to attack army positions. Loyalist forces fought back, shelling rebel strongholds in and around the town. As their control over al Qusayr loosened, they retreated into the surrounding area and began to drop improvised barrel bombs containing explosives and scrap metal from helicopters, killing and wounding civilians with burns and shrapnel. By the end of 2012 the situation had reached an impasse: neither the rebels nor the regime forces were able to take full control of the town.

Several months later, Mustafa devised an operation to clear al Qusayr of the anti-Assad forces for good. The rebels had heavily defended the town in anticipation of a regime onslaught, excavating tunnels, mining roads and laying boobytraps in buildings. In April 2013, Hezbollah fighters attacked smaller villages to the south of the town, with Syrian armed forces taking the areas to its north. By mid-May, just before the rebels announced to the world that Mustafa was in the country, most of al Qusayr had been surrounded.

Hezbollah's veteran fighters had been trained to wage war in the rural mountainous areas of southern Lebanon, not in urban environments. But following the 2006 war with Israel, its elite fighters had undergone training in urban warfare in both Iran and Lebanon.

The assault proper began with the town coming under heavy bombardment from regime mortars, artillery and airstrikes in the early hours, followed by Hezbollah fighters entering from their positions to the south. Some reports said that 1,700 Hezbollah fighters, many veterans of its special forces units, had amassed in al Qusayr. As they entered they broke into small tactical groups, moving from building to building as they retook the town street by street. During fierce fighting Hezbollah took heavy casualties, but the rebel fighters were eventually pinned into a small area in the north of al Qusayr, their food and ammunition supplies dwindling.

In early June, seventeen weeks after the assault began, the Syrian military and Hezbollah troops launched a final attack on the last enclave of the town still held by the rebels – and were victorious. The battle was over. Mustafa's men had won. Retaking al Qusayr was a statement of intent, choking off supplies to other rebel-held areas and dealing a blow to their morale. The Americans were taken by surprise by the scale and impact of Hezbollah's entrance into the Syrian civil war. Some had believed the Assad regime was close to collapse. Instead, Hezbollah had tilted the momentum back in the regime's favour.

But since that early victory for Mustafa the conflict had ground into a bloody stalemate. Now, with the loss of Idlib in 2015, it appeared that the regime was at greater risk than at any time since the civil war had begun. The rebels were being aided by arms and money sent by foreign powers including the United States, Turkey and Qatar. A covert CIA-backed programme called Timber Sycamore had been pumping hundreds of millions of dollars into training and supplying weapons to rebels operating out of a base in Jordan.

In Damascus, there were signs that all was not well in the house of Assad. Soon after the loss of Idlib, Rustom Ghazaleh, the head of Syrian political intelligence in Lebanon at the time of the Hariri assassination, was reported to have been beaten to death by men loyal to a rival Syrian spy boss. Rafic Hariri's son Saad claimed that Ghazaleh had called him up before his death, saying he wanted to appear on Lebanese television to 'announce something we don't know'. Some speculated that he had been caught planning to defect. Or perhaps he had been intending to reveal evidence that the Assad regime had ordered the car bomb that killed Hariri, which Mustafa had orchestrated a decade before.

The Syrian dictator and his allies knew they were running out of time. In July 2015, Qasem Soleimani secretly flew to Moscow to meet with Russian officials. If Bashar al-Assad was going to survive, then the efforts of Mustafa and his men weren't going to be enough. He needed more firepower, and he needed it fast. And far from the battlefields of Syria, on the streets of Europe, there were men who were working hard to ensure it would arrive.

20

TG NIKE

Livorno, August 2015

Sixteen days. Salvatore knew he had sixteen days from when the container ship left Colombia until it arrived in Italy.

Four months after he had met Castro in Rome to hand over the money, the cocaine was finally on its way. On a Sunday evening, *TG NIKE*, a 210-metre South Korean-built vessel flying a Liberian flag, left the port of Turbo and set sail across the Atlantic. Millions of euros were on the line. But so was Salvatore's future, and possibly his life. Everything now depended on that ship reaching Europe.

TG NIKE would stop first at Livorno, where some of its containers would be dropped, before continuing on to Genoa. The plan was for Salvatore's men to break into the Italian port in the middle of the night and pull off the packages before any inspection could take place.

As Salvatore glanced over the shipping schedule Jota Jota

had emailed him, he realised the complexity of the task ahead. There would be thousands of metal containers on that ship. But just one contained his bananas. He knew the port inspectors often conducted random searches. They would pick one or two containers to rifle through. Where was his positioned? At the front? In the middle? It was all in Jota Jota's hands.

At least Salvatore knew that he was working with professionals. Before *TG NIKE* departed from Turbo, Jota Jota had told the Italians in intricate detail exactly how the cocaine was going to be shipped. Yes, if they were unlucky their container could be picked out by the inspectors. But the odds were greater than a thousand to one. And even so, Jota knew how to package the cocaine to avoid it being detected.

The companies the cartel worked with in Turbo dealt only in bananas. So Salvatore's crate would have hundreds of boxes of bananas inside. Each of those boxes would be marked with a number. And twenty of those numbers would identify the boxes in which Jota had hidden the drugs.

Each of the packages inside those twenty boxes would be covered in aluminium foil that would hide it from X-ray scanners. And on top of those packages would be lots of real bananas. Any inspector would have to rummage to the bottom of the twenty boxes to discover Salvatore's packages. And even then, the foil Jota Jota had used to cover the cocaine had coloured images of life-size bananas printed on it. A quick glance would suggest that the packages were only more bananas.

Another crucial element, Jota had explained, was the weight. Port inspectors would sometimes decide to weigh each box as a quick way of establishing if contraband could be hidden inside. Each carton containing the drugs had to weigh twenty-three kilograms – exactly the same as the banana boxes.

Still, there was one final security protocol that Jota insisted on. Only he would know the numbers of the container and boxes that held the drugs. A few days ahead of the ship docking in Europe, Jota Jota would travel personally to Italy to share that critical piece of information with Salvatore's men. Even if their communications were being intercepted, it would be impossible for the police to know which container the drugs were in until the last moment.

TG NIKE was now somewhere in the Atlantic, slowly sailing towards Livorno. Salvatore could do nothing apart from wait. Sixteen days.

Salvatore was panicking. It was Saturday, just a few days until *TG NIKE* was scheduled to make port, and they still had no news of when Jota Jota was due to arrive in Italy to hand over the final details about the shipment.

They were in Oksana's flat. Salvatore and Antonio were grilling Jhon Peludo about when his boss was going to arrive.

'Listen, Jhon, you need to know as much as possible, you have to be sure about all the details,' Antonio pleaded.

'I have asked him,' Jhon said. 'Jota is saying he will arrive in Rome, he is arriving tomorrow.'

'Yes, but we don't know which airport in Rome!' Salvatore said.

'In Rome there are two airports, Jhon,' Antonio added.

'He will be coming to the international one,' Jhon replied innocently.

'Both are international!'

'Look,' Jhon said, 'if he doesn't get here by Monday—'

'No!' Salvatore interrupted. 'We don't need him to come on Monday! We need him to arrive on Sunday, tomorrow!

On Monday morning, at 5 a.m., we need to see our people, who will then start their work, you understand? The team needs to know everything by 6 a.m. Monday morning.'

Jhon was trying to keep the Italians calm. Jota had been delayed because of his visa. They had needed to pay €3,000 for Jota to get the correct papers to travel. Moving the money around to pay for the visa had taken longer than they had expected.

'You know what the problem has been—'

'Yes, three thousand euros, I know!' Salvatore said. 'For three thousand euros, we can't lose €1.2 million!'

Nothing Jhon said was reassuring him. If Jota didn't arrive with the information, they would miss the shipment. As soon as *TG NIKE* docked in Livorno, his men would only have a small window of time to get into the port area, identify the right container and pull out the correct boxes.

'It is one day before he has to be here, and we still don't know!' said Salvatore. 'The ship will arrive in three days, but we don't know what we have to do when it gets here. And we don't know anything about Jota. We don't know if it is true he has put the stuff on the ship, or if he is even coming!'

Salvatore paused for a moment, then continued his tirade:

'I don't believe it any more! It's not possible that he wants to lose this shipment! It's not possible, Jhon! There are one thousand containers on that boat, and I still don't know which one is ours ...'

Salvatore was reaching boiling point. This wasn't just about the shipment. Salvatore had taken money from dangerous people, people who he knew wouldn't hesitate to kill him if the operation went wrong.

'If this job doesn't go well,' Salvatore told Jhon, 'I will be financially destroyed. I could be shot.'

Several hours later, Jhon received the news: Jota was getting on a flight from Colombia.

'He is leaving at 10 p.m. this evening,' Jhon told Antonio. 'He arrives in Portugal at 1500 tomorrow, and then takes another flight to Rome. He will be there at 1900 tomorrow night.'

Jota was coming into Rome's Fiumicino airport. 'OK,' Antonio said. 'We will be there.'

Jhon Peludo waited patiently by the arrivals gate, hands on his hips and his large belly bulging over his light blue jeans. Standing next to him was a line of car hire drivers dressed in dark suits and ties, holding up the names of the various passengers they were there to collect.

Finally, Jota Jota stepped through the sliding doors. This time, he was wearing a white, blue and red checked cowboy shirt and pulling a large black wheeled bag behind him.

Antonio, who was dressed in white beach shorts and flip-flops for the summer heat, was waiting outside in a silver Fiat Punto. The two Colombians got in, and the three men drove onto the Rome–Florence motorway, heading north towards their rendezvous.

It was 3 a.m. by the time they reached their destination – a bar on the outskirts of Altopascio, a small town about a thirty-minute drive from Pisa.

Almost exactly as they arrived, another car pulled up and a tall bald man stepped out of the vehicle. He was going to oversee getting the shipment from the port when it docked in Livorno in twenty-four hours.

The four of them entered the bar, which was deserted apart from a lone woman sitting at the marble-topped counter, and two waiters. It may have been the middle of the night, but Antonio ordered an espresso. The walls around them were decorated with plaster paintings of empty rowing boats floating on a lake.

Jota Jota and the man they had just met headed to the back of the bar, while Antonio and Jhon remained up front. Sitting down at a large white circular table, Jota Jota pulled a folder from his bag and slid it across. He had flown five thousand miles to Rome for this single task: to give this man a piece of paper in a bar in a small town in Italy in the middle of the night. The Italian opened the folder, wrote down the information on another piece of paper and handed it back.

Moments later, they got up. Antonio paid for his espresso, and the four of them left. The final pieces had been set. Antonio and the two Colombians got back into the car and began the long drive south to Calabria.

The drive took nine hours. As soon as they arrived, Antonio took Jota Jota and Jhon Peludo to Oksana's apartment, where they had arranged to meet Salvatore.

At almost exactly the same time, *TG NIKE* docked in Livorno, and the containers it had carried across the Atlantic began to be unloaded. In just a few hours they would know if the operation had been a success. Salvatore could only wait. If everything went to plan this was going to be the start of an extremely profitable relationship. Salvatore already knew that the cartel had lots of cocaine waiting in the jungle in Colombia. It was ready to be shipped to Europe, Jota had told him.

'My people have 1.2 tonnes ready to be sent to the port of Turbo,' Jota said. 'But not all together. We can send three hundred kilograms, then five hundred kilograms, and next week another shipment.'

If Salvatore wanted to start regularly shipping large quantities, the Colombians explained, then it was important to find a fruit importation company in Europe that would permanently act as a front for the operation.

'We normally work with bananas,' said Jhon. 'We need to look for a person or a company that buys the bananas directly from us.'

Still, other fruits and ports were a possibility. 'We have people at the port who check the containers coming from Costa Rica arriving in Turbo. They go to Genoa, they go to Spain. These containers have different types of fruit, you understand?'

But they were getting ahead of themselves. First, they had to collect the shipment Jota had sent, which was waiting in a container in the port. And that evening Salvatore had to check in with Filippo Fiarè, his primary investor.

Early the next morning, the Colombians were waiting in Oksana's flat for news about the shipment. Salvatore walked through the door with a man they hadn't met before, who had some news: *TG NIKE* had docked.

'Last night,' the man reported to the group of men waiting in Oksana's living room, 'everything arrived.'

This new man was the person whom Salvatore had put in charge of relaying messages to the team monitoring the port for the arrival of the cargo. That evening they would break in, search among the floodlit rows of stacked white metal boxes, crack open the correct shipping container and rip off the boxes of bananas.

Jota Jota then repeated the information that he had shared with the man in the bar the previous night, rattling off the numbers of the banana boxes with the exact weights of cocaine in each. They had thought of everything. In one of the boxes was a replacement seal for the container, which Salvatore's men would use to replace the one they would break when opening the cargo.

'So what's it like, this stuff?' the man asked Jota. 'Is it good?'

'I can guarantee you that it is 97 per cent pure. If it is not at least 97 per cent, I will give it to you for free,' the Colombian replied. 'I went to the company in Colombia and did the packaging. We put it in anti-scanner envelopes. There will be no problems. We invested a lot of time and money in the work.'

All that remained was to collect the bananas.

'If I get the message tonight that means everything has gone well,' the man told them before he left. 'As soon as I get the news, I will come here immediately, even if it is midnight. Tonight, my guys will go to get the stuff, and by tomorrow morning you will know everything.'

But by the time Salvatore's men arrived at the port later that evening, dozens of Italian police officers were crawling over every container from *TG NIKE*. Inside container TRIU8763, across five boxes of bananas, they discovered sixty-three bricks of cocaine, just as Jota Jota had packed them. Each brick was wrapped in banana-print anti-scanning foil. Salvatore's deal had been blown.

Curiously, the police also saw that underneath the foil

the drugs had been marked with the insignia of a luxury Swiss watchmaker: Romain Jerome. Several months earlier, Colombia's National Police had carried out a raid in San Pedro de Urabá in Antioquia, around seventy kilometres outside Turbo, where in an underground bunker they discovered 170 grams of cocaine marked with the insignia 'Romain J' – along with four AK-47 assault rifles, nine 40-millimetre grenades and a large amount of ammunition. During the raid that day, they killed one member of the Clan del Golfo and arrested fifty-seven more. Among the men arrested were regional bosses of the cartel, hitmen and drug traffickers.

The Colombian police knew that drug cartels used insignias to identify ownership of cocaine. And they knew that the man who used 'Romain Jerome' was one of the most powerful drug lords in Latin America. His name was Roberto Vargas Gutiérrez, alias Gavilán, the former Maoist guerrilla who was now the second-in-command of the Clan del Golfo. But Gavilán was nowhere to be seen.

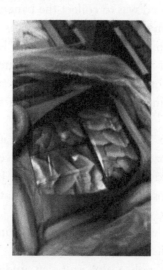

*

Back in Oksana's flat, Salvatore was panicking. None of his men could explain what had happened: they had taken every precaution. How did the police know there was cocaine on the ship? And how could they have known the exact container to search?

Jota Jota had quickly got on a flight back to Colombia, fearing arrest. Salvatore was in serious trouble – he had lost the drugs and the money. He needed answers for his investors, and fast. If they suspected that Salvatore had stolen the drugs, he knew what the consequences would be. He had to bring them some proof of the raid. 'It has to come out in the newspapers that it was seized,' he told one of his men. Salvatore could worry about the lost money later. For now, he just needed to stay alive. 'It has to appear in the newspapers!'

21

Terror Control

Leidschendam, 2015

Iain Edwards had been sitting in his office on Chancery Lane in central London when an old colleague called to ask if he wanted to represent Mustafa Badreddine.

The barrister had recently returned to the UK after several years working at an international tribunal defending clients charged with committing genocide in Rwanda. Since then Edwards had been busy trying to resurrect his criminal defence practice, representing people arrested for pub brawls or burglary.

Badreddine, Edwards's colleague explained, had been charged with a very serious crime by a United Nations-backed tribunal. His trial promised to be ground-breaking – the first time an act of terrorism had been prosecuted as a discrete crime by an international criminal court.

But there were some important things Edwards should

know before agreeing to take on the job. First, neither he, nor any other members of the defence team, would ever be able to meet or talk with the client. And though the client had been charged with committing a terrorist act – the intentional homicide of twenty-two people and the attempted homicide of more than two hundred others – he had not, in fact, been arrested. And even if the case resulted in his conviction, the client would remain at large. This was because no one had any idea where he was. In fact, the client had never asked for anyone to be his lawyer. After giving it some thought, Edwards took the job.

After Mustafa's victory in al Qusayr, the Hezbollah special forces fighters under his control were now battling to retake Aleppo. At the same time, thousands of miles away in the small Dutch town of Leidschendam, an international criminal trial was underway into the assassination of Rafic Hariri.

Four years earlier, Mustafa had been formally charged by the UN-backed Special Tribunal for Lebanon for masterminding the bombing operation that had killed the former Lebanese prime minister in 2005. Hassan Nasrallah had immediately refused to recognise the legitimacy of the tribunal, warning he would 'cut off the hand' of anyone who attempted to pursue the arrest warrants it had issued.

Because of the near impossibility of ever arresting Mustafa (along with three co-defendants), the UN court's statutes had allowed their trial to proceed *in absentia*, the first time this had happened at an international court since the Nuremberg Trials in 1945. And to ensure that Mustafa and the others received a fair trial, the court had appointed on their behalf a team of experienced defence lawyers.

Working from inside the tribunal building near The Hague that once was the headquarters of Dutch intelligence, Edwards and the rest of Mustafa's legal team faced an unenviable task. Not only were they unable to take instruction from their client, but the prosecution had gathered a mountain of evidence against him.

Mustafa, they claimed, was a highly experienced international terrorist who had already been sentenced to death for carrying out a bombing operation in Kuwait in the 1980s – and had only managed to escape the country after it was invaded by Iraq. This was a man, they said, who possessed the training and temperament to pull off a complex assassination plot.

Then there was the phone evidence, which was circumstantial but compelling. UN investigators had built on the data analysis started by Wissam Eid, the Lebanese police captain murdered in 2008. This showed that, in the months leading up to the Hariri assassination, a person they believed to be Mustafa had covertly communicated with Salim Jamil Ayyash, a more junior Hezbollah operative, using a number of different mobile phones which the prosecution had named the 'green network'.

The investigators had discovered that several of these phones were registered to a man by the name of Sami Issa. But Issa, the prosecution said, was a false identity being used by Mustafa – a man who had regularly adopted aliases during his decades of terrorist operations.

Ayyash, they claimed, relayed the instructions from Mustafa over the 'green network' to a 'red network' of phones that belonged to the assassination team. Weeks before the attack, Ayyash had called Mustafa from a location that the phone data revealed was close to the showroom where the Mitsubishi truck used in the bombing was bought, and on the same day as the purchase.

The phone evidence, the prosecution claimed, also showed that at 11.58 a.m. on the day of the assassination, Ayyash had called Mustafa from close to the St. Georges Hotel. This, they said, was the phone call that gave the operative his final instructions before the attack. Around an hour later, at 12.50 p.m., after Hariri's motorcade had set off, Ayyash received several calls from the 'red network'. These were the last calls the phone numbers in the red and green networks ever made. Five minutes later, a suicide bomber detonated the military-grade explosives hidden inside the truck.

Edwards and the rest of Mustafa's legal team examined the evidence and thought about a defence strategy. Without a client who could provide them with any type of alibi or explanation, they had decided the only way to proceed was to put every scrap of the prosecution's case under the microscope.

Yes, the mobile phone evidence suggested that a man named Sami Issa could have been involved in the plot. But were Issa and their client really the same man? Mustafa, the prosecution had said, 'passes as an unrecognisable and virtually untraceable ghost throughout Lebanon, leaving no footprint'. No recent photos of him existed. There was only one in black and white, of a young Mustafa, in his early twenties, grinning in a white shirt and suit. How, his defence team reasoned, would it be possible for any witnesses to confirm that Issa and Badreddine were the same person? And could those witnesses prove the prosecution's claims beyond reasonable doubt?

At the same time as Mustafa was put on trial by the UN tribunal, an anonymous website appeared. It was called Terror Control, and was available in English, Spanish and Arabic. At first glance, it seemed to be a blog devoted to tracking Hezbollah activity. But closer examination suggested it was something more sophisticated.

The site claimed it had been set up by 'an association of Western intelligence organizations established to fight the threat of terror'. It had already posted several grainy photos of men it claimed to be senior Hezbollah operatives and promised its readers 'a considerable sum of money' for any information they could provide about them.

'Information you send us will be verified, and cash payments will be sent,' Terror Control told its readers, instructing them to use the anonymous internet browser Tor for their own safety. 'After information has been verified, we will be in touch with the people who sent it to check how best to send the compensation, without compromising their safety in any way. We undertake to pay hundreds and even thousands of dollars to anyone sending valuable information.'

In 2012 an article appeared on Terror Control headlined 'Mustafa Amine Badreddine: Exposed!' It contained a black-and-white picture of a clean-shaven man wearing a baseball cap and a checked shirt open at the neck. The man in the photo, the website claimed, was Mustafa. It was impossible to know if the picture was genuine, but if it was then it represented a significant find. Suddenly, there appeared to be a new, recent photo of the 'untraceable ghost'. The article signed off 'More to come ...'

Further reports about Mustafa soon appeared – and more photos. There was a picture of him talking on the phone wearing dark sunglasses and a baseball cap pulled over his face. Another seemed to show him walking down a street wearing a black dress shirt, blue jeans and pointed black leather shoes.

These posts also contained what seemed like detailed intelligence reports about the secret life of Hezbollah's top military commander. Mustafa, one reported, 'tends to kick out his right leg in front of him, and while taking a step forward, he straightens the right leg completely and leans forward slightly while doing so'. Another post noted that he removed his baseball cap and sunglasses only when he was in the company of 'his most trusted subordinates', and that his 'preferred look involves wearing a closely cropped beard and military style haircut, although he at times has shaved his beard in favour of wearing a goatee'.

Mustafa, the website said, had significant business interests and property in Lebanon and abroad. He spent most of his time in Syria, working out of an office at the Dama Rose, a five-star hotel in Damascus. It also claimed that the Hezbollah commander was 'feared for his explosive temper and manipulative personality', was 'prone to angry tirades of physical violence' and had made enemies inside the organisation since he assumed Imad's position after his death. One post even claimed that at the time of Imad's assassination in Damascus in 2008, he and his cousin were no longer on speaking terms: apparently Mustafa was furious that Imad had taken a second wife, in addition to Saada.

All this was of course impossible for the lawyers in the Netherlands to verify. Perhaps the people behind the anonymous website claiming to be shadowy Western intelligence operatives were hucksters, or black propagandists. Or perhaps, as hard as Mustafa had been trying to hide, his enemies were finally catching up with him.

22

A Family Crisis

Calabria, November 2015

Salvatore was scrambling. The seizure in Livorno meant the money given to him by his business partners had gone up in smoke. He had to find a way to bring in a new shipment to make up for a loss of over a million euros, as well as to settle his debts. If he failed, he knew exactly what the consequences would be.

Jhon Peludo was still stationed in Italy, busily trying to reassure Jota Jota, now back in Medellín, that the shipment had been raided by police, and not stolen. With neither side able to explain how the police had known which shipping container to raid, Salvatore was more paranoid than ever. Had there been a leak? Had the police been listening to their conversations? As a precautionary measure the gang had already dumped all their SIM cards and mobile phones.

Salvatore knew it was critical the cartel didn't lose

confidence in his organisation if he was going to convince them to send another shipment. But Salvatore didn't have any money to pay for one. And Jhon told him that because of the police seizure the cartel was now refusing to send anything without first being paid. So desperate was Salvatore to convince Jota to front him another shipment that he offered up Giuseppe, his first-born son, to go to Medellín as a human guarantee. The Colombian refused.

As Salvatore rushed around, his partners were trying to devise different ways to transport the next shipment safely. They discussed switching ports, from Livorno to Gioia Tauro in Calabria, or to Naples. Some suggested hiding the drugs in the hull of a ship leaving Colombia, or even using an improvised submarine. But none of this would matter unless Salvatore found more cash.

The Italians were moving Jhon from house to house, frightened that the police might be watching them. For now, they had put him up in Oksana's flat, something she hated. Salvatore had come over to discuss the situation with the Colombian emissary.

'Look, that thing is now gone,' Salvatore said, referring to the lost shipment. 'The important thing is the newspaper, you understand,' he continued, stressing the need to use news reports of the seizure as evidence of his side's innocence.

Jhon, for his part, was eager to get the deal moving again, telling Salvatore that Jota Jota's 'papa', a top-level cartel boss, was putting pressure on the organisation to shift the vast amount of cocaine that was sitting in their storage facility in Colombia.

'Right now, in Turbo, we have 1,200 kilos. He is saying, come on, move, move,' Jhon said. 'We have to work hard for this. How much money is that? A lot of money.'

Still, Salvatore had to find the cash to pay for it. He left

Oksana's flat and began his rounds, anxiously trying to arrange meetings with his investors to update them on his attempts to salvage the situation and to raise new funds.

Oksana, meanwhile, was miserable. Salvatore was taking out his stress on her, she told Jhon. Jhon tried to reassure her, saying that it was normal for her boyfriend to be so agitated – he had just lost a large amount of money and drugs – and that as soon as they found a way to bring in a new shipment, life would be peaceful again. Oksana wasn't convinced. They were acting recklessly, she said, and had better watch what they were doing.

But what choice did Salvatore have?

'The "papa" said that without money we will keep all of the merchandise,' Jhon told Salvatore. 'You have to pay, you understand?'

'Yes, Jhon. I told you that I would figure it out. But he also has to understand me.'

'Jota said to go and speak with the man with white hair,' he replied, referring to one of Salvatore's investors for the previous shipment.

'He can't put in any money. Right now, he doesn't have any more money.'

The Colombians expected more effort, Jhon told Salvatore. Time was running out.

Antonella and her eldest son, Giuseppe, were driving towards the parking lot of a concrete shopping centre on the outskirts of Lamezia Terme, a city an hour's drive north of Mileto. It was around six in the evening, and they had a small but sensitive errand to complete. The car approached the shimmering lights of the enormous shopping centre.

Antonella knew she had family duties that went beyond bringing up her three boys and keeping their house in order.

The Pititto family was facing a crisis. She, too, had to play her part. Salvatore had asked her to go with Giuseppe that evening to drop off a package of cocaine he had sourced from another supplier in Italy with a man at the shopping centre. It was a small deal that would raise only a tiny amount of the money, but it would help. And perhaps it would make her husband respect her a little bit more.

Antonella had known about her husband's affair for more than a decade. It hurt. Salvatore's parents knew about Oksana, their sons knew about her, and so did his friends. Antonella and Salvatore still slept under the same roof – when he was not staying with Oksana, that is – but they no longer slept in the same bed. It was perhaps, by now, a loveless marriage, one of routine and weary convenience, and Antonella had come to accept all of this. But perhaps what upset her more was that her husband seemed to think she was an idiot, someone who could not be trusted with the simplest of tasks. Tonight, she had a chance to prove him wrong.

Antonella stopped the car and she and her son began to look for the man they were scheduled to meet.

'Are you sure he said to meet here?' Giuseppe asked his mother.

'Yes. Didn't you hear him?'

'Wasn't he meant to come in from the entrance over there?'

'No, he is meant to arrive from over there.'

Giuseppe was Antonella's first child. Once her little baby, the twenty-three-year-old man sitting beside her in the car had been raised to be a hardened criminal. Sometimes, Giuseppe and his brother Gianluca, who was four years younger, would get into trouble, and Salvatore would have to bail them out. Not long ago, a man had attempted to sell weed in the area of Mileto that the two brothers controlled. They savagely attacked the dealer, leaving him with a broken cheekbone, jaw and ribs. He was taken to hospital, where he underwent surgery. The man had told the doctors he had fallen off his motorcycle. But he had told the Mancuso family, one of the most powerful crime groups in Italy, what Salvatore's sons had done to him.

Salvatore had been forced to justify his sons' actions to the Mancusos. His two boys, he explained, had been reasonable. They had asked to talk to the dealer and had warned him twice before they beat him up. Salvatore eventually succeeded in smoothing over the situation. It was an inconvenience, but how could he not have been happy with them? His eldest boys were acting exactly the way he wanted them to. He had told Oksana how proud he was of them. Salvatore and Antonella's teenage son Alex was ten years younger than Giuseppe, but soon enough he too would be like his elder brothers.

Finally, Giuseppe and his mother spotted the car of the man they were meeting. 'Give me the thing,' he told her. Antonella took out the wrap of drugs and passed it to her son. He got out of the car and walked towards the man, but then came back. The man, Giuseppe said, didn't want to take receipt of the drugs out in the open; they would have to drive on to somewhere else.

'He is breaking my balls about this,' Giuseppe said.

'We have to go somewhere else?' Antonella asked.

'Yes.'

'But what if we lose him?'

'Drive slowly. We won't lose them.'

They drove around the corner and stopped. Giuseppe got out of the vehicle and approached the man's car. He quickly came back to his mother and told her they would have to move again. The man still wasn't happy with the location. They would now have to go to a nearby slip road and wait for him there. Antonella was getting nervous. Something didn't feel right. What she had expected to be a simple drop-off was turning into a confusing ordeal. She drove to the new meeting point.

'If he doesn't arrive here then we will leave, OK?' Giuseppe told his mother as they waited for the man to arrive.

Antonella, clearly nervous, had wanted to drive away. But Giuseppe had stopped her.

'You are making me anxious,' he said.

'Me?' she asked.

'Yes, because you don't understand what I tell you.'

'And what should I understand?' she asked her son.

'That we are meant to wait here, and you were starting to leave.'

'I didn't know.'

'And you took fifteen minutes to hand the stuff over to me.'

'That's not true,' she argued back.

Finally, the man arrived and took the wrap of cocaine from Giuseppe. Then his mother began to drive home. Salvatore rang Antonella's phone. Giuseppe picked up. He told his father the drop-off had gone ahead as planned and that they were on their way back. After he had hung up, he informed his mother that Salvatore had called because he was worried that the meeting was taking so long. Antonella told Giuseppe that she had expected his father to do that. Salvatore thought she was stupid, she said, and never trusted her to get things right. Her son said nothing.

It was a family crisis, and that meant that Salvatore, as always, had to consult Pasquale. Visiting his cousin was always a risk. In setting up the meeting, Salvatore once again used cryptic romantic text messages that called Pasquale 'my love' and 'my treasure'. Bringing an international drugs trafficker to Pasquale's door was perhaps unwise. But this was an emergency.

Jhon got into Salvatore's Volkswagen Golf and they drove down a winding country road, lined with wild trees and unkempt green fields. It was the sort of dark, secluded road where Pasquale, back when he was a young man, used to lie in wait to ambush his enemies with a machine gun.

They pulled up outside Pasquale's house. Salvatore made sure that no one was watching them.

'Jhon, stay here. I'm going inside, understand?'

'Yes, yes.'

'I'll leave the keys. I'm going to see if he is here.'

'Should I wait for you here?'

'Yes.'

For Salvatore, family was everything. How else was he to find a way out of this mess than by trying to pull his family together?

23

'Very Important Russians'

Paris, November 2015

In November 2015, Jack Kelly got a call from Paris. The French police had learned that Mohamad Nourredine, the head of the cocaine money laundering cell, was due to fly into Charles de Gaulle airport from Beirut. Jack immediately got on a plane to Europe and was soon sitting at a table on the outside terrace of the Café du Trocadéro in the centre of the French capital, jetlagged and nursing a glass of red wine in the crisp chill of an early winter evening.

For months, the French police and the DEA had been amassing hundreds of hours of wiretap evidence against Nourredine. They now had what they needed to charge him. But they knew from studying his travel patterns that Nourredine flew to Europe just once or twice a year. Tomorrow was going to be their best – perhaps their only – chance to arrest him. The French police had coordinated with forces across Europe to launch simultaneous raids to bring in all the network's money couriers.

It was still relatively early, before nine o'clock, but Jack decided to head back to his hotel room. He paid the bill and walked towards the Renaissance Trocadero hotel, a few minutes down Avenue Raymond Poincaré. Eligible for retirement in a year, he knew this operation was probably going to be the last big one of his career.

The close cooperation between the DEA and the European authorities had been unprecedented. The US and France had signed a judicial collaboration agreement, meaning Jack and the other DEA agents had the authority to monitor the evidence from phone intercepts in real time, as well as to work on French soil. A few months before, Jack had given a briefing on the money laundering case to law enforcement officials from France, Germany, Spain and Italy, as well as representatives from Europol, the European Union's joint law enforcement agency, and Eurojust, the EU agency that handles judicial cooperation between member states.

Once back in his room at the Renaissance, Jack put his phone on the side table and on silent; he sat on his bed to read a book. His mind was racing. He couldn't stop thinking over the details of the investigation, and about the arrests that were going to take place the next day.

It was a complex and sprawling international conspiracy, one that not only involved moving drug money for Colombian cartels and European organised criminals, but also reached into the darkest corners of the global shadow economy. The evidence they had gathered from the wiretaps showed that Nourredine and the people he was working with in Beirut were not merely laundering money. They were also working on procuring weapons for the Syrian regime for its battle against anti-Assad rebels.

Nourredine, the intercepts had already shown, spoke on a near-daily basis to Adham Tabaja, one of Hezbollah's most senior financiers who regularly met with the highest echelons of the party's military and political leadership. He was also in regular communication with Mustafa Badreddine's brother.

In the middle of the wiretap investigation into the Beirut cell, the US Treasury sanctioned Tabaja for maintaining 'direct ties to senior Hezbollah organisational elements, including the terrorist group's operational component, the Islamic Jihad'. On the same day, the French police listened in to a phone call in which the normally reserved Tabaja ranted at Nourredine about the sanctions and the problems they would cause his business operations.

But it soon became clear that Nourredine's calls to the associates who worked with him in the Beirut office where he coordinated the money-laundering scheme in Europe were as interesting as those with Tabaja. Nourredine, the DEA had discovered, ran the money-brokering operation in Beirut with the assistance of three other men: his brother-in-law, Hamdi Zahreddine; a businessman called Abbas Nasser; and a close friend of Mohamad Nourredine's called Mazen al-Atat. The French police had recorded a conversation between Nourredine and Hassan Tarabolsi, the money collector based in Germany, in which he said, 'I only coordinate with Abbas, Mazen and Hamdi.'

Zahreddine, who was more than a decade younger than Nourredine, would handle client relations and account management, relaying instructions to Tarabolsi and others on the ground in Europe regarding money pick-ups. Abbas Nasser, it appeared, coordinated a broader international network of clients, discussing collections from as far afield as Mexico, Hong Kong, Dubai and Singapore for amounts as large as tens or even hundreds of millions of euros.

But the man who really jumped out at the investigators was Mazen al-Atat. He seemed to have a less formal role at Nourredine's money exchange operation, picking up phones for him and speaking on occasion with couriers collecting cash in Europe. He also regularly went on business trips with Nourredine, and had proposed launching various businesses with him in Iran. But as his friend laundered tens of millions of euros from European cocaine deals through Lebanon, al-Atat was busy working to procure weapons for the Syrian government.

The DEA discovered that al-Atat had been in contact with Ali al-Salim, who, as the head of the Syrian Arab Republic's Army Supply Bureau, oversaw weapons procurement for the Assad regime during the civil war. Al-Salim, who had been sanctioned by the US, UK and EU for his role in procuring arms used to attack Syrian civilians, had sent emails to al-Atat giving him official permission to negotiate weapons deals on behalf of Syria with Russian state arms companies, and to secure so-called end user certificates to allow the weapons to be sent to Syria.

'By this letter we inform you that the inventory requested by Mr Mazen El-Atat [sic] (citizen of Lebanon), specifically 50,000 rounds of 100mm incendiary ammunition for T-55 tanks, is being procured for us,' Al-Salim wrote to a Russian arms dealer. The DEA had seen this correspondence after a US magistrates judge authorised an email search warrant.

Al-Salim also wrote a letter on behalf of al-Atat, authorising him to enquire with Belvneshpromservice, the Belarusian state arms company, about prices for grenade launchers, sniper rifles and machine guns. The same company had been sanctioned by the United States in 2012 for selling items that could be used as fuses for aerial bombs to al-Salim's Army

Supply Bureau. Those bombs had been used by the Syrian regime to attack civilian populations in Aleppo.

In another email, this time to a Vienna-based middleman working with Rosoboronexport, Russia's state-controlled arms exporting body, al-Atat listed the arms he hoped to source. The email requested, among other items, thirty thousand AK-47 assault rifles and fifty million rounds of 12.7mm ammunition for DShKs, the large-calibre heavy Russian machine guns. In a series of WhatsApp messages seen by the DEA, an Iraqi arms dealer told al-Atat that he could supply SVD Dragunov sniper rifles, PKS Soviet-era machine guns and ZU-23 Soviet anti-aircraft twin auto cannons.

It was clear to the DEA that al-Atat had extensive contacts not only in the Russian arms industry but also among the elite network of Syrian financiers operating in Russia to prop up the Assad regime during the civil war. On his phone, he had the contact details of Mudalal Khuri, a Syrian banker based in Moscow who had been sanctioned by the United States for assisting the Assad regime. Khuri, the US Department of the Treasury said, had also attempted to broker the sale of ammonium nitrate to Damascus, a deadly ingredient used in the barrel bombs being dropped on the Syrian population.

Al-Atat had sent confirmations of some of his weapons deals to Nourredine, with one email between the two showing a contract for the purchase of 930 DShK machine guns at a price of $10,500 per unit. He had also emailed Iraqi government weapons procurement lists to a man who worked at a company majority-owned by Adham Tabaja. That man was later sanctioned by the US government for being a member of Hezbollah's Islamic Jihad Organization or Unit 910, the secret unit founded by Imad that carried out its overseas intelligence and terrorist operations.

As the DEA continued to covertly observe Nourredine's

money-laundering cell, they saw evidence of even more complex and internationally sensitive deals being struck involving trading in Iranian oil, which had for years been subject to US economic sanctions. During several months of wiretaps, the French investigative team had intercepted calls in which the groups discussed transactions with people in Russia and Iran.

In one of the recorded calls, Mazen al-Atat rang Nourredine's mobile phone, and Hamdi Zahreddine picked up.

'This is Mazen,' he said.

'Mazen, I have heard this name before,' Hamdi joked.

'I called you three or four times already . . . Reassure me, you are in Tehran? Or are you still in Iraq?'

'No, in Tehran,' Hamdi replied.

'You have started to use a Tehran accent,' al-Atat teased him.

'What is your news?' Hamdi asked.

'I'm in Moscow. We will have news soon. They started working yesterday. I just arrived today . . . We are doing our best to find stock. We found a big stock, but the characteristics are different from what they asked for. The group tells us that within one or two days we will have the characteristics they need.'

'Inshallah . . . How long are you going to stay there?'

'I will stay for a week. Then I will go to Belarus.'

'Everything is fine here. Things are picking up.'

It wasn't clear to the investigators what the 'big stock' the two men were discussing was but, from the previous interceptions and the fact that Mazen al-Atat was in Moscow, it seemed probable they were talking about weapons. But then the two men began discussing an Iranian oil deal.

'The Russians are chasing me about the oil tariff,' Mazen reported to Hamdi.

'What do they want?'

'They want two million barrels of heavy crude, and two million barrels of light crude, and they would collect them ship to ship in Oman.'

'I will give you the price,' Hamdi responded, 'but if they ask me for the final destination, what do I tell them?'

'Tell them it is going to Europe,' Mazen said.

'You need to tell me a specific country.'

'I swear, they didn't tell me one. You tell them Europe. The main thing is that the papers say it is from Oman.'

'OK,' said Hamdi. 'I will see what I can do.'

During the call, Hamdi broke off to crack a joke with someone in the room. 'We are Hezbollah,' he said. 'Don't mess around with us.' Mazen laughed.

Before ending their conversation, Mazen pressed upon his colleague the importance of making sure they found the oil for his Russian buyers. 'God forbid, this is a serious thing,' Mazen told him, 'and the people are important Russians.'

Several hours went by before Jack, his head still fuzzy from the jetlag and the wine, put down his book and glanced at his mobile phone. Outside he could hear police sirens ringing through the streets. He saw a string of messages and calls from members of his family back in the United States. His immediate concern was that someone had died or been in an accident. One of the text messages was from his niece in Baton Rouge, Louisiana. 'Uncle Jack, are you OK?' Jack messaged back, asking her why she was asking. 'Because of the attacks,' she replied. 'Haven't you seen what is happening on the television?'

Paris was under fire. Outside the streets were crackling with panic, and police were swarming the city. Starting at 9.20 p.m., three suicide bombers had blown themselves up outside the Stade de France during an international football match between France and Germany. At the same time, in the 10th arrondissement, a group of men had emerged from a rented SEAT Leon car and begun shooting, gunning down thirteen and injuring ten others before jumping back in the vehicle and driving several streets away to fire at diners outside a restaurant on rue de la Fontaine au Roi.

Near the Bataclan theatre, three men equipped with assault rifles and explosive vests had been waiting in a black car. Shortly before 10 p.m., they got out of the vehicle and began shooting at people outside the venue, then bursting into the concert hall and firing on the crowd. They barricaded the doors and took the concertgoers hostage. Just after midnight, following attempted negotiations with the attackers, the French police burst into the theatre and shot one of the gunmen, whose suicide vest detonated. The siege ended with two other gunmen blowing themselves up. A total of 130 people died, and hundreds were wounded. Several of the terrorists were discovered to be young jihadists who had returned to Europe after travelling to fight in the Syrian civil war.

The country was in shock. Flights in and out of France were cancelled. The next day, Jack learned from French police that Nourredine had postponed his trip to Paris. The operation to arrest him was called off.

BOOK THREE

BOOK THREE

24

'Your Country Has Screwed Up'

Lebanon–Syria Border, December 2015

Somewhere near the Syrian border, the five Czechs were told by the masked men that it was time to leave their windowless cell. It had been almost a hundred days since the hostages had last seen sunlight, but now they had been given a ray of hope.

The kidnappers hooded the hostages, bundled them into a vehicle and drove them to a new location. They had been moved between makeshift prisons several times already, their captors careful never to keep them in one place for too long. But this time seemed different. After they arrived, the masked men shaved the hostages' scraggly beards, cut their hair and gave them clean clothes. It was as if they were being cleaned up for release.

The Czech government still had no idea where the

hostages were being held, but they had at least confirmed they were alive. Shortly after the five men had disappeared in Lebanon, diplomats and security officials opened a secret line of communication with men who claimed to represent the kidnappers. The talks had been progressing, but they continued to hinge on a single, unbendable demand: Ali Fayad, the arms dealer arrested in the DEA's sting operation in Prague, must be set free.

For Adam, the group's translator, the situation was bewildering. He had come to Lebanon to assist Ali Fayad's lawyer and two television journalists as part of a fact-finding mission for their imprisoned client. Somehow, he had been dragged into a diplomatic crisis where nothing was what it seemed.

He still didn't know who had ordered the kidnapping, or who the masked men were ultimately working for. He could tell they were professional, well-trained soldiers and that they appeared to be sympathetic to Hezbollah. Adam had seen Shia military tattoos on some of their arms. Sometimes the kidnappers would drop small, teasing hints about their true identity. One showed Adam an ID card for the Lebanese military, suggesting that the kidnappers were somehow connected to the state, but it was impossible to know if it was real.

If the outside world didn't know where Adam and his fellow hostages were being held, they certainly didn't either. They could still be in Lebanon, or they could be in Syria. Even the true identities of his fellow prisoners were unclear.

Malem, the lead kidnapper, had already dramatically outed one hostage as an undercover agent working for Czech military intelligence. Over time the agent had told the others that he had been dispatched to Lebanon as part of a scheme to gather information about another kidnapped Czech citizen, a cook who had been seized by militants in Libya. Perhaps the kidnappers, Adam thought, had identified the spy as a valuable target they could use to pressure the Czech government over the Fayad case, and he and the other hostages had just been in the wrong place at the wrong time.

From his prison cell in Prague, Ali Fayad was claiming he wasn't really the man the DEA said he was. Fayad told the Czech authorities that he was no terrorist arms trafficker, but a spy working for Lebanese intelligence hunting for foreign criminals. His arrest in the DEA sting operation, he said, had been nothing more than a terrible case of mistaken identity. Before he was kidnapped, Fayad's lawyer had made a trip to Lebanon on his client's instruction to meet a senior domestic intelligence official. The Lebanese spy acknowledged that the arms dealer was a friend of his, but he stopped short of confirming he was a paid agent. And the Czech police had uncovered a prison phone call made between Fayad and his brother, discussing how to brief the Lebanese spy.

For Adam, none of this mattered. He just wanted to go home. The masked kidnappers had told the hostages that the secret negotiations to exchange them for Fayad were progressing. If all went to plan, then soon they would all be flying back to their loved ones on a military plane sent over from Prague. Czech officials had even started to tell some of the hostages' wives and girlfriends that they would be home soon. But several weeks later the mood of their captors suddenly darkened. One of the masked men broke the news: 'Your country has screwed up.'

There had been important news from Prague. A Czech court had ruled for a second time that Ali Fayad could be extradited to the United States.

Finally, more than a year after he had first been arrested, it appeared that Ali Fayad was going to be extradited to face trial in the United States. The Czech government was now on high alert. Its foreign minister requested additional security for the country's embassies in Beirut and Damascus. But the Americans and the kidnappers knew that the Czech government still had the power to overturn the court's decision if it wanted to. The final decision on Fayad's fate – and, it seemed, the fate of the five kidnapped men – would be decided by the Minister of Justice.

As Adam waited anxiously for news inside his prison cell, Russian military personnel were quietly surveying an abandoned Syrian airstrip. In August 2015, cargo planes loaded with equipment and construction materials landed at Khmeimim Air Base, outside the Syrian coastal port of Latakia. Soon workers began to re-lay the asphalt. A new aircraft control tower sprang up, as well as housing units and missile defence systems.

Within weeks satellite images alerted Western governments to the scale of what was underway at the barren air strip. A Pentagon spokesman announced that the Russians appeared to be constructing 'a forward air operating base'. Russian aircraft and tank landing ships were now sailing from the Black Sea towards the Mediterranean. Under the noses of the world, Vladimir Putin was preparing to launch Russia's first military deployment outside the former Soviet Union since the end of the Cold War.

The Assad regime was on the brink. It had lost Idlib to the rebels in the north, and ISIS had ransacked the ancient desert city of Palmyra. As hard as they had fought, the Hezbollah fighters under the command of Mustafa and the Iranian forces led by Qasem Soleimani had been unable to decisively shift the war back in Bashar al-Assad's favour. The Syrian dictator had admitted for the first time since the war began that his troops had experienced 'setbacks' on the battlefield.

Then the bombing began. Russian fighter jets used

Khmeimim Air Base to unleash thousands of attacks on anti-Assad rebels. Moscow claimed it was focusing its attacks on ISIS jihadists but evidence on the ground suggested it was primarily targeting non-ISIS rebels.

In the middle of October, emboldened by the Russian intervention, an army of Iranian and Hezbollah fighters began a new assault on Aleppo. Mustafa Badreddine had left for Syria vowing he would either return victorious or in a body bag. And now, for the first time since he had arrived, victory was in sight.

25

Hunted Like a Dog

Calabria, January 2016

It was 6 a.m. when the men arrived at Salvatore's front door to demand money. He had known for days that they were looking for him. As soon as he heard the buzzer, he raced down the stairs to meet them.

Salvatore's problems were now licking around his feet like fire. He had thrown everything into trying to find more cash to buy a new shipment from the cartel. It was the only way Salvatore was going to be able to pay off his debts. But it had come to nothing. His creditors were circling, and the Colombians were losing patience.

Several days earlier, Jhon Peludo, who was still posted in Italy waiting for the Italians to get things in order, messaged Jota Jota in Colombia. Their deal, he reported to his boss, was going nowhere.

'I'm not going to make you wait any longer, because I

think that would be cheating you,' he wrote. 'I don't think these people have any more financial possibilities right now. I went with them to several meetings, and they came back with nothing.'

Salvatore was now sitting in Oksana's kitchen. The men who had come looking for him that morning, he told his girlfriend, had eventually left after he reasoned with them. But he knew that he was running out of options – and time. He had been reduced to selling some of his agricultural land to raise cash. And if the debts and interest didn't catch up with him, then he feared the police would instead.

Salvatore had been paranoid about the police spying on him for months. He had taken precautions, speaking in code on the telephone and being careful to switch off his phone when travelling to avoid electronic tracking. But there had been multiple warning signs. There was the electronic device he and Antonio had discovered in their car on their way to pick up Jota Jota from the airport in Milan. And, of course, there had been the seizure of the cocaine shipment.

Now Salvatore had learned that a man he had recently collected money from had been arrested shortly afterwards. What if the police had been recording or photographing their meeting? And to make matters worse, that man had owed Salvatore significant amounts of money from some previous business – money that he desperately needed and which he now might never see again. It was becoming too much.

Salvatore was convinced that the police had been taking pictures of the meeting with a long-lens camera. If they had come for the man, why wouldn't they arrest Salvatore, too?

'Won't they now come for you, too?' Oksana asked.

'One day I am going to kill myself,' he said. 'I can't take it any more … There had to have been someone there watching us.'

'Who knows how many photos they took?' she said.

'They are just waiting for the right moment ... They are like dogs hunting me. And you know if they catch me, they will throw away the key.'

He needed her now, perhaps more than ever. And Oksana was there, not only to listen and console, but also to advise. She would gently tell him how he should go about trying to negotiate with the Colombians over the money he owed for the lost shipment.

'How much did you give him?' she calmly enquired about the man who owed Salvatore money, even as her boyfriend exploded into another rant. And she would listen, seemingly without blinking, as he threatened to murder an entire family. 'I'm going to go to Milan and bring him here and I am going to kill him,' he would say about one of his creditors. 'I am willing to go to everyone, to his wife, his sister, so I can get back the €120,000 I have lost.'

Later that evening, Oksana told Salvatore that he could still get out, that he could walk away. He could leave Mileto until things calmed down. It would be OK. Salvatore stopped her. If he left, he asked, would she stay faithful to him? Oksana reassured her lover: she would never betray him.

26

The Champagne Reception

Paris, January 2016

In late January 2016, two months after the terrorist attacks in Paris, the French police and the DEA learned that Mohamad Nourredine was planning another trip to the city. Operation Cedar was suddenly back on, and the French police were going to have to move fast.

Shortly after 7 p.m. on Sunday 24th, Nourredine touched down at Charles de Gaulle airport accompanied by his friend Mazen al-Atat. At 7.45 p.m. they were arrested. Nourredine was travelling light, holding $1,174 in cash, a Rolex watch and Mastercard Platinum credit card. The next morning police in Germany, Italy, the Netherlands and Belgium executed simultaneous European arrest warrants, raiding the houses of the money couriers Hassan Tarabolsi in Düsseldorf and Jimmy in a small town outside Milan. As they searched Tarabolsi's home the police discovered multiple mobile phones, SIM cards, a bag containing a Rolex watch, and the keys to his Land Rover, which had a gas-powered replica pistol inside.

Jack Kelly and his colleagues from the DEA and US Customs and Border Protection raced to get on flights to Europe. The mood at the US embassy in Paris the morning after the arrests was triumphant. The operation against Nourredine and the others was still secret, but Jack knew that when the news broke it was going to make headlines around the world. The DEA bosses began to work on a draft press release, which they were going to send out jointly with the French authorities and the other national law enforcement agencies working on the case.

Jack almost couldn't believe it. The press release was going to make everything he had been working on for years public, and reveal the existence of Project Cassandra. Headlined 'DEA And European Authorities Uncover Massive Hezbollah Drug and Money Laundering Scheme', it was going to announce that Hezbollah's Business Affairs Component had been working alongside Colombian drug cartels to move cocaine into Europe for years, and had been using the proceeds 'to purchase weapons for Hezbollah for its activities in Syria'.

Even more explosively, the DEA was going to publicly reveal previously highly classified US intelligence about how far up in the organisation the conspiracy went. The Business Affairs Component, it said, had been 'founded by deceased Hezbollah senior leader Imad Mughniyah and currently operates under the control of Abdallah Safieddine and recent US-designated Specially Designated Global Terrorist (SDGT) Adham Tabaja'. Naming Imad Mughniyeh, Hezbollah's most celebrated military commander, represented an unprecedented shift in the US government's public statements about the terrorist group's connections to international criminal schemes. Naming Abdallah Safieddine, Hezbollah's envoy to Iran, Hassan Nasrallah's maternal cousin and brother of Hashem Safieddine, the party's second most powerful official, was even more incendiary. An American law enforcement agency had for the first time directly criminally implicated family members of the leader of Hezbollah.

With the Americans now on the ground in Paris the US embassy began preparations for a joint press conference with the French authorities. For Jack this was finally it, the knock-out blow he had been working towards for years. And it had all been done in collaboration with the French, Europol and several other European countries. It was the most important case of Jack's career. He thought of the sceptics in the US agencies, the pushback he had suffered in Florida, and the intelligence analysts who had doubted him for years. Finally, after all the blood, sweat and tears he had put into his investigations, he would be proven right.

On the evening of the arrests Jack and the others from the DEA and American embassy were invited to a champagne reception at the Ministry of Justice to celebrate their joint success. Jack, as usual, was jetlagged, but the atmosphere was electric. French judges exchanged pleasantries with the Americans and Captain Quentin Mugg and his team from the anti-money-laundering unit were in high spirits. But as they sipped champagne the feeling inside the room changed. The top French official who had arranged the reception hadn't turned up. Jack and the other Americans began to ask where she was. There had been some complications inside government, an official explained.

The next morning Jack got a call from a colleague. They told him the press conference had been called off. The French president's office had said the announcement couldn't happen – maybe in a few months, but not now. The US embassy, where some of the DEA's top bosses had gathered, still wanted Jack to come in that morning.

His head began to spin. They had to issue a joint statement, to show international coordinated action. It was going to be the culmination of his decade of work at the Special Operations Division. But now the entire thing was hanging by a thread.

'We can try and fix this,' his colleague said.

'I'm not coming in,' Jack replied. 'This is done. They are done. What am I going to come in for? So we can have a series of calls? You know, fuck it. This is done.'

Jack couldn't bear to move. At the hotel bar he could feel a migraine begin to throb through his skull. There was a television above him. It was still mid-morning, but he ordered a glass of red wine. He looked at the television. The French President François Hollande was greeting the Iranian President Hassan Rouhani at the Élysée Palace.

Rouhani had arrived in Paris the day before as part of the first visit to Europe by an Iranian president in almost twenty years. The trip was part of a reset in relations between Iran and the West as a result of the nuclear deal that had been hammered out between Tehran and the United States, France, the UK, Germany, Russia and China. Two weeks earlier, diplomats in Vienna had formally allowed crippling international sanctions on Iran to be lifted.

The Iran nuclear deal had been hailed by both sides as a landmark in diplomacy: Rouhani celebrated what he called 'a glorious victory'. For the first time in decades, Iran was going to be reconnected to the global economy. Tehran had already announced plans to buy 118 aircraft from Airbus to replace its decrepit fleet of commercial planes in a deal worth €25 billion.

It dawned on Jack that the timings of the arrests couldn't have been worse. While Rouhani was in Paris there was no way the French government would announce a major criminal investigation involving Hezbollah. That would have exploded into a hugely embarrassing diplomatic incident. The plan for the press conference had been doomed from the moment the arrests were made at the airport. The exhilaration Jack had felt the night before evaporated into the Paris morning. Politics and bureaucracy had won again. Should he really be surprised?

There was one bit of good news: the French sensitivity around the Rouhani visit was not going to stop the Americans from making the operation public. Back in Washington, the US Treasury had been working on sanctions against Nourredine, which would name him as a Hezbollah-connected financier. On 28 January – the same day Rouhani met with French business leaders in Paris and the Airbus deal was inked, and four days after Nourredine had been arrested at Charles de Gaulle airport – the US Treasury put out the announcement.

It said it had 'targeted Hezbollah's financial support network by designating Hezbollah-affiliated money launderers Mohamad Nourreddine and Hamdi Zaher El Dine' for 'providing financial services to/or in support of Hezbollah, which has long been designated by the US as a terrorist organization'.

The DEA then put out its own press release, announcing that 'working closely with foreign counterparts in France, Germany, Italy and Belgium' it had arrested 'top leaders of the European cell of the Lebanese Hezbollah External Security Organisation BAC last week'. Jack Riley, the DEA's acting deputy administrator, who had led the operation to catch the notorious Mexican drug lord Joaquín 'El Chapo' Guzmán, told the world that the arrests had uncovered 'a revenue and weapons stream for an international terrorist organization responsible for devastating terror attacks around the world'.

Nourredine, Mazen al-Atat and the other members of the money-laundering cell were now in custody, being questioned by French police and DEA agents. The operation was over. By most measures, it had been a huge success. Jack should have felt elated. Instead, he was exhausted and furious. Then he heard the news about Ali Fayad.

At the same time, unknown to the DEA agents working on the operation in Paris, the five Czech hostages were being bundled into the back of a van. After driving for some time the vehicle stopped, dropped them off, and sped away. They found themselves staring at some kind of mine, off in the distance and down a hill.

Adam began to trudge down the slope. He needed to find a phone. Finally, he knew where he was. The kidnappers had told him they were in Lebanon, and to contact the Lebanese General Security Directorate, who would be expecting his call and would come and pick them up. But as soon as they had been dumped on the road some of the Czech hostages, confused and traumatised, started to panic, running and sliding down the hill in fear that they were about to be kidnapped again.

Adam reached the mine and began calling out for help. A worker rushed up to him and asked, 'What the hell happened to you?'

Several days later, after being debriefed by Lebanese security officials and Czech diplomats in Beirut, Adam and the others were put on a plane to Prague. Finally, after two hundred days in captivity, they were free – and so, it turned out, was Ali Fayad. The US attempt to extradite the arms dealer had failed. The Czech government had secretly nego-tiated to release Fayad in exchange for the five hostages. The American embassy in Prague was outraged, claiming there was 'no justification' for Fayad being released, and that the Czech decision would 'only encourage criminal groups and terrorists all over the world'.

The back-and-forth began. The Czech defence minister gave a newspaper interview in which he at first acknowledged that Fayad had been swapped for the five hostages. Then the country's foreign minister reverted to the government's official line that it did not negotiate with terrorists, suggesting that the simultaneous release of Fayad and the five hostages was a mere coincidence.

After the hostages had arrived safely back home, the Czech military intelligence officer who had been unmasked in Lebanon received a text message. 'Hi, how are you my friend? We miss you.' It was signed 'MALEM'.

Walking through the streets of Paris, Jack knew it was over. Project Cassandra, the operation he had devoted a decade of his life to – the operation that was supposed to make clear how crimes once hidden deep in the recesses of a lawless world could be connected and their perpetrators made to face justice – was finished.

Not long after the press conference debacle, Jack received an email from the office of the DEA's Chief of Operations. He knew it was important right away. This was one of the most senior people in the entire organisation. The email said his time at the Special Operations Division was over. He was going to be transferred to a job at headquarters.

27

'A State and Condition of Death'

Damascus Airport, May 2016

In the early hours of Friday 13 May 2016, Iain Edwards was woken by his wife as he snoozed in a maternity ward in The Hague. Hours before, she had given birth to the couple's first child and was cradling their sleeping baby in her hospital bed.

'Iain,' she said, holding her phone. 'I think you should have a look at this ...'

There had been a huge explosion in Damascus. The news alert read: 'Senior Hezbollah commander killed in Syria'.

Edwards began to examine the story. There was a statement from Hezbollah: 'The initial investigation shows that a large explosion targeted one of our centres near Damascus International Airport and led to the martyrdom of the commander Mustafa Badreddine.' Little other information seemed to be known.

Mustafa had managed to survive in the shadows for thirty years. But that evening his luck finally ran out. The man Edwards had devoted the last four years of his life to defending, a man he had never met, was dead.

Mustafa's corpse was rushed from Damascus to Beirut. Just as after his cousin Imad's death, the existence of a man who had lived as a grainy spectre his entire adult life suddenly burst into full Technicolor. Immediately Al Manar, Hezbollah's media arm, published eulogies to a man it declared to have been one of the movement's greatest military operatives, the man who it said had been the lifelong 'partner in jihad' of Imad Mughniyeh.

Solemn bearded men wearing green military berets and camouflage carried Mustafa's coffin, draped in the bright yellow Hezbollah flag, through the streets of Beirut as a brass band played, and women in black veils threw confetti from their balconies onto the procession below. Some mourners rushed to touch the coffin as it passed, while others punched the air in response to martial chanting amplified by megaphones.

Spies and investigators had been trying to track down photos of Mustafa for decades. Now his smiling face appeared all over the south of Beirut. Mourners carried large colour prints of the dead man, wearing spectacles and dressed in camouflage fatigues.

Surrounding Mustafa's coffin were his mourning family and a cadre of Hezbollah's most important figures. Wafiq Safa, one of its top security officials, was there, as well as Hashem Safieddine, a powerful member of the executive council and brother of Abdallah Safieddine, the group's Tehran envoy named in the DEA's Paris arrests three months earlier. Mustafa's son, Ali, was flanked by his grieving uncles, including Mustafa's older brother, Mohamed. He, the DEA knew, had been in regular contact with Mohamad Nourredine, the cocaine money launderer now languishing in a prison cell in Paris and who had been sanctioned as a Hezbollah financier by the US government.

Syria's ambassador to Lebanon sent condolences on behalf of Bashar Al-Assad, predicting that 'this great martyrdom is an announcement of victory, God willing, a coming victory'. That evening, Mustafa's coffin was buried alongside Imad in Hezbollah's Rawdat al-Shahidayn cemetery.

'As usual, when we talk about martyrs during their lives, we almost always use their jihadi codenames,' Hassan Nasrallah said in a memorial speech. 'For example, we say

"Sayyed Zuylfiqar" [Mustafa's codename], "El-Hajj Radwan" [Imad's codename], et cetera. But after their martyrdom, we almost always go back to using their real names. Thus we say: Sayyed Mustafa, El-Hajj Imad. For this reason, I will now use this name: Sayyed Mustafa.'

Secrets, once tightly held, were being revealed. Mustafa, Nasrallah said, had been one of the 'first men of this resistance'; he was severely wounded fighting in the early 1980s, and he had been left with scars on his body and one of his legs, which had hindered his ability to walk for the rest of his life. Nasrallah spoke of the secret military operations Mustafa had worked on with Imad, the attacks he had masterminded against Israel, and the spies he had caught operating inside Lebanon after the 2006 war.

When the conflict in Syria had broken out, Nasrallah said, 'Sayyed Mustafa was in charge of leading and commanding the Hezbollah military and security units inside Syrian territories.' He had never wanted Mustafa to go to Syria, he confessed, knowing that it was a dangerous risk for the commander to take. But Mustafa had insisted. Now, just like his cousin Imad seven years before, Mustafa had met his end in Damascus.

Back at the UN tribunal in Leidschendam, the assembled judges and legal teams began a crisis meeting. A dead man could not remain on trial. Everyone in the courtroom knew that if Mustafa had died then the case against him for masterminding the assassination of Rafic Hariri would have to be closed for ever.

It was a paradox. If Mustafa had been killed in Damascus airport then the case against him would end. But the barrage of information released since his death – his crimes, his secrets – meant that the proof of his guilt was stronger than ever.

The prosecution needed to keep the case open. And so it began to wonder, could Mustafa's death in Damascus be proved beyond reasonable doubt? They were dealing with a master terrorist, and a master of disguise and deception – 'an untraceable ghost'. Nothing had been independently verified. Hezbollah had taken full control of the investigation into Mustafa's death, the movement of his remains and his burial. The court had seen the media announcements, the funeral parade, the grieving relatives and the speeches eulogising his military operations. But they had not seen a death certificate, and certainly not a corpse.

Sami Issa, the mysterious playboy jeweller whose mobile phones had been used to coordinate the assassination, had long been a critical part of the prosecution's case. The evidence showed, the prosecution had argued, that Sami Issa had always been an identity used by Mustafa to carry out the killing. The defence had countered by saying it was impossible for any of the witnesses who had met Issa to definitively link him to their client. The only images they could use to compare the two men were decades old, or questionable snaps leaked into the public domain by the website Terror Control.

But now Hezbollah had for the first time confirmed that Mustafa was a top military commander in Syria, with decades of operations under his belt; it had also released up-to-date images of him grinning in green military fatigues at his command post. The prosecution had eight eyewitnesses to confirm that the new pictures of Mustafa showed Sami Issa and he were the same person. And without a corpse, he could still be out there.

'Is there any evidence, other than that which comes directly from Hezbollah, that Mr Badreddine is in fact dead?' David Re, the Australian presiding judge, asked at the first hearing.

Graeme Cameron, a Canadian lawyer acting for the

prosecution, said there was not. 'All I can do in this proceeding is to present all of the evidence that I have, which is consistent with death,' he explained. 'Now really it is up to you to decide whether you are satisfied.'

Janet Nosworthy, another judge on the bench, wasn't comfortable. There was no evidence yet, she said, of 'a body [that] was seen in a state and condition of death'. A funeral alone wasn't going to cut it. 'I am not certain you can actually say because there was a condolence ceremony, and because pursuant to that condolence ceremony there was a procession . . . that you can reach the type of finding you're asking for.'

Peter Haynes, a British barrister acting for the families of the twenty-one other victims who died in the Beirut truck bomb, told the court that his clients wanted bulletproof evidence that Mustafa was really dead before they could accept closing the case. At the very least they needed DNA evidence or a death certificate before they could be satisfied. 'It's our submission, really, that a death certificate is a minimum requirement,' he said.

Judge David Re then asked Haynes about the grieving members of Mustafa's family, who had been recorded at the funeral. Could they really be faking it? Or had they been tricked? 'Are you suggesting that they could have been duped, and led to believe that Mr Badreddine was dead but in the absence of any real proof that he is dead?'

Haynes said the pictures of Mustafa's grieving brothers weren't enough – they needed the death certificate. 'If there were direct evidence from the person expressing that grief that he had seen the body of Mustafa Badreddine, that would be a wholly different thing,' he said. 'But a mere still photograph of someone looking upset at his brother's funeral is not the most potent piece of evidence, with the greatest respect.'

*

While the lawyers at the UN court argued, questions were beginning to be asked elsewhere about the explosion that was meant to have killed Mustafa.

On the night of the blast, Damascus International Airport was fully under the control of the Syrian regime. Hezbollah did not immediately attribute the explosion to anyone, but said that it was conducting an investigation to find out 'if it is the result of an airstrike, a rocket, or artillery attack. We will announce more results in the investigation soon.'

A pro-Hezbollah Lebanese television station had initially attributed the attack to Israel, but then quickly pulled its article from its website. The US government soon confirmed that no coalition planes had been flying in the area, and said it had been unable to verify the reports of Mustafa's demise.

The day after the funeral, Hezbollah released another statement attributing the Damascus attack to 'Takfiris' – jihadist rebels in Syria – but providing no further details. The nearest rebel positions on the night of the blast were believed to have been seven kilometres away – a distance that would have required weaponry they didn't possess, immense good fortune, or devastatingly accurate intelligence, to take someone out with such precision. There was no information to suggest anyone else died in the explosion. None of the jihadist and other rebel groups operating around Damascus claimed credit for the attack that killed one of the most important commanders of their enemy.

On the same day, the Syrian Observatory for Human Rights, a UK-based opposition monitoring group, published a statement that it had been 'informed by reliable sources' among the rebel groups close to the area that no shells or rockets had been fired into Damascus airport on the days around Mustafa's death. 'There is no truth about what has been published by Hezbollah about the assassination of its military commander in Syria,' it said.

A report published by Al Arabiya, a Saudi-owned media group hostile to Hezbollah, claimed that aerial images showed no damage to the building that was supposed to have been hit. The report cited witnesses saying they had heard gunfire that night, not an explosion. Mustafa, the report concluded, had not died in a rebel artillery strike. He had been shot.

Then the chief of staff of the Israeli military, Lieutenant General Gadi Eisenkot, took the rare step of commenting publicly on the circumstances surrounding Mustafa's death. Following previous targeted assassinations of Hezbollah leaders attributed to Israel, including the car bomb that had killed Imad in Damascus, the country had a policy of never confirming or denying its involvement. This time was different. Eisenkot said that the Arab media reports 'corresponded with the information we have and with our assessment'. Mustafa had not been blown up by a rebel bomb: he had been killed by his own side. It was, Eisenkot said, evidence of 'an internal crisis over what they are fighting for, an economic crisis and a leadership crisis'.

Israeli intelligence had long regarded Mustafa as a hothead and a womaniser. But perhaps he had his principles too. The battle he had been fighting in Syria had cost many lives. Lebanese Shias who had staunchly supported Hezbollah now faced their sons returning home in body bags – not because they'd been fighting Israel, the group's founding purpose, but because they'd been used as cannon fodder to prop up a dictator.

According to this telling, Mustafa had been in growing conflict with Qasem Soleimani over the strategic direction of the war in Syria. He had met with the Iranian general to try to resolve their differences.

Soleimani wasn't just an ally: he was a family friend. He had broken bread with Saada and zipped around on motorcycles with Imad during the 2006 war. After Jihad Mughniyeh, Imad's twenty-three-year-old son and Mustafa's nephew, was killed by an Israeli drone strike close to the Golan Heights, Soleimani read the Quran by the young man's grave in a midnight ceremony. The Iranian commander then joined the family in mourning at the home of Mustafa's father.

After many years of fighting, Mustafa was said to have been angry about the large number of casualties his men had suffered and wanted to reduce their presence in Syria. Soleimani had refused, demanding that the Hezbollah men under Mustafa's control stay on the front line. That evening they drank tea and discussed the matter. Then Soleimani left the room. His bodyguards pulled out their pistols and, at close range, shot Mustafa.

It was a story of betrayal recounted by Mustafa's bitterest enemies and, like so much about his shadowy life, was impossible to verify.

Sami Issa, his old alias, had written on his application to the Lebanese American University about his desire to 'deeply understand the dynamics and the rules that control the political world, and to be able to plan for change'. The world the ageing Mustafa found himself in had become unrecognisable. He was an analogue warrior in a digital age, a throwback to a time where passports could be easily forged and electronic surveillance was limited. He lived through secrets in the name of piety, but his decadence and womanising had been revealed in an international tribunal for the world to see. And perhaps, to his own side, he had become a liability.

Back at the UN tribunal, after several weeks of debate, the matter was finally settled. Iain Edwards and Mustafa's other lawyers returned with a Lebanese death certificate signed by two people whose identities the court redacted. The defence said it 'respectfully submits that these two witnesses are close enough to Mr Badreddine to provide cogent and reliable evidence of his post-mortem identification'. The court had no choice but to be satisfied. Regardless of how exactly it had happened and who had pulled the trigger, Mustafa was dead.

28

No Options Left

Calabria, 2016

Salvatore and Oksana were in her kitchen. It was just after nine in the evening and the television was on. He was agitated. She knew how much trouble he was in and that every time he left her, she might never see him again. In the dark, lonely hours of the night, she would lie down on her bed and pray for him, begging God to protect her lover wherever he went.

'I fell asleep praying today,' she said.

'You have to stop it. Every time you throw it in my face.'

'I don't throw it at you. I pray every time you leave,' she said. 'If you don't want to believe me then don't believe me.'

Salvatore seemingly owed money to everyone and was running out of friends. He had stolen, murdered and lived outside the law his entire adult life, working in a system that ordered the world around him. But that evening, sitting in Oksana's kitchen, the system no longer protected him. Nothing could help him now – not his cousin, nor the powerful bosses that stood above all of them. If not for Oksana, he'd be alone.

Days later Oksana was preparing dinner for Salvatore. He was clearly stressed by something.

'I can't take it any more . . . I have to leave again tomorrow.'

'You have to leave tomorrow night?' she asked.

'Tomorrow.'

'But where do you have to go?'

'Albania.'

Oksana knew exactly how dangerous such a trip would be.

'You must be joking. You don't have to go.'

Salvatore had been scrambling to arrange various drug deals to try to make back the money he had lost. But none of them were going well. One involved taking delivery of a large shipment of marijuana from a group of Albanian gangsters, and then paying them once Salvatore and his more senior partners had sold it in Italy. But Salvatore's collaborators had failed to find a buyer. And now the Albanian boss wanted the money. Both Oksana and Salvatore knew that if he went to Albania there was a risk that he would never come back.

She pleaded with him again.

'You don't have to go.'

'Because they will kill me?'

She hated him saying that. 'What the fuck? Won't you stop this?'

Salvatore tried to reassure her. He told her he would get Antonio to look after her while he was away. But this did little to calm Oksana's nerves.

'That doesn't help me at all . . . I'm ready to leave you! I told you that you don't have to go, but not for me . . . Everyone looks after himself except you. I'm saying this for your own good. Go where you want and do what you want, but I assure you that you won't find me when you come back!'

Oksana was trying to use the tiny amount of leverage she had to change his mind, but Salvatore didn't seem to take her threats seriously. Instead he once again began to list with weary resignation why he had no choice but to go.

'I hope you get sick, so you then can't get up from the bed and then you won't be able to go,' she told him, probably half joking.

'Sorry – you don't care what happens to me,' he replied. In Salvatore's mind, Oksana wasn't worried about his safety, but what it would mean for her financial wellbeing if he never returned from Albania. 'The important thing for you is nothing happens to the person who you want to provide a future for you.'

It was hopeless. After arguing for almost an hour Oksana had become resigned to the fact that Salvatore would be leaving the following morning, no matter what she said or did. All she could do was tell him how worried she was and to lament his stubbornness.

'But how can I be calm if I don't know where you are and what you are doing?'

'I have to solve a problem. I will immediately return if they don't keep me there.'

The next morning Salvatore travelled to Bari, on Italy's Adriatic coast, and from there caught a ferry to Albania. He arrived alone in the port with only a phone number he had been told to call, and with no idea about where he had to go. He hailed a taxi and struggled to explain to the driver that he needed to call the number to find out the address.

Salvatore was nervous. As soon as he arrived he would have to apologise for the missed payments – and tell the Albanians how ashamed he was about what had happened. He sat down on a sofa with the boss, an intimidating figure even for a man like Salvatore. He noticed the Albanian had a pouch on his lap containing a pistol as well as numerous mobile phones, all of the same model.

To Salvatore's relief, the Albanian was pleased that he had come over to explain the missing payment. 'Be calm, you are at home here,' he told the Italian. This didn't mean the boss wasn't upset; but he wasn't going to spill blood over the misunderstanding, at least not yet.

'I didn't expect this from you,' he told Salvatore in disappointment. But he pinned the blame on Salvatore's business partners, not him.

Salvatore later recounted the Albanian's words to Oksana: 'I know you had nothing to do with it,' he had told him. 'You should tell your partner that he should have come here to talk to me and not you. But I'm glad you came.' The Albanian trusted that Salvatore would resolve the problem, but asked him in future to speak with him directly and cut out his unreliable business partners.

'He told me, "Salvatore, you know what I tell you . . . you are neither a thief nor a crook, but you have to listen to my advice. Your partner treats you like a toy . . . and for that I'm sorry. You have to do one thing for the future. You can come here whenever you want, and we negotiate ourselves."'

With that the Albanian bought Salvatore's ticket back to Italy, and one of his men accompanied him to the port. Salvatore had managed to smooth over the problem in Albania, for now, but he still had no money coming in and enormous debts to pay.

As the days went by, Salvatore would spend hours sharing his problems with Oksana. She would listen to him rehearsing the lines he was going to use on his creditors. His situation didn't seem fair to him. Going through his accounts, which he kept on scraps of paper, he could see how much work he had put in, making money for others.

'Do you know how much money I brought to you?' he would say to an imaginary business partner. 'I wrote it all down, I burned the papers the other day. TWO MILLION and EIGHT HUNDRED THOUSAND euros! – I will tell him that,' he told Oksana, '– in less than two years!'

During their long conversations, Salvatore would veer between rage and dejection. Oksana could not comfort him. Salvatore knew the chance of a new shipment from Colombia was close to zero. Jhon Peludo had left some time ago. The dream had died.

In the final months of Jhon's stay with them in Calabria they had all been sitting in Oksana's flat together. Salvatore had lunged at Jhon and tried to throttle him. In that moment, Salvatore believed only one of them was going to survive: either he would kill Jhon with his bare hands, or the Colombian would kill him.

'What the fuck are you doing?' Oksana had yelled. 'You each go to your houses and kill each other wherever you want. This is my house!'

Eventually, Antonio managed to break the two apart. But, as Salvatore continued to fight for his survival, the bitterness remained. Oksana had come to feel the same way. 'First the Colonel came, and then after that the dickhead philosopher,' Oksana said, referring to Jhon. She started to imitate the lines he used to roll out to Salvatore about the fortune that awaited him. '"Trust me my friend, you will become rich, rich!" But he sent the money back home, and here he ate like a pig. I washed and ironed everything for him.'

'I bought him petrol,' Salvatore weighed in. 'I bought him pasta, I put meat in the refrigerator, I bought him pastries—'

'Don't even talk to me about that.'

'Here is everything,' Salvatore continued, recalling the hospitality he had lavished on the Colombians as if he were a hotelier. 'Here is your bed, here is the bathroom . . . '

He began to fantasise about what he would do if he ever saw Jhon again. 'I will take out my gun, and the moment he starts speaking that same evening I will shoot him,' Salvatore said. 'You know what he wants to do: he wants to come back again to ask for money.'

'You mustn't care about that,' she replied. 'Don't give him anything more. And if he starts talking about me . . . he is gone.' Was Oksana advising Salvatore to kill Jhon? It was hard to know for sure.

The cruellest joke, in Salvatore's eyes, was the fact that he had found out that the Colonel – the idiotic guarantee the Colombians had sent to Italy at the start of the whole affair, the man who had almost ruined everything before it had even begun – was still alive. Jhon and Jota Jota had assured the Italians that the Colonel would pay for his incompetence by being 'taken to the mountains'. But they had lied.

'If that son of a bitch Jhon ever comes back here, the first thing I want to know from him is this: why did you tell me the Colonel is dead?'

Raging about the Colombians perhaps made Salvatore feel better. But anger would fade into despair. He was a killer, a cold-hearted and ruthless gangster, but he was in that moment vulnerable. Oksana could see that no matter how angry he was about the Colombians there was a growing acceptance inside him that his fate was sealed. Salvatore was ruined.

'I'm telling you, and not as a joke, I have no options left,' he told her. 'I really don't.'

*

Six thousand miles away, at 2 a.m. on 16 May 2016, Colombian police commandos, supported by two Black Hawk helicopters, raided the banana plantation outside Turbo.

After arresting three people, the police discovered inside a wooden shack the entrance to an underground bunker, covered with a layer of cement. When they broke the seal, a strong chemical smell wafted out of the tunnel. Inside they found 359 white tarpaulins containing more than nine tonnes of cocaine.

This was the cocaine that Jota Jota, Jhon Peludo and the Colonel had been trying to sell to the Italians – the cocaine that Salvatore had dreamed would make him a millionaire. Now the packages were lined up one by one on the ground outside, stretching as far as the eye could see.

Later that evening Juan Manuel Santos, President of Colombia, tweeted his congratulations to the police, announcing the seizure as the largest in his country's history, estimated to be worth as much as $250 million.

Three months before the raid, an agent from the Colombian national police had gone undercover by posing as a day labourer seeking work on the banana plantation. He began to quietly gather intelligence, leaving the compound to drop coded messages to his colleagues at pre-agreed spots in the nearby town.

The agent had learned that the banana plantation was well known in the area for the higher wages it paid, intended to keep its staff quiet. And keeping quiet was wise. The workers knew that they were working for people who wouldn't hesitate to order their murder. Soon the agent observed the trucks arriving in the middle of the night, bringing food for the workers and also hundreds of kilograms of camouflaged cocaine.

As the agent continued to speak with the other labourers,

he learned that the drugs being hidden belonged to Gavilán, the second-in-command of the Clan del Golfo and one of the most wanted men in Colombia. The rumour on the plantation, the undercover policeman told his bosses, was that the kingpin had become increasingly paranoid that the reward on his head would tempt his underlings to betray him. But when the commandos arrived to raid the plantation, Gavilán was not there.

Some weeks after Salvatore returned from Albania, he told Oksana he needed to go on another trip to raise some money. But this time she wouldn't be left on her own to worry about him. They could go on a road trip to the mountains. It would be romantic, a chance for the two of them to spend time together.

Four days before Christmas, Salvatore had made an appointment with a man from a small town in Calabria to sell him three hundred grams of cocaine and ten kilograms of marijuana. It was a tiny amount, almost pathetic for a man who had dreamed of importing tonnes of cocaine alongside one of the most powerful cartels in Latin America. But he was desperate.

Salvatore's client had been delayed during a trip to Lombardy in the north of Italy, so the meeting was pushed back to two days after Christmas. Oksana was nervous, telling Salvatore that she had a bad feeling about travelling in a car carrying drugs. But he convinced her. He always did.

On the day of the meeting, Salvatore put on a pair of jeans, a dark jacket and a cap, and got into a burgundy Fiat 220 van. He had told Oksana he would be picking her up at around 8 a.m. near her apartment. As he approached her the dull yellow beams of his headlights bore through the darkness of the winter morning. She got inside the van, and they began to move.

As they travelled along a motorway junction near Lamezia Terme, Salvatore spotted a police roadblock up ahead. Nothing to worry about – it was only a routine inspection. But after Salvatore had stopped his van and rolled down his window, the police officers asked him to let them inspect the vehicle. Inside, taped to the lining of the bonnet, was the marijuana and a wrapper containing 295.7 grams of cocaine (slightly less than Salvatore had promised his client), wrapped in a plastic bag to which was taped a scrap of paper with the number 300 written on it. The police told Salvatore and Oksana they were under arrest.

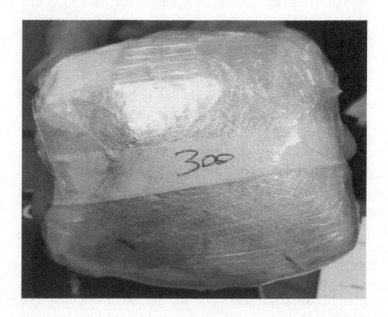

29

The Retirement Party

Virginia, May 2016

The news that he was being transferred out of the Special Operations Division hit Jack hard. For more than a decade the SOD had been his life. For in spite of all the stress, all the battles and the toll it had taken on him, he had the best job in the world. He could never understand the agents who just turned up, sat at their desks looking at the internet and left early to go to their kid's Little League game.

To make matters worse, Jack had been told that his bosses were planning to move him into a regional gang crime unit at the DEA headquarters in Arlington. Just a month before, he had been in Paris taking down a drug money laundering conspiracy that reached across continents. Now he was being sent back to the daily grind of street-corner busts and small-time crooks.

Jack's first day working for the DEA had been just before

Memorial Day weekend in 1991. That meant he would soon have completed twenty-five years of service and be eligible for retirement. After the disappointment of Paris and the shock of the transfer news, and without telling his team, Jack had put in his papers.

None of Jack's colleagues had believed he was going to retire. He would sometimes drop into conversations that his twenty-five years was coming up. But they probably thought it was a joke. Jack was too obsessed, too devoted. He had never really believed it himself. Yes, he had put the calendar up on the wall of his condo, marking off each day in a private ritual. But retirement had been an escape hatch, if needed. He was burned out, true, but part of him had wanted to never leave. Now, he felt like his hand had been forced.

After Paris there was a big shake up at the SOD. Derek Maltz, who had always been fiercely protective of his agents, had been gone for more than a year and a half. A new Chief of Operations had begun shifting veteran agents out of the SOD to bring in fresh faces. The bosses had sent a formal email to several top agents telling them their time was up.

Jack was pissed off. Pissed off about what had happened in Paris and pissed off about Ali Fayad being released by the Czechs. And now he was pissed off about his transfer and what was happening at the SOD.

If he was going to retire, he was at least going to retire in place. Moving to a new unit a few months before leaving the DEA seemed like a pointless cruelty, an insult. The SOD was being ripped apart. Emails sent around by management announced bulk transfers of agents to new jobs, sometimes ten or twenty going at a time. Agents who had worked on some of the biggest, most important cases in the history of the DEA were being moved into regional field divisions across the US. They had been rock stars. Now men and women who had chased international supervillains were being told to shuffle papers in desk jobs. Rob Zachariasiewicz, one of Jack's closest friends, and the DEA agent who had read Viktor Bout his rights in a Thai hotel room, was shifted to a field group in the Washington DC office. Jack compared it to putting Michael Jordan on a high school basketball team.

He had always known that the SOD was vulnerable after Maltz retired. The department's success had bred resentment. Rank-and-file agents doing boring jobs at headquarters could be resentful of the select few, like Jack, who had been picked to join the elite unit. Senior DEA leadership had also become wary of the SOD. It not only stole many of the headlines, but Maltz had also fought hard to ensure his team received significant funding, and his pick of the very best agents. During Jack's time at the SOD, it had also gained significant influence over how investigations were run. This had generated spectacular results. But some managers believed it had to be cut down to size.

It felt to Jack like the end of an era. He was a charter member of the swashbuckling Special Operations Division, built in a brief, flickering moment of post-9/11 America, which gave a group of drug cops working the streets the licence to go after the biggest bad guys in the world. In those years the SOD had been given the resources and the political backing to embark on some of the most audacious criminal cases in history. They were, at their heart, street agents taking down arms dealers like Monzer al-Kassar and Viktor Bout. Perhaps it was crazy that Jack and his colleagues had ever been able to get as far as they did.

At the same time, the DEA began to be hit by damaging scandals and a leadership crisis. For six years, from 2015 to 2021, it went without a Senate-confirmed administrator, leaving it rudderless. It also suffered a string of departures, losing nearly 1,300 employees, of which seven hundred were agents. Many took early retirement to move into higher-paying private sector work.

More painful were revelations that some agents working abroad had become corrupted at a time when the DEA was under fire for failing to halt a deadly fentanyl epidemic at home. One agent attended sex parties with prostitutes hired by Colombian drug cartels, while another laundered money for traffickers and used the cash to buy luxury homes and attend yacht parties. In 2021 an audit by the US Department of Justice's Office of the Inspector General found that the DEA failed to effectively monitor its foreign operations and agents overseas, prompting the DEA to order an outside review.

After several weeks of arguments, Jack's bosses relented: he could stay at the SOD to see out the last few months of his career. They also said they were going to organise a retirement party. It was going to be a classic send-off, with the DEA's tartan-clad pipers rolled out and much whisky consumed. But Jack didn't want a party. He never liked big social events. And what was there to celebrate? They insisted and Jack reluctantly agreed, as long as it was near his condo. They chose a generic sports bar called the American Tap Room. But after a few days Jack changed his mind again. He told his boss to cancel the party. And then he booked a holiday, alone, in Cancún.

Before his holiday, he got a message from his friend Nugget, an agent in the DEA's Miami office. 'Jack, I am flying up for your party.' Jack was confused. 'Nugget, there is no party,' he said. 'If there is a party then I won't be there.' Jack made sure to tell all his close friends and family not to come down, in case there was any confusion, and flew to

Cancun. A few nights after he arrived, he got a string of text messages: 'Jack, walk up the hill to the American Tap Room.' 'Jack, we are waiting for you.'

He typed back: 'I am in Mexico.'

They thought he was joking. The bosses had thrown the party without telling him.

Back in Virginia, Jack began to clear his desk. It was surrounded by piles of papers and documents relating to Project Cassandra, enough to fill fifty boxes. There were thousands of pages of reports on their targets, complex organisational charts, financial documents and newspaper clippings. It was going to take days, even weeks, to get rid of it all.

Because of the risk that some of the papers were classified, Jack would have to have them all destroyed. At first he tried to shred them, but it soon became clear there were too many. They would instead have to be burned. He got hold of a large dumpster and began to toss away the best years of his career, his life, to be wheeled away and incinerated.

He began to think back over old operations. There had been big successes and painful failures. Many targets had been prosecuted. Some, like Ali Fayad, had got away. Perhaps it was the right time to leave. He knew he could be a pain in the ass, constantly pushing his colleagues and his bosses to go further, to work harder. They had probably done as much as they could. The job was done. It was time to let go.

On his final day, he drove into the office to return some things to the security guards. As he was walking out, the SOD's new top boss grabbed him and said he wanted to take him out for lunch. Jack had known him since his New York days. But they had never talked about the attempt to transfer him. At the restaurant Jack ordered a margarita. Part of him wanted to let rip, to tell him how disappointed he was with what was happening at the SOD. But it wasn't worth it. After lunch, the boss walked him to his car and gave him a hug. Jack got inside his Jeep and drove away from the SOD building for the last time.

30

'My Name is Oksana'

Paliano Prison, February 2017

A lone woman entered the interview room and sat down at a table. Sitting opposite her was a man in a dark suit and tie, and a recording device. He started the tape, and she began to speak.

It began as a trickle of words. 'My name is Oksana Verman, I was born in Cherkasy in Ukraine on the twenty-third of November 1976,' she said. 'I have made mistakes, and I want to change my life.'

Her hands were trembling, and tears streamed down her face. Listening to her intently was Camillo Falvo, the public prosecutor of Vibo Valentia who lived under constant police protection for pursuing cases against men like Salvatore Pititto. Falvo was always dressed in a dark suit and tie, but had the sympathetic, reassuring face of a man who had spent a career gently reaching into the souls of the damned.

Oksana was exhausted. They were inside a maximum-security prison in the town of Paliano, about an hour's drive from Rome. Three other men from Italy's anti-Mafia investigative police unit were in the room with her, and so was her lawyer. Prisons are usually designed to protect society from criminals. This prison, on a hill five hundred metres high, protected by a double row of ramparts and overlooking the green fields of central Italy, protected the prisoners from people who wanted them dead.

In the fifteenth century, Paliano had become the seat of a branch of the House of Colonna, a noble Italian dynasty which had warred with papal armies, winning, losing and winning back control of the fortress town over several centuries. Following Italian unification in 1871, the newly established state began to use a large building in the centre of the fortress as a prison. During the twentieth century, it became the location for prisoners known as 'collaborators of justice', or state's witnesses. In Italy's years of partisan terror some of the prisoners were turncoats from the Red Brigades. Now, the eighty or so prisoners were almost exclusively Mafia informants who had decided to break their vow of silence and testify against their organisation.

The word in Italian for a Mafia state's witness is pentito, or 'repentant'. This was what Oksana was here to do – repent. 'I met Salvatore Pititto the first day I arrived in Italy. He came to pick me up when I got off the train,' she told the prosecutor. She had never known life in Italy without him. She had cared for him, prayed for him. She had loved him. She had dreamed for him.

Oksana was now far away from Salvatore, who was in prison in the south of Italy, and she was far away from Calabria. But even being protected inside the bowels of a stone fortress could not calm the terror that gripped her. She had been physically sick, shaking with fear and unable to stop crying as she thought about the consequences of her betrayal.

She told them how she had had nothing, almost no possessions to her name. Salvatore had controlled almost every aspect of her life. He and his family were murderers who had acted without remorse. And if they ever had the chance to kill her, they wouldn't hesitate. 'I am so scared for my safety. I have been suffering from constant panic attacks,' she said. 'I am scared of them, in the sense that I am scared of their gang, the Pititto gang, because Salvatore always told me that Pasquale Pititto, his cousin, is very dangerous. Salvatore said that Pasquale had committed all these murders. He spoke to me about these acts, telling me that he had killed various people.'

Oksana then began to tell them how she came to be in Italy, and how she came to be with Salvatore. She told them about her past, and her dreams of moving to Italy for a new life. She told them about Salvatore's jealousy, how he had beaten her, and the secret meetings he had held in her apartment. About the nights when he sent her away as he discussed with his friends the crimes he was going to commit, and the low voice he would speak in because he feared that he was being recorded.

She told them more about Pasquale, the cousin she had never met who sat alone in his house all day, and how much she feared him. She talked about Salvatore's sons, and the pride he had in them: pride that they were becoming with each day more like their father. And she told them about the drug trafficking, the master plan Salvatore had hatched with the Colombians. She told them about the Colonel coming to Italy and Osvaldo being sent to Colombia, about Jhon Peludo and Jota Jota. And she told them about the guns, and the murder in Mileto that Salvatore had confessed to her.

It was several weeks after Oksana and Salvatore had been pulled over by police. Salvatore would have known the three hundred grams of cocaine the police had found hidden in the bonnet of his car meant he was in trouble. But he soon discovered that his problems were far greater than he could have imagined. Just weeks later, the Italian anti-Mafia police launched dawn raids across the country, arresting fifty-four people who had been involved in Salvatore's drug-trafficking scheme. They arrested Antonella, Giuseppe and Gianluca, as well as Filippo Fiarè. They charged Pasquale with new crimes relating to his role in the conspiracy, and several of his other cousins.

Salvatore had spent his days in a state of intense paranoia about being watched or recorded. He had sent cryptic text messages to his business partners and his cousin, pretending to be their girlfriends, and driven in silence to olive groves deep in the countryside to speak in private with other gangsters. But after the raids took place, Salvatore discovered that the police who had been watching his every move had managed to place a listening device in the one place he had felt free to speak without fear: in Oksana's kitchen. The investigation had amassed hundreds of hours of Salvatore confessing his hopes, fears and crimes to his lover. They had tapped Salvatore's phone, and those of dozens of others involved in the drug plot. They had photos of his movements across the country, his meetings with the Colombians and his secret liaisons with Pasquale.

Camillo Falvo, the public prosecutor leading the case, knew that the confession he was about to hear from Oksana was the final piece of the investigation. Her words would seal her lover's fate. Falvo showed her pictures of Salvatore's family and associates for her to identify. One by one, she fingered every single person involved in the conspiracy. There was the photo of the Colonel, of Jhon Peludo and even Jota

Jota. There was Filippo Fiarè, and others from Mileto. They showed her pictures of Antonella, Giuseppe and Gianluca. Oksana recognised them all.

In the months leading up to their arrest, Oksana had spent her evenings praying for Salvatore. Now she was not just condemning her lover, but obliterating everything he held dear. The Pititto gang would no longer be able to stalk the streets of Mileto, ruling over it like kings. And with Salvatore's two eldest sons also behind bars the future of the family, which had terrorised their town for more than two decades, could simply vanish. This was what would cause Salvatore more pain than any prison sentence, or even betrayal by his lover.

Oksana had loved him, but had he ever really loved her? Was she ever more than his possession, a trinket that gave him relief in moments of stress or difficulty, but that could be tossed away at any time? Moments after the arrest, he had slipped the secret phone he had been using to arrange the drug deal into her handbag. Later, he denied to the police that the phone was his. Salvatore had betrayed her before she betrayed him.

As the weeks went by, Oksana did more interviews, telling prosecutors everything she knew. Slowly, she became more confident, more defiant in rejecting the world that had trapped her. The grip Salvatore had held her in began to fade. Far away, he wasn't powerful and frightening, but a sad and broken figure.

'I knew that Salvatore had lots of debt, he was ruined because of all the drug trafficking he had invested in that had gone wrong,' she told them. The luxury wedding with horse-drawn carriages that had been planned for Giuseppe and his girlfriend would now never happen. And if they hadn't been arrested, would his father's lover even have been allowed to go?

Salvatore had destroyed himself and everything that he had cared about. But he hadn't destroyed Oksana.

In Holy Week, three months after Oksana had arrived in Paliano, there was an unexpected visitor to the prison. Pope Francis came to deliver a private Easter Mass, washing and kissing the right foot of each of twelve inmates in imitation of Jesus's gesture of humility towards his apostles the night before the crucifixion. In an impromptu sermon to the prisoners who were being housed there – including Oksana – Francis spoke about betrayal and forgiveness.

'Jesus was at supper with his disciples in the Last Supper and, as the Gospel says, he knew that his hour had come to pass from this world to the Father,' the Pope told the prisoners. 'Jesus knew he had been betrayed, and that he was to be handed over that very night by Judas. Having loved his own, who were in the world, he loved them to the end ... "To love to the end." It's not easy because all of us are sinners; we all have limitations, defects, so many things. We are all able to love, but we are not like God.'

Oksana knew that regardless of the information she was providing to the state prosecutor, she would be charged with being Salvatore's co-conspirator and likely spend significant time behind bars. But imprisoned behind the walls of Paliano was perhaps the first time since she had met Salvatore that she felt free.

31

The Speech at the Stone

Calabria, April 2017

Back in Mileto, the small grey house on the corner where Salvatore had lived with his wife and his three sons was quiet. Four of the five who had lived at the address had been arrested. Only one remained.

Alex had recently turned fifteen. He had celebrated his birthday without his parents or his older brothers. The little garden to the side of the house with the orange trees where Antonella had grown vegetables – and where she had pointed a gun at Salvatore's head in a fit of jealousy – was silent.

Salvatore had raised Giuseppe and Gianluca to be just like him. Giuseppe, who drank grappa with Pasquale, had been groomed to lead the family one day. But Alex, ten years younger than Giuseppe and six years younger than Gianluca, was still a child. He lived a life similar to the other teenagers in Mileto, hanging out with his friends, smoking joints and eating pizza in the local squares.

Alex was a short, slightly pudgy boy who had shaved the side of his head and wore tracksuits. Since the arrest of his parents and brothers he had been placed in the care of his grandparents. Alex's friends had noticed he had started to act erratically, getting into arguments and repeatedly breaking up and getting back together with his girlfriend Noemi. During one of their break-ups, Noemi had discovered that Alex had been spending time with other girls. Wanting to make him jealous, she had flirted with some of the boys in his group of friends. It had worked: Alex was becoming increasingly paranoid that she was spending time with them behind his back.

On the evening of 29 May, at around 7 p.m., Alex was hanging out with two friends in a piazza in the centre of Mileto. A friend, Domenico, had driven over in his father's car and was going to drop them all home. After they had said goodbye to the other two, Alex asked Domenico to drive him to another place as he wanted to meet one of his best friends, a boy called Francesco. Domenico stopped the car near the Mileto elementary school, and Alex rang Francesco, telling him to meet them in the town centre. Francesco was a year older than Alex, a popular and handsome boy who was captain of the Mileto youth football team. Francesco arrived about five minutes after Alex had called him. Alex said he wanted Domenico to drive them into the countryside so he could show them something special he had hidden. On the way, Francesco asked Alex for a cigarette and both of them smoked.

They arrived at a remote dirt road leading into an olive grove. Alex told Domenico to turn the car around and wait for him and Francesco. They went into the field. Suddenly, Domenico heard several loud bangs. Scared, he started the engine but then saw Alex running towards the car. There was no Francesco. Clearly something terrible had happened.

Back in Mileto, Francesco's mother and sister were getting increasingly concerned. Her son had left home several hours earlier, saying he was going to meet some friends for dinner. It was now after 10 p.m. and he wasn't picking up his phone or responding to messages. His WhatsApp profile showed that he hadn't been online for hours.

Out on the dirt road, as Alex got back into the car Domenico noticed he was holding something in his hand. It was a small, dark pistol. Where was Francesco? Where was Francesco? 'I killed him,' Alex replied. The boy holding the gun appeared emotionless. In a state of shock, Domenico asked him why he had killed him, and Alex said that Francesco had 'done things he wasn't meant to do'. He then told Domenico to drive them back to Mileto. When they reached the town, Alex asked to be let out on one of the main streets.

Francesco's mother heard a car pull up outside their home. Maybe her son was back. But when she looked out their window, she didn't see Francesco but the police. She began to panic. 'Where is my son?' she asked them. 'Where is my son?' The police told her that he had been shot.

At 10.10 p.m. Alex Pititto arrived alone at the police station. He told them there had been a terrible accident. Alex had gone with his friend Francesco into the countryside to recover a gun buried in a field. He told them that once they had found it Francesco had snatched it from his hand and pointed it at Alex's head. In an act of self-defence, Alex had lunged at his friend, the two of them struggling and rolling around on the grass. Suddenly, the gun went off. Francesco was shot. In a panic, Alex said he had run away without checking on his friend, and thrown the gun into a bramble hedge.

The police rushed to send out a search team. It took less than half an hour for them to find Francesco's body. It was slumped on the ground with a gunshot wound to the head.

The next morning the police sent a search team with metal detectors and sniffer dogs to recover the pistol Alex had said he had thrown away. But it wasn't there. Back at the station, Alex said he wanted to tell the police something. What he said was very different from the night before. There had been no struggle, Alex said, and he'd deliberately killed Francesco. 'I falsely claimed that I had a fight with a boy,' he said, 'that we had struggled and two gunshots had been fired.' He then went quiet, refusing to answer any more questions.

That same morning Domenico turned up at the police station with his father and uncle. He had heard that mourners were arriving at Francesco's house and had decided to confess what had happened the night before.

Soon the police called in more of Alex's friends to be interviewed. Another boy, Simone, told them that he had dropped Alex off at the police station on the night of the murder. He had been driving through Mileto and had seen Alex walking alone on Corso Umberto, one of the main streets. Alex flagged him down and got into his car. Simone said he could immediately see something was up. He asked Alex what was wrong. 'I have fucked up,' he said. 'I have fucked up big time.' Without any apparent emotion, he told him he had shot Francesco and that he was going to run away. But Simone convinced him to go to the police station and turn himself in.

As the police interviews continued, it became clear that Alex had been an angry, frustrated boy. His friends reported that in the months after the arrest of his parents he would erupt into rages, threatening people who he suspected had been messaging Noemi behind his back.

The police also discovered that Alex had probably been using the gun for a while. Several weeks before the night he shot Francesco, Alex had sent a WhatsApp message to two boys he believed had been sending Noemi messages. He asked to meet them in an alleyway. Once they arrived, they found Alex with a gun in his hand. He ordered them to kneel on the ground and began beating them with an iron bar, smashing one of them in the face before the two ran away. One of the boys later messaged Francesco, trying to get him to mediate. Francesco said he had spoken to Alex, who was apparently sorry for what had happened.

At some point during the weeks running up to the murder, Alex had become suspicious of Francesco himself. Simone said that Alex had interrogated him about Francesco and Noemi. 'Simone,' he recalled Alex telling him, 'there are too many things going on. I know Francesco wants my girlfriend, and you are helping him.' Simone told Alex he was crazy: neither he nor Francesco would ever do that to him. Alex flashed Simone a pistol he had tucked into his trousers. He then started to swear, calling him and Francesco bastards. Simone tried to reason with his friend. 'If you have to shoot me, then at least I want to speak with whoever is telling you this stuff first. If he is right about it, then you can shoot me, but if he is wrong, what are you going to do? Shoot yourself?'

Alex seemed to respond, and his rage started to cool. He asked Simone to find out if it was Francesco who was pursuing Noemi, or her pursuing him. But he also warned him not to mention anything about their conversation to Francesco. Simone, though, told Francesco about Alex's anger and paranoia. Francesco hadn't taken it seriously: he had nothing to hide, and this was nothing more than an everyday teenage drama.

One afternoon, Alex called Simone, demanding answers about what was going on between Francesco and Noemi. Simone again told Alex that there was nothing happening between them. Alex said he didn't know who to believe.

That evening Alex arranged to meet Francesco. His friend felt he had nothing to fear. So he got in the car and went with Alex to the olive grove.

News of the murder stunned even Mileto. How could a boy of fifteen murder his best friend? Inside the police station, Alex Pititto was still refusing to talk. His mother was in prison. His father was in prison. His brothers were in prison. His uncle was serving a life sentence for murder. The last of Salvatore's sons now seemed destined for prison, too.

The public prosecutor sent a psychologist to speak with Alex. Under sixteen, he was not yet an adult in legal terms. Could he really understand the consequences of his actions? Could a child be a cold-blooded murderer? The psychologist concluded that the imprisonment of his father Salvatore and the rest of his family would have caused him suffering and made him depressed, but that 'does not affect his capacity to understand, and to make decisions'.

Alex had been surrounded by violence from the moment he was born. He would have known when his older brothers beat other boys on the streets. He would have heard the stories about his uncle Pasquale. It was a sickness, passed from father to son, from brother to brother. Over the decades, they had wrecked countless lives, killing innocent children like Nicholas Green. And they had done it all in the name of their family, and to sustain the grip they held over the poor town they ruled over. But in his desperation to make his family great, Salvatore had destroyed everything he had cared about.

Helpless in prison, he now learned the fate of his youngest child. What had it all been for?

The day of Francesco's funeral, Mileto was silent apart from the church bells. Every shop and home was closed; posters of the dead child were pasted on the shutters and banners were hung across the streets with the words 'Ciao Ciccio' – Francesco's nickname.

Slowly, hundreds of mourners walked through the streets. At the front of the procession were three priests wearing white robes, with purple stoles draped around their shoulders. Male members of Francesco's family carried the white coffin, with flowers laid on top, towards the cathedral; mourners touched it as it moved past.

Above the entrance to the cathedral hung a banner that read 'You are a new star that shines in heaven. This is not goodbye, but see you later. You will rest inside our hearts for ever.' Father Salvatore Cugliari began his sermon. The priest knew about the sickness that had taken root in his town. After he had given sermons against the Mafia, the door to his home had been doused with petrol and set on fire. Francesco's parents sat in silence as Father Cugliari spoke.

'It is difficult to find words in circumstances like this. Perhaps silence would be better as a sign of respect for the pain.' He ended with some words from Alyosha's 'Speech by the Stone' at Ilyusha's funeral in *The Brothers Karamazov*. 'Francesco,' he said, 'today you unite us . . . your memory will make us all better.'

As the coffin was brought out of the cathedral, the mourners released blue and white balloons, threw white confetti and clapped to say a final goodbye. Francesco's male relatives carried the coffin on their shoulders, pausing to lift it high towards the heavens as the balloons floated into the sky. They then lowered the coffin onto a platform. Francesco's mother pressed her face into the coffin, embracing her son for the last time before the pallbearers carried him to the silver hearse.

After Francesco's murder, hundreds of mourners held a candlelit vigil in the town centre. It was a commemoration of the life of a murdered boy – but it was also a sign of defiance. The Pitittos had ruled over them for decades but now they were gone. The people of Mileto were not scared of them any more.

Epilogue

New Jersey, 2017

Jack Kelly had never planned to move back to New Jersey. But his elderly mother's health was getting worse and he decided he would come home to help look after her. It was only going to be for a few months. Jack barely even packed, putting his cats in a carrier and throwing some clothes in the car before driving away from his condo in Virginia.

Some of his friends had been worried how he would adjust to civilian life. But the first morning after he'd left the Special Operations Division, Jack felt a wave of relief wash over him. He was full of the kind of quiet excitement he'd felt as a kid on the last day of the school year, those long summer days stretching out in front of him.

It was in August 2016, three months after leaving the DEA, that he moved back close to East Brunswick, the town he had grown up in. Twenty-five years on, his part of New Jersey felt stuck in a time warp: the same tree-lined suburban streets of wooden slatted houses, Stars and Stripes flags fluttering on poles above neatly cropped front lawns.

Each morning, he would still go for his daily run, pounding the concrete pavements past the Catholic church, the Italian delis and the nail bar. Some days he would run past the local youth football team, out practising in the summer holidays just as he had three decades before. On others, he would run past a chain-link fence that surrounded a ten-acre field. Back in the early 1940s, it had been used by the US government to store uranium ore shipped in from the Belgian Congo – radioactive metals that would be used to develop nuclear weapons during the Manhattan Project. Since then the once top-secret facility had been demolished and the site sealed off to be decontaminated, the large expanse of patchy grass now a spectral memorial to a past age of American power.

He still got calls from his old colleagues asking him when he was coming back. No one believed he would be able to stay out in Jersey for long. It was only a matter of months, they told him, before he took a contracting job for a US government agency. Some friends told him his name sometimes came up in interagency meetings. One of the intelligence analysts from another agency apparently reflected on their past battles with weary admiration, referring to him as 'that fucking Jack Kelly'.

His old cases ground on without him. In France, Mohamad Nourredine was sentenced to ten years for laundering drug money for Colombian cartels. His associate Mazen al-Atat was sentenced for two years for criminal association with the laundering operation. Both men denied any connection to Hezbollah, and al-Atat said his attempts to procure weapons from Russia for the Syrian regime was legal. The French judge presiding over the Cedar case declared, 'I cannot say that there is a direct link with terrorism and Hezbollah, but I cannot say that there is not either.' By contrast, Gilles de Kerchove, the European Union's Counter-terrorism Coordinator, described the Cedar case as involving 'millions, if not hundreds of millions, of euro being laundered between cartels in America, Latin America, Europe, and Africa [which] were traced and linked to the Lebanese Hezbollah group'.

In 2018, the US Department of Justice indicted al-Atat for providing material support to Hezbollah and breaking US sanctions. (Al-Atat's French lawyer said the case was flawed and politically motivated.) Based on the evidence gathered during the investigation, the US government won French legal approval to extradite al-Atat to the United States to face trial. But he later fled France and, according to his lawyer, nobody knew where he was. Ali Fayad, the arms dealer released by the Czech government in the hostage swap, remained a fugitive.

In Syria, Bashar al-Assad, having brutally crushed opposition with the support of Iran, Hezbollah and Russia, was still in power. Even after committing countless human rights abuses and atrocities against Syrian civilians, he and other regime officials appeared unlikely to ever face justice. Some of Project Cassandra's super facilitator targets, some of whom the DEA believed had smuggled materials for chemical weapons to the Assad regime during the civil war, remain at large. In February 2022, emboldened by his military success in Syria, Vladimir Putin would invade Ukraine. In 2023 Syria was readmitted into the Arab League, more than a decade after being thrown out for its brutal suppression of pro-democracy protests.

Hassan Nasrallah labelled the allegations of Hezbollah's involvement in drug trafficking as US and Israeli propaganda. Hezbollah also continued to deny that it or Mustafa Badreddine played a role in the assassination of Rafic Hariri. But the Appeals Chamber of the United Nations Special Tribunal for Lebanon eventually ruled in March 2022 that 'the evidence proves beyond reasonable doubt that during the period of the indictment Mr Badreddine was the leader of both the preparation and performance of the conspiracy'. This overturned an earlier judgment that had acquitted three of the four suspects who were still alive. But coming seventeen years after Hariri's murder, the decision attracted little international attention.

Four years earlier, in 2018, the US Department of the Treasury sanctioned Mustafa Badreddine's brother Mohamed, noting his association with Mohamad Nourredine. Mustafa Mughniyeh, the first son of Imad Mughniyeh and Saada Badreddine, whom they named after his uncle during

Mustafa's imprisonment in Kuwait in the 1980s, followed his father and uncle into becoming a senior Hezbollah commander. In 2017, aged thirty, he was sanctioned by the US State Department for being a 'specially designated global terrorist'. Qasem Soleimani, the Iranian general, Mustafa's family friend and – according to some – his murderer, was himself killed in a US drone strike in Iraq in 2020.

In Italy, Salvatore Pititto was sentenced to eighteen years for his attempts to import cocaine from Colombia. Antonella was sentenced to four years, Giuseppe nine. In a separate drug-trafficking case, Gianluca was sentenced to three and a half years. Alex was sentenced to fourteen years for the murder of Francesco. Pasquale, however, was acquitted on drug-trafficking charges and allowed to return to house arrest to see out the remaining years of his old murder conviction.

Prosecutors knew that very little of this would have been possible without the cooperation of Oksana Verman. Her eight-year sentence was reduced to three years and eight months on appeal, and after serving her time she entered Italy's witness protection programme.

The men from the Colombian cartel who had come to Mileto, including Jota Jota and Jhon Peludo, seemingly disappeared into thin air. In 2016, the Colonel was arrested in the Antioquia region of Colombia for impersonating an official from the Swedish embassy in a scam involving construction contracts. His current whereabouts are unknown.

Since Nicholas Green's death his parents have used his memory to transform Italian attitudes to organ donation. The woman who received his liver aged nineteen went on to have two children, one of whom she named Nicholas. Another boy, who received Nicholas's heart, lived for twenty-two years and passed away in 2017. The family of Francesco have continued to campaign against the Calabrian Mafia, visiting local schools to tell children about their son.

Some months after Jack got home to New Jersey, he received a call telling him that the Director of National Intelligence had awarded him and his DEA team a prize for the Paris operation. Jack's old colleagues were ecstatic. The National Intelligence Meritorious Unit Citation was to be presented by James Clapper, the US's top intelligence official, for the operation against 'Lebanese Hezbollah Transnational Organized Crime' and 'the culmination of its analytic effort contributing directly to a series of law enforcement actions in Europe during January 2016 against elements of the network'.

After years of fighting with US intelligence analysts, Jack was finally being given an award. It was his career's crowning moment. But he decided to give the ceremony a miss. Jack didn't care about being proven right any more. After he received the gold-embossed certificate in the post, he put it on the wall in the garage where he lifted weights and listened to music. Some nights he would go to his local bar and over a beer chat to firefighters and construction workers. When asked what he did for a living, he would tell them, 'I used to work for the DEA.'

Acknowledgements

This book would not have been possible without the help of a vast number of people from across the world. Some of those who helped me cannot be named, and I will forever be grateful to those who took risks in speaking with me. Many of them have displayed immense bravery in their professional and personal lives and they are the heroes of this tale.

I started on the trail that would end in this book when I was working in Rome as a foreign correspondent for the *Financial Times*. I was reporting on the finances of Italian organised crime, which was making large profits from the booming European cocaine trade. As I began to speak with law enforcement officials and study criminal cases, it became clear that the story went well beyond Italy. The explosion of cocaine smuggling into Europe was bringing about new and surprising overlaps, collaborations and alliances between transnational criminal organisations.

I also quickly realised that while these alliances crossed borders many criminal investigations stopped at national boundaries. Yet the ever-expanding geographical scope and complexity of global criminal activity meant that events in one place could have a huge effect on others unfolding far away. Drug money laundered in Europe could fund arms purchases for a civil war in Syria.

I trained as a business journalist and have always been interested in how money – both licit and illicit – moved around the world. I have also always been fascinated by the dark side of globalisation. Business publications and books illuminate the lives of CEOs and tell the dramas of high-stakes mergers and late-night crisis meetings. I wanted to do the same for the parallel dimension of the global criminal economy, a place that remains largely hidden from view. Through this research, grounded in the work of multiple overlapping criminal investigations in different countries, I came across the human stories contained in this book.

Jack Kelly was generous and patient in sharing his own story and wisdom over many hours, and hugely helpful in introducing me to others. David Asher, a pivotal figure in Project Cassandra, provided his vast expertise and guidance. I would also like to thank Derek Maltz, Rik Bashur, Jimmy Grace, Quentin Mugg, John Fernandez and Rob Zachariasiewicz for their help, as well as the men and women of Italy's Guardia di Finanza, its GICO unit, and Camillo Falvo.

Jonny Geller at Curtis Brown spotted the potential in a fledgling idea from the very start. It would never have become a reality without his guidance, encouragement and vision. Thank you, too, to Viola Hayden, Ciara Finan and Sophie Storey.

It has been a pleasure to work with Sameer Rahim and Holly Harley at Little, Brown UK, who expertly edited and hugely improved a complicated manuscript. My thanks also go to Tim Whiting, Zoe Gullen, Henry Lord, Lilly Cox and Charlie King.

Mike Peed provided invaluable advice about the structure of the book. Anna Stephens did a wonderful job tirelessly fact-checking vast numbers of pages of documents and speaking to many people I had interviewed (of course, any errors that remain are entirely my own). Thank you also to Pietro Comito for his help on the ground in Calabria, and Davide Ghiglione for his assistance with translations.

It has been an honour to work at a newspaper as brilliant as the *Financial Times* for the last fifteen years, where I have been able to live and work in several different countries and meet, collaborate with and learn from many wonderful and talented people. I would like to especially thank Roula Khalaf and Tobias Buck for allowing me the time away to report and write this book.

It is a daily pleasure to work alongside my colleagues on the *FT*'s investigations team, and especially Paul Murphy who is always there to remind us that what we try to do is serious, but that it should also always be fun. Matt Vella has been the source of many inspiring conversations about long-form writing. Thanks, for various reasons, go to Robert Smith, Arash Massoudi, Lionel Barber, Geoff Dyer, Chloe Cornish, Dan McCrum, Alec Russell, John Thornhill, Nigel Hanson and James Fontanella-Khan.

Several academic experts have been generous in sharing their thoughts and time with me. Thanks especially to Emanuele Ottolenghi, Chris Phillips, Anna Sergi, Federico Varese, Matthew Levitt and Olga Kavran, former head of outreach and legacy at the Special Tribunal for Lebanon. Josh Meyer led the way with his groundbreaking reporting on Project Cassandra.

There are also many people who provided their advice, thoughts and support on this book's journey from a sprawling proposal to words on a page. Juliet Nicolson's encouragement and guidance from the start has been immense. My thanks go out to James Macmillan-Scott, Simon Sylvester-Chaudhuri,

Sophia Goulandris, Craig Coben, Billy Smith, William Boyd, John Lau, Tom, Karen, Clemmie, Bean, Eliza, Olivia, Nuria and Charlie.

My parents have been reading my first drafts since I was a kid. I owe them everything. And, most importantly of all, I would like to thank my wife Flora. This book is dedicated to her, and to Gus.

A Note on Sources

The title of this book, *Chasing Shadows*, has also been an apt description of the process of reporting it. Several of the people I have reported on are fugitives and have been impossible to trace. Others are serving long prison sentences for serious crimes, or are in witness protection programmes. Some are dead.

This is a work of narrative non-fiction. No details are invented or imagined. The people, dialogue, descriptions, places and events are all real. When I describe the thoughts or feelings of a person this is because they have described them to me, have been described by a witness or someone who knew them, or they have expressed them in interviews, witness statements or in conversations captured by wiretap recordings.

A large amount of the reporting in this book has been made possible by access to evidence gathered during multiple criminal investigations that were later submitted to a court and resulted in a criminal conviction. There are comprehensive endnotes, giving the sources for the reported events and dialogue.

I have conducted more than one hundred interviews with law enforcement and intelligence officials, lawyers, judges and eyewitnesses in many countries over a three-year period. Almost all the interviewees are named but some have remained anonymous. Where this is the case, it is referenced in the endnotes. Many of the subjects of this book are currently in prison and declined to speak with me, while some communicated via their lawyers.

Memories can be fickle, and therefore I have made every effort to cross-check their recollections with other people and sources, and against documentary evidence where available. The book has been independently fact-checked, but any errors remain entirely my own.

In addition to interviews, this book has also been reported through extensive archival research, including thousands of pages of judicial documents, witness testimony, affidavits, declassified intelligence reports, documents released through freedom of information requests, newspaper reports, academic journals, archive footage, photographs and site visits. The endnotes make clear which court documents, police reports and other evidence have been used for different sections of the book, which include cases from the United States, Italy, France, Colombia, the Czech Republic and the Special Tribunal for Lebanon (STL) in the Netherlands.

This book is not intended to provide a comprehensive account of the horrors of the Syrian civil war or the history of Hezbollah. I have made it clear where I have made use of the invaluable expertise, scholarship and reporting of others.

For the sections on Mustafa Badreddine's early life, I am grateful for the scholarship of Dr Shimon Shapira, as well as an interview given by Saada Badreddine. Later parts of Badreddine's life have been constructed using thousands of pages of evidence submitted by witnesses to the STL, as well as other primary and secondary material. Iain Edwards, one of Badreddine's defence lawyers, provided an expert understanding of the dynamics and challenges of the case against him.

For Salvatore and Oksana's story I have relied heavily on witness statements given to the Italian police by Oksana herself, and judicial investigative material that contains many hours of conversation and communication between Salvatore and other members of his criminal organisation. I have also made use of numerous other criminal cases against the Pititto family and its associates dating back to the trial of Nicholas Green's murder in the 1990s up to the conviction of Alex Pititto in 2018, as well as the testimony and recollections of the state's witness Michele Iannello.

This is a book about individuals and their choices. I have intentionally avoided using collective terms such as 'Ndrangheta to describe Calabrian organised crime. There are several excellent books available in English for readers wanting to learn about the history and traditions of the various Italian mafia groups, including John Dickie's *Mafia Republic: Italy's Criminal Curse.*

Notes

Prologue: The Cousins

1   **took out their binoculars:** Hala Jaber, *Hezbollah: Born with a Vengeance* (London: Fourth Estate, 1997), p. 83, and Ronen Bergman, *Rise and Kill First: The Secret History of Israel's Targeted Assassinations* (London: John Murray, 2018), p. 374.

1   **enjoy a late brunch:** Timothy J. Geraghty, *Peacekeepers at War: Beirut 1983 – The Marine Commander Tells His Story* (Sterling, VA: Potomac Books, 2009), p. 91.

1   **studied everything about their target:** Jaber, *Hezbollah*, p. 83.

2   **were already on guard:** United States Department of Defense, 'Report of the DOD Commission on Beirut International Airport Terrorist Act, October 23, 1983', p. 8.

2   **Six months before:** Herbert H. Denton, 'Toll in Beirut Bombing Rises to 46', *Washington Post*, 20 April 1983.

2   **the real truck had been ambushed:** 'United States District Court for the District of Columbia. Evan Fain, et al. vs Islamic Republic of Iran, et al. Memorandum Opinion', p. 7.

2   **drank several cups of sweet tea:** Jaber, *Hezbollah*, p. 83.

2   **'Get the fuck outta here':** Geraghty, *Peacekeepers at War*, p. 96.

2   **ripped through the barracks:** Ibid.

2   **the largest non-nuclear explosion:** 'United States District Court for the District of Columbia. Evan Fain, et al. vs Islamic Republic of Iran, et al. Memorandum Opinion', p. 8.

3   **a Scud missile attack:** Geraghty, *Peacekeepers at War*, p. 92.

3 **Mangled body parts:** Ibid., p. 99.

3 **'Large numbers of dead and wounded':** Ibid., p. 94.

3 **still in its sleeping bag:** Ibid., p. 99.

3 **harrowing groans:** Ibid., p. 100.

4 **in the morning sun:** Several kilometres away in West Beirut a second truck bomb ripped through a nine-storey building housing French peacekeeping troops, killing fifty-eight people on the same morning.

4 **left countless others wounded:** 'United States District Court for the District of Columbia. Evan Fain, et al. vs Islamic Republic of Iran, et al. Memorandum Opinion', p. 1.

1: 'The Navy SEALs of the DEA'

7 **'cooked by the time you are twenty-nine':** Except where separately noted, all personal details and dialogue in this chapter are taken from interviews with Jack Kelly and Derek Maltz.

13 **grown into eighty-three offices in sixty-two countries:** Statement of Derek S. Maltz Special Agent in Charge of the Special Operations Division Drug Enforcement Administration Before the Subcommittee on Terrorism, Nonproliferation, and Trade Committee on Foreign Affairs United States House of Representatives Entitled 'Narcoterrorism and the Long Reach of US Law Enforcement', 17 November 2011, accessed at [https://www.dea.gov/sites/default/files/pr/speeches-testimony/2012-2009/111117_testimony.pdf].

13 **information, tips and leads:** Drug Enforcement Administration, 'History: 1994–1998', accessed at [https://www.dea.gov/sites/default/files/2021-04/1994-1998_p_76-91.pdf].

13 **21 U.S.C. § 960a:** John E. Thomas, Jr, 'Narco-Terrorism: Could the Legislative and Prosecutorial Responses Threaten Our Civil Liberties?', *Washington & Lee Law Review* 66 (2009).

14 **smashing down information barriers:** Melanie M. Reid, 'NSA and DEA Intelligence Sharing: Why it is Legal and Why Reuters and the Good Wife Got it Wrong', *SMU Law Review* 68:2 (January 2015), p. 436.

14 **formally admitted into the United States intelligence community:** Drug Enforcement Administration, 'History:

2003–2008', accessed at [https://www.dea.gov/sites/default/
files/2021-04/2003-2008_p_118-153.pdf].

14 **extradited to the United States:** 'International Arms Dealer
Extradited on Terrorism Offenses', US Department of Justice, 13
June 2008.

15 **tried to block his extradition:** 'US Embassy Cables: Russia Tries
to Block Viktor Bout's Extradition', *Guardian*, 1 December 2010.

16 **'the Navy SEALs of the DEA':** Johnny Dwyer, 'The DEA's
Terrorist Hunters: Overreaching Their Authority?', *Time
Magazine*, 8 August 2011.

16 **'At least drug dealers have ethics':** Nicholas Schmidle,
'Disarming Viktor Bout', *New Yorker*, 27 August 2014. Viktor Bout
was released from US custody in December 2022 in a prisoner
swap with the Russian government in exchange for the basketball
player Brittney Griner.

17 **terrorist group and Shia political party:** Hezbollah has
been designated as a foreign terrorist organisation by the
United States since 1997. See US Department of State,
Foreign Terrorist Organizations', [https://www.state.gov/
foreign-terrorist-organizations/].

17 **exploiting these networks to circumvent US sanctions:**
Written Testimony of Adam J. Szubin, Acting Under Secretary
for Terrorism and Financial Intelligence United States House
Committee on Foreign Affairs, 'Iran Nuclear Deal Oversight:
Implementation and its Consequences (Part II)', 25 May 2016.

18 **'super facilitators':** 'Attacking Hezbollah's Financial Network:
Policy Options', Hearing Before the Committee on Foreign
Affairs House of Representatives, One Hundred Fifteenth
Congress, First Session, 8 June 2017.

18 *In the Garden of Beasts:* Erik Larson, *In the Garden of Beasts:
Love, Terror, and an American Family in Hitler's Berlin* (New York:
Crown, 2011).

20 **selling weapons being used by Hezbollah to fight in Syria:**
The DEA's assessment that Ali Fayad was brokering weapons
sales to the Syrian regime was made public by John Fernandez,
then assistant special agent in charge of the DEA's Special
Operations Division's Counter-Narcoterrorism Operations

Center, in his January 2020 presentation to the Washington Institute, 'The DEA's Targeting of Hezbollah's Global Criminal Support Network'. Fernandez said: 'Ali Fayad ... he was involved in shipping arms to LH [Lebanese Hezbollah] forces that were fighting in Syria.' In 2022, Fayad's former US defence attorney, Louis Adolfson, wrote that Fayad 'sold arms to Iraq and to Syria' but said these sales were lawful and legitimate. See Louis Adolfson, 'Terrorism, "sting" operations, prisoner swaps and Brittney Griner', *JD Supra*, 7 September 2022, accessed at [https://www.jdsupra.com/legalnews/terrorism-sting-operations-prisoner-4829266/].

2: 'Elias Saab'

22 **'May holy God bless your deeds':** Words and images of Badreddine in Syria are taken from 'From Khaldeh to Sayyeda Zainab (P) Shrine: 55 Years of Sayyed Zulfikar's Jihad', *Al Manar TV*.

22 **denied any of its men were even in the country:** Rick Gladstone and Anne Barnard, 'US Accuses Hezbollah of Aiding Syria's Crackdown', *New York Times*, 10 August 2012.

22 **the funerals were held in the dead of night:** Shimon Shapira, 'Iran's Plans to Take Over Syria', Jerusalem Center for Public Affairs, 5 May 2013.

22 **waging urban warfare near the Lebanese border:** 'Treasury Sanctions Hizballah Leaders, Military Officials, and an Associate in Lebanon', US Department of the Treasury, 21 July 2015.

23 **brokering crisis meetings:** Ibid.

23 **had never been issued a passport in his own name:** 'The Prosecutor v Salim Jamil Ayyash Hassan Habib Merhi Hussein Hassan Oneissi Assad Hassan Sabra – Judgment', Special Tribunal for Lebanon, 18 August 2020, p. 1304.

23 **considered leaving the country:** This is according to the Iranian Revolutionary Guard commander Hossein Hamadani, at the time head of a delegation of Iranian 'military advisors' to Assad in Syria, cited in Shimon Shapira, *Hezbollah: Between Iran and Syria* (Tel Aviv: Moshe Dayan Center for Middle Eastern and African Studies, 2021), p. 323.

23   **send their families into hiding:** Ibid.

24   **unable to regain lost territory:** Charles Lister, 'Dynamic Stalemate: Surveying Syria's Military Landscape', Brookings Doha Center, 19 May 2014.

24   **attacked the opposition-controlled suburbs of Damascus with Sarin nerve gas:** The governments of the United States, United Kingdom, France, Germany and Israel have conducted investigations that concluded the Assad regime was responsible for the Ghouta chemical weapons attack on 21 August 2013. The Organisation for the Prohibition of Chemical Weapons in 2023 concluded that the Assad regime dropped chemical weapons on civilians during the civil war.

24   **Hundreds of thousands:** In April 2016 the United Nations Special Envoy for Syria estimated four hundred thousand Syrians had by that point died in the conflict.

24   **'will go to hell, and cannot be considered martyrs':** 'Hezbollah Fighters Killed in Syria Will "Go to Hell," Says Former Leader', *Al Arabiya*, 26 February 2013.

24   **Assad could not be allowed to fall:** 'S. Nasrallah: Hezbollah Will Reinforce Troops in Aleppo to Achieve Major Victory', *Al Manar*, 28 June 2016.

25   **'I won't come back from Syria':** 'Senior Hezbollah Leader Mustafa Badreddine Martyred', *Al Manar*, 13 May 2016.

25   **always excited when Imad came to visit:** Interview with Saada Badreddine, 'In God's Eye, I Saw Nothing but Beauty', *Al-Ahed News*, 15 February 2020.

25   **cinder block house with no running water:** Robert Baer, *See No Evil: The True Story of a Ground Soldier in the CIA's War on Terrorism* (London: Arrow Books, 2002), p. 148.

25   **long hours together debating politics and religion:** Interview with Saada Badreddine, 'In God's Eye, I Saw Nothing but Beauty'.

26   **stray bullets and shrapnel:** Baer, *See No Evil*, p. 148.

26   **theocratic ideas that had inspired the 1979 Iranian revolution:** Central Intelligence Agency, 'Lebanon, Prospects for Islamic Fundamentalism', July 1987, p. 2.

26   **Saada felt something important:** Interview with Saada Badreddine, 'In God's Eye, I Saw Nothing but Beauty'.

26   openly challenging the older generation: Ibid.

26   They were ambitious: Ibid.

26   reading texts by Leon Trotsky: Shapira, *Hezbollah*, p. 154.

26   ran into groups of Palestinian militants: Ibid.

26   drawn into the orbit of Yasser Arafat's Fatah: CIA, 'Lebanon,
      Prospects for Islamic Fundamentalism', p. 11.

26   taken under the wing of Ali Salameh: Ronen Bergman, *Rise
      and Kill First: The Secret History of Israel's Targeted Assassinations*
      (London: John Murray, 2018), p. 373.

26   carefully studying military tactics: Shapira, *Hezbollah*, p. 154.

27   she had secretly fallen in love with her cousin: Ibid., p. 214.

27   the son of a sweet seller, was poor: Interview with Saada
      Badreddine, 'In God's Eye, I Saw Nothing but Beauty'.

27   she was not particularly religious: Shapira, *Hezbollah*, p. 214.

27   Mustafa and Imad took up arms: Ibid., p. 215.

27   Saada begged her father: Ibid.

27   who employed Imad as his bodyguard: Ibid.

27   enough money for a party: Ibid.

27   living in a makeshift room: Interview with Saada Badreddine,
      'In God's Eye, I Saw Nothing but Beauty'.

27   planning their next operation: Ibid.

27   a new, more dangerous force: Robin Wright, 'The Demise of
      Hezbollah's Untraceable Ghost', *New Yorker*, 13 May 2016.

27   quietly established a training camp: Mark Perry, 'The Driver',
      Foreign Policy, 29 April 2013.

28   the party of God: Naim Qassem, Hezbollah's Deputy Secretary
      General and a founding member, dates the party's founding to
      the so-called 'Manifesto of the Nine' in the wake of Israel's 1982
      invasion of Lebanon. See Qassem, *Hizbullah: The Story from Within*
      (London: Saqi, 2007), p. 65. Augustus Richard Norton notes that,
      although most Hezbollah officials trace the group's formation to
      1982, it remained 'less an organization than a cabal' up until the
      mid-1980s. See Norton, *Hezbollah: A Short History* (Princeton:
      Princeton University Press, 2018), p. 23.

28   a normal marriage: Interview with Saada Badreddine, 'In God's
      Eye, I Saw Nothing but Beauty'.

28   following the attacks that slaughtered hundreds: Hezbollah

has denied responsibility for the 1983 marine barracks attack. No one has ever been indicted in relation to the bombing. Subhi al-Tufayli, the first Secretary General of Hezbollah and now a vocal critic of the organisation, later said the group was responsible. See Nicholas Blanford, *Warriors of God: Inside Hezbollah's Thirty-Year War Against Israel* (New York: Random House, 2011), p. 59. Shimon Shapira, former Military Secretary to the Prime Minister of Israel and chief of staff to the Foreign Minister, has said that 'It was Mughniyeh who dispatched both bombers.' Fatima Mughniyeh, Imad and Saada's daughter, was asked by a Western journalist in 2008 about the attack on the barracks and replied: 'America was invading our country, like Israel . . . my father's duty was to defend Lebanon'. See Trish Schuh, 'Inside Hezbollah Leader Imad Mughniyeh's Funeral', *Esquire*, 21 February 2008.

28 **slipped into Kuwait:** 'The Prosecutor Special Tribunal for Lebanon vs Mustafa Amine Badreddine et al.', Indictment, 10 June 2011, p. 4.

28 **'a masters degree in explosives':** Thomas L. Friedman, 'State Sponsored Terror Called a Threat to the US', *New York Times*, 30 December 1983.

28 **a truck stacked with gas cylinders:** Wright, 'The Demise of Hezbollah's Untraceable Ghost'.

29 **missing his head by inches:** Robin Wright, *Sacred Rage: The Wrath of Militant Islam*, 2nd edn, (New York: Touchstone, 2001), p. 112.

29 **other strategic targets:** Ibid., p. 113.

29 **failed to go off close enough:** Ibid.

29 **to ensure the culprits couldn't hide:** Ibid., p. 122.

29 **'export the revolution':** Friedman, 'State Sponsored Terror Called a Threat to the US'.

29 **headquartered in Tehran:** Wright, *Sacred Rage*, p. 124.

29 **hidden in oil barrels:** Ibid., p. 121.

29 **as they laughed and joked:** Ibid., p. 112.

29 **sentenced to death:** 'The Prosecutor Special Tribunal for Lebanon vs Mustafa Amine Badreddine et al.', p. 4.

29 **Imad Mughniyeh was not going to sit idly by:** Ronald

Reagan Presidential Library Digital Library Collections. Oliver North Files. Terrorism: Imad Mugniyah. Box: 49. Document, EO13526, point 5.

3: A Loaded Gun

30 **'Because you are in love with her':** 'Indictment, Operazione Stammer', Fermo di indiziato di delitto del pubblico ministero, Procura della Repubblica di Catanzaro, Direzione Distrettuale Antimafia. Proc. Pen. N.9444/14 R.G. notizie di reato/Mod. 21 DDA, p. 1698.

30 **on the advice of a friend:** Statements of Oksana Verman in 'Ordinanza sulla richiesta di applicazione di misura cautelare', Tribunale di Catanzaro, Sezione GIP/GUP, N. 1166/7 R.G.N.R., 12 March 2018, p. 43.

31 **she knew through work:** Ibid.

31 **he got her a job:** Ibid.

31 **who lived next door:** Ibid.

31 **gazing at her:** Ibid.

31 **off-the-books checkout girl:** Ibid.

31 **who had three sons:** Ibid.

31 **walks together:** Ibid.

32 **had warned the boy's uncle:** Ibid.

32 **'nobody can':** Statements of Oksana Verman in 'Verbale illustrativo della collaborazione', Procura della Repubblica di Catanzaro, Direzione Distrettuale Antimafia, N. 9444/14 RG Mod. 44, 15 June 2017, p. 7.

32 **'bring you the cheese':** Ibid., p. 8.

32 **a TV drama:** The TV series was *Solo*, titled *Mafia Undercover* in English. 'Indictment, Operazione Stammer', p. 1698.

32 **'I have two of those':** Ibid., p. 1699.

33 **blue Converse trainers:** Ibid., p. 1684.

33 **thought she was stupid:** Ibid., p. 1426.

33 **like he spoke to her:** Ibid., p. 417.

33 **no longer shared a bed:** Statements of Oksana Verman in 'Verbale illustrativo della collaborazione', p. 34.

33 **watch him play bowls:** Ibid., p. 49.

33 **who nobody ever saw:** Ibid., p. 29.

34   **in the same year, one month apart:** 'Indictment, Operazione Stammer', p. 4.

34   **suffered a gunshot wound:** Statements of Oksana Verman in 'Ordinanza sulla richiesta di applicazione di misura cautelare', p. 8.

34   **lived under house arrest:** Pasquale Pititto was convicted in Operation Tirreno for the murder of Pietro Cosimo in 1990. See: ''Ndrangheta: l'ergastolano di Mileto Pasquale Pititto passa ai domiciliari', *Il Vibonese*, 13 June 2022.

34   **M12 submachine guns:** Statements of Michele Iannello in 'Verbale di interrogatorio di persona sottoposta ad indagini', Procura della Repubblica di Catanzaro, Direzione Distrettuale Antimafia, N. 624/97 R.G.N.R. Mod. 21 DDA, 22 May 1997, p. 79.

34   **how similar they were:** Statements of Oksana Verman in 'Verbale illustrativo della collaborazione', p. 29.

34   **seemed to know everything:** Ibid.

34   **a bottle of cognac and an ornamental boat:** Ibid.

34   **started out as young hoodlums:** Statements of Michele Iannello in 'Verbale di interrogatorio di persona sottoposta ad indagini', pp. 4–5.

34   **a chilling threat:** Statements of Michele Iannello in 'Verbale di interrogatorio', Raggruppamento operativo speciale carabinieri, Sezione Anticrimine Catanzaro, 7–9 June 1997, p. 2.

35   **homemade explosive device:** Ibid.

35   **a dog's severed head:** Statements of Michele Iannello in 'Verbale di interrogatorio di persona sottoposta ad indagini', p. 16.

35   **'receiving a flower':** John Dickie, *Mafia Republic – Italy's Criminal Curse: Cosa Nostra, Camorra and 'Ndrangheta from 1946 to the present* (London: Sceptre, 2013), p. 187.

35   **in cell number 18:** Statements of Michele Iannello in 'Verbale di interrogatorio di persona sottoposta ad indagini', p. 85.

35   **to be just like him:** Statements of Oksana Verman in 'Verbale illustrativo della collaborazione', p. 33.

35   **helping their father out:** Ibid., p. 55.

36   **horse-drawn carriages:** Ibid., p. 49.

36   **drinking grappa:** Ibid., p. 50.

36   **shaved his hair:** 'Alex Pititto, il figlio del boss che a 15 anni

uccide l'amico coetaneo per un like su ragazzina', *Blitz Quotidiano*, 31 May 2017.

36   **eating pizza:** Sentencing of Alex Pititto, Tribunale per i Minorenni di Catanzaro, N. 56/18 R.G. Sent., 8 June 2018, p. 16.

36   **distant and depressed:** Ibid., p. 28.

36   **'break up your family':** 'Indictment, Operazione Stammer', p. 1967.

36   **tending the vegetables:** Ibid.

36   **'fucking idiot':** Ibid.

37   **losing everything:** Statements of Oksana Verman in 'Verbale riassuntivo di interrogatorio di persona sottoposta ad indagini', Procura della Repubblica di Catanzaro, Direzione Distrettuale Antimafia, N. 9444/14 RG Mod. 44, 8 February 2017, p. 8.

37   **'the deadliest stroke of luck':** Ibid., p. 83.

38   **dominant cocaine cartels:** United States Department of Justice, Dario Antonio Usuga David, Narcotics Rewards Program [https://www.state.gov/narcotics-rewards-program-target-information-wanted/dario-antonio-usuga-david/].

38   **a $5 million bounty:** Ibid.

38   **hidden cameras in the woods:** Statements of Oksana Verman in 'Verbale illustrativo della collaborazione', p. 22.

39   **a concealed door:** Statements of Oksana Verman in 'Ordinanza sulla richiesta di applicazione di misura cautelare', p. 9.

39   **using coded text messages:** 'Indictment, Operazione Stammer', p. 592.

4: The Prague Sting

40   **outside the Sheraton Hotel:** Except where separately noted, details of the account of the DEA's arrest of Ali Fayad are taken from interviews with Jack Kelly, Jimmy Grace and Adam Homsi.

40   **selling weapons now being used by Hezbollah:** John Fernandez, 'The DEA's Targeting of Hezbollah's Global Criminal Support Network', Washington Institute, January 2020.

40   **to discuss a deal:** United States of America v. Ali Fayad, Faouzi Jaber, Khaled El Merebi, Indictment, Case No. 1:13-cr-00485, United States District Court Southern District of New York, 4 June 2016, p. 13.

41 **Moscow-aligned president of Ukraine:** Report into kidnapping of Czech nationals by National Headquarters Against Organized Crime of the Criminal Police and Investigation Service – Terrorism and Extremism Section, Reference no. NCOZ-1370/ TC˅-2016-410093, 15 November 2017, p. 15.

41 **he had met Vladimir Putin:** Interview with Ali Fayad's US attorney, Louis Adolfsen.

44 **provide false documentation:** United States of America v. Ali Fayad, Faouzi Jaber, Khaled El Merebi, Indictment, p. 12.

44 **no problem reaching their target:** Ibid.

5: 'Time is of the Essence'

46 **hair shaved off:** Fred Burton and Samuel M. Katz, *Beirut Rules: The Murder of a CIA Station Chief and Hezbollah's War Against America* (New York: Berkley, 2018), p. 240.

46 **had quickly developed a reputation:** 'Top Suspect in Hariri Murder Familiar Name in Kuwait Jail', *Kuwait Times*, 2 July 2011.

46 **reeling off the names:** Ibid.

46 **blow his cell door off:** Ibid.

47 **pressed against his neck:** Robin Wright, *Sacred Rage: The Wrath of Militant Islam*, 2nd edn (New York: Touchstone, 2001), p. 134.

47 **bloodied, unrecognisable body:** Ibid., p. 136.

47 **Hôtel de Crillon:** Nicholas Blanford, *Warriors of God: Inside Hezbollah's Thirty-Year War Against Israel* (New York: Random House, 2011), p. 76.

48 **'Imad Mugniyah has recently arrived in France':** Letter from John Poindexter to General Jean Saulnier, 24 October 1985. Ronald Reagan Presidential Library Digital Library Collections. Oliver North Files. Terrorism: Imad Mughniyah. Box: 49. Document No. 109670.

48 **'ample evidence':** Ibid.

48 **had a narrow escape:** Abdel-Jalil Mustafa, 'Kuwaiti Ruler Survives Suicide Car Bomb That Kills Three Others', Associated Press, 25 May 1985.

48 **'the thrones of the Gulf will be shaken':** Jonathan C. Randal, 'Kuwaitis Tested Growing Tension Seen After Attack on Leader', *Washington Post*, 14 June 1985.

49   **from inside his cell:** 'Hezbollah: Portrait of a Terrorist
Organization', Meir Amit Intelligence and Information Center,
18 December 2012.

49   **Imad orchestrated:** James Risen, 'US Traces Iran's Ties to Terror
Through a Lebanese', *New York Times*, 17 January 2002.

49   **onto the tarmac:** Gwen Ifill and Sue Anne Pressley, 'Hijack
Victim Was Navy Diver', *Washington Post*, 17 June 1985.

49   **wrapped in a white shroud:** 'Islamic Jihad Says It Killed Buckley,
Shows Picture of a Body', Associated Press, 12 October 1985.

50   **a passport in his own name:** Declassified National Security
Council intelligence report on Imad Mugniyah. Ronald Reagan
Presidential Library Digital Library Collections. Oliver North
Files. Terrorism: Imad Mugniyah. Box: 49. Document No.
13526, point 11.

50   **'the Fox':** 'Profile: Imad Mugniyah', Council on Foreign
Relations, 17 August 2006.

50   **a fierce debate broke out:** Robert Oakley, 'The Failed Attempt
to Get a Terrorist Mastermind', Association for Diplomatic
Studies and Training, 5 February 2015.

50   **approved a request from the CIA:** Ibid.

50   **best to ask the French:** Ibid.

50   **'Time,' Poindexter warned:** Letter from John Poindexter to
General Jean Saulnier, 24 October 1985.

50   **ever been in the French capital:** Oakley, 'The Failed Attempt to
Get a Terrorist Mastermind'.

50   **before he slipped away:** In the months after the failed raid *Le
Figaro* and *France-Soir* reported that the French government had
intentionally allowed Mughniyeh to escape as part of ongoing
hostage negotiations. The French government denied this.

50   **A team of commandos abseiled:** Robert Baer, *The Perfect Kill:
A Personal History of Modern Assassination* (London: Weidenfeld &
Nicolson, 2014), p. 166.

50   **fifty-year-old Spanish tourist:** Oakley, 'The Failed Attempt
to Get a Terrorist Mastermind'.

50   **stuffing dollar bills:** Robert Baer, *See No Evil: The True Story
of a Ground Soldier in the CIA's War on Terrorism* (London: Arrow
Books, 2002), p. 190.

50   He had removed any trace: Jeffrey Goldberg, 'In the Party of
      God', *New Yorker*, 28 October 2002.

51   just a faded photograph: Ronen Bergman, *Rise and Kill First: The
      Secret History of Israel's Targeted Assassinations* (London: John Murray,
      2018), p. 375.

51   'a fierce-looking, bearded young man': Declassified National
      Security Council intelligence report on Imad Mugniyah.

51   'cunning, resourceful, coldly calculating': Matthew Levitt,
      Hezbollah: The Global Footprint of Lebanon's Party of God (London:
      Hurst, 2013), p. 28.

51   never left a building the same way: Baer, *See No Evil*, p. 190.

51   never appeared in the press: Declassified National Security
      Council intelligence report on Imad Mugniyah.

51   fluent in Arabic, English, French: Levitt, *Hezbollah*, p. 28.

51   undergone plastic surgery: These rumours were later proved to be
      false. See 'Profile: Imad Mugniyah', Council on Foreign Relations,
      17 August 2006.

51   funded by the CIA: The American journalist Bob Woodward
      claimed in his book *Veil: The Secret Wars of the CIA* that former
      CIA Director William Casey told him on his deathbed that,
      among other revelations, the US foreign intelligence agency had
      commissioned the 1985 car bomb attack against Sheik Mohammad
      Hussein Fadlallah. Casey's widow said Woodward's account was 'a
      fabrication'.

52   declined the offer: Baer, *See No Evil*, p. 191.

52   a memo quizzing one of his ambassadors: US State Department
      diplomatic cable sent by Secretary of State George Shultz to the US
      ambassador in Paris, January 1988. Released under the Freedom of
      Information Act.

52   her and Imad's first son: Mustafa Mughniyeh's date and place of
      birth is cited in 'State Department Terrorist Designations of Ali
      Damush and Mustafa Mughniyeh', US State Department, 9 January
      2017, [https://2009-2017.state.gov/r/pa/prs/ps/2017/01/266729.htm].

53   left at the side of a road: 'Body of Higgins Identified, Taken to
      Embassy in Beirut', Associated Press, 24 December 1991.

53   dumped in a rubbish bag: 'Remains in Beirut Believed Those of
      Captive Agent', *Washington Post*, 28 December 1991.

6: Prayers in the Night

54   **large family of peasants:** Michael Nanko, 'A Report on the Case Investigation of Natuzza Evolo', *Journal of the Southern California Society for Psychical Research* 3, (1985), p. 7.

54   **ran away to Argentina:** 'Oggi è il compleanno di Mamma Natuzza', *Avvenire di Calabria*, 23 August 2021.

54   **performed an exorcism, locked away in an asylum:** Elanora Francica, 'A Great Mystic of Our Time: The Story of Natuzza Evolo and the Church', Religion Unplugged, 15 July 2022.

54   **During her confirmation:** Nanko, 'A Report on the Case Investigation of Natuzza Evolo', p. 8.

55   **results were inconclusive:** Ibid., p. 9.

55   **Aramaic or Greek:** Ibid., p. 12.

55   **two places at the same time:** Francica, 'A Great Mystic of Our Time'.

55   **she appeared inside his house:** Nanko, 'A Report on the Case Investigation of Natuzza Evolo', p. 16.

55   **written in French:** Ibid., p. 13.

55   **begin 'travelling':** Armando De Vincentiis, 'Nuovi approfondimenti sul fenomeno di Natuzza Evolo', Comitato Italiano per il Controllo delle Affermazioni sulle Pseudoscienze, 22 February 2011.

55   **widows in black headscarves:** Descriptions of Paravati in the middle of the twentieth century are taken from archive footage in 'La grande storia: Natuzza la mistica di Paravati', *RAI 3*, aired on 10 June 2015.

55   **superstitious folk Catholicism:** Citation of Professor Piero Cassoli in Nanko, 'A Report on the Case Investigation of Natuzza Evolo', p. 7.

55   **Gardner-Diamond syndrome:** This conclusion is made by Armando De Vincentiis in 'Nuovi approfondimenti sul fenomeno di Natuzza Evolo'. For a summary of Gardner-Diamond Syndrome see Mohammad Jafferany and Gaurav Bhattacharya, 'Psychogenic Purpura (Gardner-Diamond Syndrome)', *The Primary Care Companion for CNS Disorders*, 22 January 2015.

56   **fall asleep in bed praying:** 'Indictment, Operazione Stammer', Fermo di indiziato di delitto del pubblico ministero, Procura della

Repubblica di Catanzaro, Direzione Distrettuale Antimafia. Proc. Pen. N.9444/14 R.G. notizie di reato/Mod. 21 DDA, p. 1574.

56   **They made him angry:** Ibid.

56   **blood streamed from her face:** Statements of Oksana Verman in 'Verbale illustrativo della collaborazione', Procura della Repubblica di Catanzaro, Direzione Distrettuale Antimafia, N. 9444/14 RG Mod. 44, 15 June 2017, p. 55.

56   **started to have fainting spells:** Ibid.

56   **dissolved their victims in acid:** 'Mafia Informant's Body Was Dissolved in Acid, Italian Police Say', Reuters, 18 October 2010.

56   **shot in both legs:** 'Anziana gambizzata nel Vibonese', *CN24i*, 20 August 2014.

56   **firing Kalashnikovs:** 'Auto affianca una Peugeot e parte la raffica di kalashnikov, 45enne ferito di striscio', *CN24i*, 15 June 2017.

56   **tossed homemade bombs:** 'Ordigno esplode nei pressi di autosalone a Mileto', CN24i, 30 April 2011.

57   **a sign of respect:** Giuseppe Baldessarro, '"No alla 'ndrangheta in processione" e gli affiliati sparano sulla casa del priore', *La Repubblica*, 5 April 2010.

57   **'clean people':** Statements of Oksana Verman in 'Verbale illustrativo della collaborazione', p. 24

57   **rented Lancia Y10:** Sentence against Michele Iannello and Francesco Mesiano. Corte di Assise di Appello di Catanzaro, Sezione Seconda, N. 14/97 RG, 5 June 1998, p. 4.

57   **temples of Paestum:** Ibid.

57   **he spotted a car:** Ibid., p. 5.

58   **black ski masks, screamed at them in Italian:** Ibid.

58   **firing shots at the car:** Ibid., p. 6.

58   **window burst:** Ibid.

58   **the empty motorway:** Ibid.

58   **shielded them from the cold:** Ibid.

58   **them to operate:** Ibid., p. 7.

58   **thirty-four-day manhunt:** Alan Cowell, 'Italy Detains 2 in Highway Killing of US Boy, 7', *New York Times*, 2 November 1994.

59   **case of mistaken identity:** Piero Catalano, 'L'omicidio di Nicholas Green, la Calabria abbraccia i genitori 25 anni dopo', *Il Quotidiano del Sud*, 1 October 2019.

59   **'Our shame':** Alan Cowell, 'Italy Moved by Boy's Killing and the Grace of His Parents', *New York Times*, 4 October 1994.

59   **'An absurd death':** Ibid.

59   **The killers:** Michele Iannello and Francesco Mesiano, the two men convicted of the murder of Nicholas Green, have always denied committing the crime. In 2005 Iannello wrote a letter to *Espresso* claiming the killer was in fact his older brother. See 'Parla l'omicida di Nicholas Green "A ucciderlo fu mio fratello"', *La Repubblica*, 29 September 2005.

59   **his brother-in-law:** ''Ndrangheta, carcere duro per il boss in carrozzina', *La C*, 13 March 2018.

59   **pinkish terracotta church:** Description taken from site visit and images in 'Indictment, Operazione Stammer', p. 422.

59   **a short, silver-haired man:** Ibid.

59   **complex networks of shell companies:** ''Ndrangheta, bar e negozi sequestrati nel centro di Roma', *La Repubblica*, 13 March 2014.

60   **fluffy blue fleece:** The description of Fiarè on the bench is taken from surveillance photos in 'Indictment, Operazione Stammer'.

61   **any enclosed space:** Ibid., p. 442.

61   **a rare criminal status:** According to the Italian state's witness Andrea Mantella. See ''Ndrangheta: il pentito Mantella e le alleanze fra i clan di Vibo e Sinopoli', *La C*, 23 May 2018.

61   **the children of all the men they had ever murdered:** Alessia Truzzolillo, 'Rinascita Scott, Arena: Razionale ha rapporti con poteri più forti della 'ndrangheta', *Corriere della Calabria*, 28 September 2021.

7: A Funeral

63   **'distinguished visitors':** Except where individually noted, details in this chapter are taken from interviews with Jack Kelly.

64   **a golden opportunity:** For the DEA senior leadership view on the Tampa meeting see Jack Riley quoted in Josh Meyer, 'The Secret Backstory of How Obama Let Hezbollah Off the Hook', *Politico*, 19 December 2017.

64   **alternative ways of raising cash:** Written Testimony of Adam J. Szubin, Acting Under Secretary for Terrorism and Financial

Intelligence United States House Committee on Foreign
Affairs 'Iran Nuclear Deal Oversight: Implementation and its
Consequences (Part II)', 25 May 2016.

65 **super facilitators:** The 'Super Facilitator Initiative' is described by
David Asher in congressional testimony given as part of 'Attacking
Hezbollah's Financial Network: Policy Options', Hearing before
the Committee on Foreign Affairs, House of Representatives, 8
June 2017.

65 **with other US agencies:** Multiple former US officials, law
enforcement agents and academic experts confirmed these
tensions between the DEA and other agencies at a rank-and-file
level. Michael Hayden, director of the National Security Agency
between 1999 and 2005 and director of the Central Intelligence
Agency between 2006 and 2009, said the DEA's 'human
intelligence skills were second to none, and there was a growing
nexus between drugs and other intelligence targets'. See Hayden,
Playing to the Edge: American Intelligence in the Age of Terror (New
York: Penguin, 2016), p. 167.

65 **bank in Beirut:** The Lebanese Canadian Bank. Statement of Derek
S. Maltz Special Agent in Charge of the Special Operations Division
Drug Enforcement Administration Before the Subcommittee
on Terrorism, Nonproliferation, and Trade Committee on
Foreign Affairs United States House of Representatives Entitled
'Narcoterrorism and the Long Reach of US Law Enforcement', 17
November 2011, accessed at [https://www.dea.gov/sites/default/
files/pr/speeches-testimony/2012-2009/111117_testimony.pdf].

65 **a civil forfeiture case:** 'Manhattan US Attorney Announces $102
Million Settlement of Civil Forfeiture and Money Laundering
Claims Against Lebanese Canadian Bank', US Department of the
Treasury, 25 June 2015.

65 **'Welcome to the island':** Interview with Derek Maltz.

65 **Business Affairs Component:** Matthew Levitt, 'Hezbollah's
Procurement Channels: Leveraging Criminal Networks and
Partnering with Iran', *CTC Sentinel*, 21 March 2019.

66 **Imad Mughniyeh:** 'DEA and European Authorities Uncover
Massive Hizballah Drug and Money Laundering Scheme', Drug
Enforcement Administration, 1 February 2016.

66 **a single organisation:** The 'hub and spoke' argument for launching a RICO case against Hezbollah officials was outlined by David Asher to the US House Committee on Financial Services in his testimony 'A Dangerous Nexus: Terrorism, Crime, and Corruption', 21 May 2015.

67 **Some strongly disagreed:** For an in-depth examination of what is called the US interagency 'food fight' over targeting Hezbollah-connected criminal activity see Matthew Levitt, 'In Search of Nuance in the Debate over Hezbollah's Criminal Enterprise and the US Response', *Lawfare* research paper series, vol. 5, 20 March 2018.

67 **black propaganda:** 'Hezbollah Denies US Accusations of Drug Trafficking', Reuters, 19 January 2018.

67 **had directly connected:** 'Strategy to Combat Transnational Organized Crime', US National Security Council, 25 July 2011.

71 **lost his only brother: Certificates of death, Bureau of Vital Records and Statistics, Department of Health, City of New York, seen by author.**

74 **had unnerved some people:** US intelligence officials' concerns about the DEA's Fayad case are described in Levitt, 'In Search of Nuance in the Debate over Hezbollah's Criminal Enterprise and the US Response'.

76 **'lack of action on this issue':** Meyer, 'The Secret Backstory of How Obama Let Hezbollah Off the Hook'.

8: 'Sami Issa'

79 **'plan for changes':** Transcript of hearing of the Prosecutor v. Salim Jamil Ayyash, Mustafa Amine Badreddine, Hussein Hassan Oneissi and Assad Hassan Sabra, Special Tribunal for Lebanon, 2 December 2015, pp. 41–2.

79 **'Safi':** Ibid., p. 52.

80 **'family in Dubai':** Ibid., p. 51.

80 **'my incomplete grades':** Ibid., p. 55.

80 **American government and politics:** Ibid., p. 48.

80 **politics of Germany:** Ibid., p. 56.

80 **BMW convertible:** Transcript of hearing of Ayyash et al., Special Tribunal for Lebanon, 10 December 2015, p. 83.

80 **luxury hotels and restaurants:** Ibid., p. 55.

81 **where his yacht was moored:** Transcript of hearing of Ayyash et al., Special Tribunal for Lebanon, 1 December 2015, p. 92.

81 **one of his girlfriends:** Transcript of hearing of Ayyash et al., Special Tribunal for Lebanon, 2 December 2015, p. 68.

81 **he would be with another:** Transcript of hearing of Ayyash et al., Special Tribunal for Lebanon, 3 December 2015, p. 70.

81 **'my soulmate, my darling':** Transcript of hearing of Ayyash et al., Special Tribunal for Lebanon, 8 December 2015, p. 83.

81 **share personal information:** Transcript of hearing of Ayyash et al., Special Tribunal for Lebanon, 10 December 2015, p. 73.

81 **discuss politics:** Ibid., p. 74.

81 **the apartment was bare:** Ibid., p. 77.

82 **He didn't seem to know much:** Transcript of hearing of Ayyash et al., Special Tribunal for Lebanon, 8 December 2015, p. 71.

82 **not to ask:** Transcript of hearing of Ayyash et al., Special Tribunal for Lebanon, 3 December 2015, p. 78.

82 **'a circuitous road':** Ibid., p. 30.

82 **a walkie-talkie:** Transcript of hearing of Ayyash et al., Special Tribunal for Lebanon, 2 December 2015, p. 97.

82 **Lebanese military intelligence:** Transcript of hearing of Ayyash et al., Special Tribunal for Lebanon, 1 December 2015, p. 90.

82 **extremely paranoid individual:** Transcript of hearing of Ayyash et al., Special Tribunal for Lebanon, 2 December 2015, p. 82.

83 **to try to stop them:** Ibid., p. 69.

83 **goatee or a moustache:** Ibid., p. 84.

83 **lowering his cap:** Ibid.

83 **a beauty contest:** Transcript of hearing of Ayyash et al., Special Tribunal for Lebanon, 10 December 2015, p. 68.

83 **wipe away his fingerprints:** Transcript of hearing of Ayyash et al., Special Tribunal for Lebanon, 2 December 2015, p. 81.

83 **asked his bodyguard:** Ibid., p. 83.

83 **dip a tissue in water:** Ibid., pp. 86–7.

83 **bring his own pipe:** Ibid., p. 73.

83 **rarely touched money:** Ibid., p. 62.

83 **a Samsonite briefcase:** Ibid., p. 77.

84 **flip it face down:** Ibid.

84   touch the briefcase again: Ibid.

84   demand to know: Transcript of hearing of Ayyash et al., Special
        Tribunal for Lebanon, 3 December 2015, p. 100.

84   'Don't give my number': Ibid., p. 93.

84   making a rapid change: Transcript of hearing of Ayyash et al.,
        Special Tribunal for Lebanon, 2 December 2015, p. 94.

84   piles of spare licence plates: Ibid., p. 93.

84   number 100000: Ibid., p. 92.

84   Lebanese military intelligence: Ibid., p. 93.

85   a lieutenant colonel: Ibid., p. 88.

85   had been deactivated: Ibid., p. 67.

85   diktats from Damascus: Detlev Mehlis, 'Report of the
        International Independent Investigation Commission Established
        Pursuant to Security Council Resolution 1595 (2005)', United
        Nations International Independent Investigation Commission, 19
        October 2015, p. 5.

86   'I will break Lebanon over your head': Ibid., p. 7.

86   'you would be very upset': Ronen Bergman, 'The Hezbollah
        Connection', *New York Times Magazine*, 10 February 2015.

86   At around 12.50: 'Public Redacted Amended Indictment', The
        Prosecutor v. Salim Jamil Ayyash, Mustafa Amine Badreddine,
        Hussein Hassan Oneissi and Assad Hassan Sabra, Special Tribunal
        for Lebanon, 10 June 2011, p. 7.

86   to search for explosives: Nicholas Blanford, *Killing Mr Lebanon:
        The Assassination of Rafik Hariri and Its Impact on the Middle East*
        (London: IB Tauris, 2009), p. 3.

87   four-gigabyte jammers: Ibid.

88   'Get completely out of Lebanon': Brian Whitaker, 'Bush tells
        Syrians: Get Out of Lebanon Altogether', *Guardian*, 20 April 2005.

88   'Syrian officials': Mehlis, 'Report of the International
        Independent Investigation Commission Established Pursuant to
        Security Council Resolution 1595 (2005)', p. 9.

88   hunt down and murder: Witness statement of Gebran Tueni in
        ibid., p. 7.

88   killed by a car bomb: Michael Slackman, 'Beirut Car Bomb Kills
        Lawmaker, a Critic of Syria', *New York Times*, 13 December 2005.

88   called thousands of times: The phone analysis showed Sami

Issa had called a landline registered in the name of Saada over 20,000 times. See 'Judgment', The Prosecutor v. Salim Jamil Ayyash, Mustafa Amine Badreddine, Hussein Hassan Oneissi and Assad Hassan Sabra, Special Tribunal for Lebanon, 18 August 2020, p. 1319.

88   **belonged to a woman called Saada:** Ibid.

88   **sent birthday greetings:** 'Prosecution Pre-Trial Brief Pursuant to Rule 91', The Prosecutor v. Salim Jamil Ayyash, Mustafa Amine Badreddine, Hussein Hassan Oneissi and Assad Hassan Sabra, Special Tribunal for Lebanon, 15 November, 2012, p. 14.

88   **received calls from a** number in **Saudi Arabia:** 'Judgment', The Prosecutor v. Salim Jamil Ayyash, Mustafa Amine Badreddine, Hussein Hassan Oneissi and Assad Hassán Sabra, p. 1339.

89   **been Mustafa Badreddine all along:** The STL judgment concluded from phone analysis and witness statements that 'The evidence that Sami Issa was an alias of Mustafa Badreddine is direct and overwhelming' – see ibid., p. 1331.

89   **pick up his certificate:** Ibid., p. 1305.

9: The Mafia Goes to Medellín

90   **gentle and affectionate:** Statements of Oksana Verman in 'Verbale illustrativo della collaborazione', Procura della Repubblica di Catanzaro, Direzione Distrettuale Antimafia, N. 9444/14 RG Mod. 44, 15 June 2017, p. 7.

90   **cascades of pink bougainvillea:** Details taken from site visit by author.

90   **given her everything:** Sentencing, Operazione Stammer 2, La Corte d'Appello di Catanzaro, Seconda Sez. Penale, N. 1964/20, 19 November 2020, p. 141.

91   **was really hers:** Statements of Oksana Verman in 'Verbale illustrativo della collaborazione', p. 6.

91   **the keys to the apartment:** Statements of Oksana Verman in 'Ordinanza sulla richiesta di applicazione di misura cautelare', Tribunale di Catanzaro, Sezione GIP/GUP, N. 1166/7 R.G.N.R., 12 March 2018, p. 44.

91   **hated these intrusions:** Statements of Oksana Verman in 'Verbale illustrativo della collaborazione', p. 30.

91   **veteran Italian drug trafficker:** 'Indictment, Operazione Stammer', Fermo di indiziato di delitto del pubblico ministero, Procura della Repubblica di Catanzaro, Direzione Distrettuale Antimafia. Proc. Pen. N.9444/14 R.G. notizie di reato/Mod. 21 DDA, p. 33.

91   **flip-flops:** Ibid., p. 750.

92   **known as a guarantee:** Ibid., p. 80.

92   **Osvaldo:** Ibid., p. 3.

92   **'The important thing':** Ibid., p. 80.

92   **'send people blindly':** Ibid.

93   **transatlantic narcotics salesman:** Ibid., p. 79.

93   **various bungles and mishaps:** Ibid.

93   **a Swedish passport:** Ibid.

93   **Jota Jota:** Ibid., p. 78.

93   **the General:** Ibid., p. 64.

93   **just after 5.30 p.m.:** Ibid., p. 94.

94   **'I am fine here':** Ibid.

94   **operational security protocols:** Ibid., p. 96.

94   **into the Colombian jungle:** Ibid., p. 94.

94   **'as soon as possible':** Ibid.

94   **anxiously enquired:** Ibid.

95   **'2,5000 kilometres':** Ibid., p. 96.

95   **'What do you need the money for?':** Ibid., p. 98.

95   **'three weeks':** Ibid.

95   **late-night drinking sessions** Ibid., p. 99.

95   **'try to eat at home':** Ibid., p. 100.

96   **military fatigues:** 'Leader of the Violent Clan del Golfo Multi-Billion Dollar Drug Trafficking Organization Extradited from Colombia to Face Federal Indictment', United States Attorney's Office, Eastern District of New York, 5 May 2022.

96   **the Finca Aurora:** 'Un policía se infiltró en Turbo para ubicar caleta de "los Úsuga"', *El Tiempo*, 16 May 2016.

96   **stench of cocaine hydrochloride:** 'Así se infiltró una policía en el corazón del narcotráfico', *El Tiempo*, 28 June 2016.

96   **batches of white powder:** Ibid.

96   **under the direct control of Gavilán:** 'Un policía se infiltró en Turbo para ubicar caleta de "los Úsuga"'.

96 **Hidden in an underground bunker:** 'La policía colombiana decomisa 8 toneladas de cocaína en Urabá', *Euronews*, 16 May 2016. Video accessed at [https://www.youtube.com/watch?v=KQJUo1scC5Y].

96 **connecting flight:** 'Indictment, Operazione Stammer', p. 103.

97 **No phone call, no message:** Ibid.

97 **'already heard about it':** Ibid.

97 **'get on Skype':** Ibid.

97 **turned off his phone:** Ibid.

98 **'the only problem I have':** Ibid.

10: Babyface

99 **one spark to ignite the case:** Except where separately noted, the following chapter has been reconstructed from interviews with Jack Kelly, 'Michael', former intelligence officials and a report by Colombia's Departamento Administrativo de Seguridad.

101 **Don Pacho:** Not the 'Don Pacho' of *Narcos* fame, who died in 1998. See: 'Treasury Designates Medellín Drug Lord Tied to Oficina de Envigado Organized Crime Group', US Department of the Treasury, 9 July 2009.

102 **a young DEA agent called Michael:** This is not the undercover agent's real name, which has been withheld for security reasons.

103 **Abdul:** The businessman's name has been changed for security reasons.

105 **Syria's Air Force Intelligence Directorate:** For a contemporaneous description of Syrian involvement see Jo Becker, 'Beirut Bank Seen as a Hub of Hezbollah's Financing', *New York Times*, 13 December 2011.

107 **Air France flight:** Chris Kraul and Sebastian Rotella, 'Drug Probe Finds Hezbollah Link', *Los Angeles Times*, 22 October 2008.

107 **DEA leadership were delighted:** 'Operation Titan Recognized by Police Chiefs', Drug Enforcement Administration, 1 November 2010.]

107 **over $42 million in assets, 3.7 tonnes of cocaine etc:** Ibid.

108 **Imad Mughniyeh:** The claim that Mughniyeh met with Chekry Harb was made by Udi Levy, a former senior agent in the Israel Defence Force intelligence, former head of Mossad's Asset Tracing Unit and an advisor to the prime minister of Israel, in an interview

with the author. Other US law enforcement sources said that their intelligence suggested that Harb was operating under the protection of Imad Mughniyeh. A report produced at the time of the investigation by Colombia's now defunct Departamento Administrativo de Seguridad and seen by the author claimed that its telephone intercepts showed an 'Arab cell' connected to La Oficina had worked 'to transport drug proceeds in bulk cash, or to receive wire transfers directly from Hezbollah's External Security Organisation. The ESO is headed by Imad Fayez Mughniyeh.'

11: Midnight in Damascus

109 **forty-two countries:** Ronen Bergman, *Rise and Kill First: The Secret History of Israel's Targeted Assassinations* (London: John Murray, 2018), p. 596.

109 **by the codename Maurice:** Ibid.

110 **'no one of that name':** Shimon Shapira, 'Hizbullah Commander Imad Mughniyeh: 10 Years since His Assassination', Jerusalem Center for Public Affairs, 13 February 2018.

110 **in disguise:** David Crist, *The Twilight War: The Secret History of America's Thirty-Year Conflict with Iran* (New York: Penguin, 2012), p. 130.

110 **a thirty-one-year-old Lebanese police captain:** Neil Macdonald, 'CBC Investigation: Who Killed Lebanon's Rafic Hariri?', *CBC News*, 21 November 2010.

110 **a significant breakthrough:** Ibid.

111 **murdered by a car bomb:** Ibid.

111 **two very important men:** Adam Entous and Evan Osnos, 'Qassem Suleimani and How Nations Decide to Kill', *New Yorker*, 3 February 2020.

111 **He pulled up on a motorbike:** Interview with Saada Badreddine, 'In God's Eye, I Saw Nothing but Beauty', *Al-Ahed News*, 15 February 2020.

111 **Saada was always fearful:** Ibid.

111 **they settled in one place:** Ibid.

111 **friends could sense:** Nicholas Blanford, *Warriors of God: Inside Hezbollah's Thirty-Year War Against Israel* (New York: Random House, 2011), p. 466.

111 **travel around openly:** Shapira, 'Hizbullah Commander Imad Mughniyeh'.

111 **Kafr Sousa:** Entous and Osnos, 'Qassem Suleimani and How Nations Decide to Kill'.

111 **good-looking local women:** Bergman, *Rise and Kill First*, p. 600.

112 **two undercover spotters:** Adam Goldman and Matthew Levitt, 'Inside the Killing of Imad Mughniyah', *Washington Post*, 1 February 2015.

112 **ripping his body into pieces:** Entous and Osnos, 'Qassem Suleimani and How Nations Decide to Kill'. Neither the US nor the Israeli government has formally acknowledged responsibility for the assassination of Mughniyeh.

113 **raced towards the scene:** Fred Burton and Samuel M. Katz, *Beirut Rules: The Murder of a CIA Station Chief and Hezbollah's War Against America* (New York: Berkley, 2018), p. 334.

113 **blaming each other:** Ian Black, 'WikiLeaks Cables: Syria Stunned by Hezbollah Assassination', *Guardian*, 7 December 2010.

113 **that Syrian negligence was responsible:** Ibid.

113 **greatest martyrs:** Blanford, *Warriors of God*, p. 466.

113 **Imad's refrigerated coffin:** Ibid., p. 467.

113 **'the downfall of the state of Israel':** Ibid.

113 **he had taken them all away:** Uzi Mahnaimi and Hala Jaber, 'Israel Kills Terror Chief with Headrest Bomb', *Sunday Times*, 17 February 2008.

114 **Tears poured down the faces:** Blanford, *Warriors of God*, p. 468.

12: Human Guarantees

115 **to stay with Pepe:** 'Indictment, Operazione Stammer', Fermo di indiziato di delitto del pubblico ministero, Procura della Repubblica di Catanzaro, Direzione Distrettuale Antimafia. Proc. Pen. N.9444/14 R.G. notizie di reato/Mod. 21 DDA, p. 113.

116 **to enrage Antonella:** Ibid., p. 983.

116 **fed their victims alive to pigs:** 'Italian Mafia Fed Man Alive to Pigs, Police Say', Reuters, 29 November 2013.

117 **'I don't see anyone':** 'Indictment, Operazione Stammer', p. 106.

117 **run out of medicine:** Ibid., p. 101.

117 **calm things down:** Ibid., p. 103.

117   'I can't stay here like this': Ibid., p. 101.

118   'people don't trust what you say': Ibid., p. 106.

118   'I have nothing to do with it': Ibid.

118   'a lot of respect': Ibid.

119   'they will kill me here': Ibid., p. 90.

119   This shouldn't be happening to him, he thought: Ibid., p. 91.

119   got a call back: Ibid.

119   'make a bad impression': Ibid.

119   'By swimming?': Ibid.

120   'you have changed the plan': Ibid., p. 92.

120   'I would cut my own head off': Ibid.

120   'everything will be solved': Ibid., p. 93.

120   'not even for my own funeral': Ibid., p. 109.

120   'balls as big as a lorry': Ibid.

121   'that isn't good for us': Ibid.

121   'Uncle Scrooge': Ibid., p. 110.

121   'can't be said on the phone': Ibid., p. 113.

121   'kick his ass': Ibid.

121   'I will cut his head off': Ibid., p. 109.

122   'under the cameras in the street': Ibid., p. 111.

122   'They've broken my balls': Ibid.

122   'I guarantee it': Ibid., p. 112.

123   the Colonel told Antonio: Ibid., p. 154.

123   'Give me an order': Ibid., p. 151.

123   'Throw him in the sea': Ibid., p. 149.

123   'They don't work with us any more': Ibid., p. 152.

123   'he knows too much': Ibid., p. 154.

123   'I'll let you know': Ibid.

124   'and me too': Ibid., p. 136.

124   'if I am a shit': Ibid., p. 137.

124   'They must not know': Ibid.

125   'I'll cut their heads off': Ibid.

13: Murder in the Blue Moon Café

126   the day he told her about the murder: In August 2022 the
Corte Di Assise di Catanzaro named Salvatore Pititto as the
'material executor' of the murder of Antonio Corigliano, and

Pasquale Pititto as the 'organiser' of the murder. The court said they were being tried in separate proceedings, and both men have not yet been put on trial for this crime. The judges said that the 'reliability' of Oksana Verman's detailed testimony about Salvatore's confession to her for being the murderer 'is not in doubt'. Salvatore Pititto, through his lawyer, declined to comment about Oksana Verman's testimony about his role in the murder. Francesco Mesiano and Salvatore's cousin Rocco Iannello were both acquitted.

126   **during the night:** 'Miletos' indictment, 'Ordinanza sulla richiesta di applicazione di misura cautelare', Tribunale di Catanzaro, Sezione GIP/GUP, N. 1166/7 R.G.N.R., 12 March 2018, p. 44.

127   **returned to Mileto:** Ibid., p. 6.

127   **two decades behind bars:** Ibid., p. 10.

127   **'the madman':** Ibid., p. 332.

127   **they had been close:** Ibid., p. 72.

127   **ruining their crops:** Ibid.

128   **'There are many of us':** Ibid.

128   **no longer buy bread:** Ibid., p. 318.

128   **blue Piaggio Ape:** Ibid., p. 40.

128   **to file an official complaint:** Ibid., p. 42.

128   **lying on his back:** Ibid., p. 46.

128   **a thin gold medallion:** Ibid., p. 47.

128   **bottles of German beer:** Ibid.

129   **had been invited:** Ibid., p. 122.

129   **daily routine:** Ibid., p. 162.

129   **He rushed to the front:** Ibid., p. 161.

129   **the front windows were down:** Ibid., p. 163.

129   **a spattered pack of Marlboro cigarettes:** Ibid.

129   **serial number punched out:** Ibid.

129   **Salvatore told Oksana what had happened:** Ibid, p. 14.

130   **set fire to their farmhouse:** Ibid., p. 44.

130   **decided to ambush:** Ibid., p. 282.

130   **seven 9x21 pistol rounds:** Ibid., p. 44.

130   **'owed it' to:** Ibid.

14: Cookies in Paris

132   **a new phase of the investigation:** Except where separately
       noted, the reporting in this chapter is taken from interviews with
       Jack Kelly.

133   **towards Europe:** Jeremy McDermott, James Bargent, Douwe
       den Held and Maria Fernanda Ramírez, 'The Cocaine Pipeline
       to Europe', Global Initiative Against Transnational Organized
       Crime, February 2021.

133   **a far higher price:** The above report noted that in 2021 'a
       kilogram of cocaine in the US is worth up to US$28,0000
       wholesale. That same kilogram is worth around US$40,0000
       on average and as much as nearly US$80,0000 in different parts
       of Europe.'

133   **slip through:** Anna Sergi, *The Port-Crime Interface: A Report
       on Organised Crime & Corruption in Seaports* (London: ebook,
       2020), p. 18.

134   **'My grandfather':** His grandfather was not a Lebanese prime
       minister. DEA/Department of Justice Reports of Investigation
       filings connected to Miami-Dade criminal case F-16-019398,
       obtained through an open records request to the Miami-Dade
       State Attorney's Office. The actual message reads 'primer
       minister' (*sic*).

134   **'better I don't say who':** Ibid.

135   **On Islamic holidays:** Ibid.

15: The Translator

139   **notorious for its violence and overcrowding:** Kate Connolly,
       'Czech Prisoners Treated Worse Than Dogs – and Made to Pay
       £8 a Day', *Guardian*, 16 January 2000.

139   **conspiracy to provide material support:** United States of
       America v. Ali Fayad, Faouzi Jaber, Khaled El Merebi, Indictment,
       Case No. 1:13-cr-00485, United States District Court Southern
       District of New York, 4 June 2016.

140   **reversed the decision:** 'Czech Appeals Court Cancels Extradition
       of Terror Suspects to USA', *CTK Daily News*, 23 June 2015.

140   **silver Kia minivan:** Report into kidnapping of Czech nationals
       by National Headquarters Against Organized Crime of the

Criminal Police and Investigation Service – Terrorism and Extremism Section, Reference no. NCOZ-1370/TCˇ-2016-410093, 15 November 2017, p. 1.

140 **called Jan:** Ibid., p. 2.

140 **to film a video:** Ibid., p. 9.

140 **an exclusive interview:** Ibid., p. 6.

141 **they had been told:** Interview with Adam Homsi.

141 **surrounded the vehicle:** Report into kidnapping of Czech nationals by National Headquarters Against Organized Crime of the Criminal Police and Investigation Service – Terrorism and Extremism Section, p. 9.

141 **managed to text his girlfriend:** Ibid., p. 2.

141 **hoods over their heads:** Interview with Adam Homsi.

141 **if they were still in Lebanon:** Ibid.

141 **freshly cemented room:** Ibid.

141 **'Welcome to Daesh':** Ibid.

142 **passports, wallets and mobile phones:** Report into kidnapping of Czech nationals by National Headquarters Against Organized Crime of the Criminal Police and Investigation Service – Terrorism and Extremism Section, p. 2.

142 **Estonian cyclists:** 'Czechs Feared Kidnapped in Lebanon', BBC News, 18 July 2015.

142 **'huge security operation':** Ibid.

142 **to claim responsibility:** 'CzechRep Not Contacted Over Five Men Missing in Lebanon – Minister', Czech News Agency, 21 July 2015

142 **the email said:** Report into kidnapping of Czech nationals by National Headquarters Against Organized Crime of the Criminal Police and Investigation Service – Terrorism and Extremism Section, p. 2.

143 **slapped Adam across the face:** Ibid., p. 10.

143 **'your country and ours':** Interview with Adam Homsi.

143 **connected in some way to Hezbollah:** Interview with Adam Homsi and Report into kidnapping of Czech nationals by National Headquarters Against Organized Crime of the Criminal Police and Investigation Service – Terrorism and Extremism Section, p. 10.

144   **Was he really a lawyer:** Report into kidnapping of Czech
       nationals by National Headquarters Against Organized Crime of
       the Criminal Police and Investigation Service – Terrorism and
       Extremism Section, p. 10.

144   **under cover:** Ibid.

144   **own passport:** Ibid.

145   **two Turkish pilots:** Martin Chulov, 'Turkish Airlines Pilot and
       Co-pilot Kidnapped in Beirut', *Guardian*, 9 August 2013.

145   **Hannibal Gaddafi:** 'Gaddafi's Son Hannibal Freed after Kidnap in
       Lebanon', BBC News, 12 December 2015.

145   **the translator couldn't discern:** Interview with Adam Homsi.

145   **to look outside for a moment:** Ibid.

145   **his extradition hearings:** Report into kidnapping of Czech
       nationals by National Headquarters Against Organized Crime of
       the Criminal Police and Investigation Service – Terrorism and
       Extremism Section, p. 10.

146   **long before the sting:** 'USA Denies Provoking Terrorists
       Detained in Czech Republic', Czech News Agency, 14
       September 2015.

146   **an undercover agent working for Lebanese military
       intelligence:** Report into kidnapping of Czech nationals by
       National Headquarters Against Organized Crime of the Criminal
       Police and Investigation Service – Terrorism and Extremism
       Section, p. 4.

16: To Do the Impossible

147   **paused in front of the palm trees:** Photos of Salvatore at
       the airport from 'Indictment, Operazione Stammer', Fermo
       di indiziato di delitto del pubblico ministero, Procura della
       Repubblica di Catanzaro, Direzione Distrettuale Antimafia. Proc.
       Pen. N.9444/14 R.G. notizie di reato/Mod. 21 DDA, p. 185.

148   **His next flight:** Ibid., pp. 190–1.

148   **'still in Bogotá:** Ibid., p. 179.

148   **'this situation':** Ibid., pp. 179–80.

149   **'here on Monday':** Ibid., p. 179.

149   **'in Milan':** Ibid., p. 181.

149   **'Tuesday max':** Ibid.

149   'No Pepe': Ibid.

149   'do the impossible': Ibid.

150   small light inside the dashboard: Ibid., p. 186.

150   'it's connected': Ibid., p. 188.

150   an old investigation: Ibid.

150   'Do you understand, asshole': Ibid.

151   'a power supply': Ibid., p. 189.

151   'A recorder': Ibid.

151   'This is him': Ibid., p. 190.

152   a large black suitcase: Ibid., p. 198.

152   briefly stood together: Ibid.

152   on his way home: Ibid., p. 201.

152   Colombian guest: Ibid., p. 35.

152   update them on the deal: Ibid., p. 236.

153   to confirm the route was secure: Ibid., p. 235.

153   their people in Europe: Ibid., p. 253.

154   wrote to Antonio: Ibid., p. 240.

154   'Jota, don't worry': Ibid.

154   blue jeans and black gloves: Photos of Jhon at the airport from
        ibid., p. 298.

154   to call Jota: Ibid., p. 300.

154   overgrown teddy bear: Ibid., p. 297.

155   'I can't be on their backs': Ibid., p. 338.

155   'It makes people angry': Ibid., p. 302.

155   to be murdered: Ibid.

155   'It is best to leave that man': Ibid.

155   rushed to hospital: Ibid., p. 136.

17: A Home Run

157   containers of cocaine: 'Cedar Judgment', Cour d'Appel de Paris,
        Tribunal de Grande Instance de Paris, N° parquet 15037000675,
        28 November 2018, p. 46.

157   The attaché: Interview with former DEA Paris attaché
        Ric Bahsur.

157   Jack had first met: Interview with Jack Kelly.

157   worked in domestic intelligence: Interview with Quentin Mugg.

157   at 5.20 p.m.: 'Cedar Judgment', p. 46.

157   **faced a difficult decision:** Interview with Quentin Mugg.

157   **'garbage':** 'Cedar Judgment', p. 46.

157   **drove the cash he had collected to Monaco:** Ibid., p. 42.

157   **Hassan Tarabolsi:** Ibid., p. 46.

158   **Mohamad Nourredine:** Ibid., p. 45.

158   **an office in Beirut:** 'Treasury Sanctions Key Hizballah
        Money Laundering Network', US Department of Treasury, 28
        January 2016.

158   **Adidas sports bag:** 'Cedar Judgment', p. 45.

158   **leaving for Rome:** Ibid.

158   **the only one he could think of:** Interview with Quentin Mugg.

158   **'home run':** Interview with Ric Bahsur.

159   **'a truck':** 'Cedar Judgment', p. 49.

159   **'the oven', 'the mill':** Ibid., p. 50.

159   **a transportation company in Germany:** Ibid., p. 65.

159   **Jimmy:** Ibid., p. 51.

159   **remove the screwdriver:** Ibid.

160   **'get a new one':** Ibid., p. 50.

160   **€14 million of watches:** Ibid., p. 46.

160   **waved through by customs:** Ibid., p. 47.

160   **almost daily phone contact:** Frequent contact between
        Nourredine and Tabaja is documented in Cedar ruling, but
        frequency of contact is from interviews with law enforcement
        officers with first-hand knowledge of the case.

160   **one of the organisation's most important financiers:** The US
        Government's Rewards for Justice programme has offered 'up to
        $10 million' for information about Tabaja. See 'Adham Husayn
        Tabaja', Rewards for Justice, [https://rewardsforjustice.net/
        rewards/adham-husayn-tabaja/].

160   **smuggle large sums of money:** 'Treasury Sanctions Key
        Hizballah, IRGC-QF Networks in Iraq', US Department of the
        Treasury, 13 November 2018.

161   **Mohamed Badreddine:** 'Treasury Targets Hizballah Financial
        Network in Africa and the Middle East', US Department of the
        Treasury, 2 February 2018.

18: The Eternal City

162   **took out his phone:** 'Indictment, Operazione Stammer', Fermo di indiziato di delitto del pubblico ministero, Procura della Repubblica di Catanzaro, Direzione Distrettuale Antimafia. Proc. Pen. N.9444/14 R.G. notizie di reato/Mod. 21 DDA, p. 468.

162   **operations room screen:** Site visit to the headquarters of the Gruppo di investigazione Criminalità Organizzata (GICO), Italy's specialised anti-Mafia investigations unit run by the country's financial crimes police, the Guardia di Finanza.

163   **Rome Termini:** 'Indictment, Operazione Stammer', p. 470.

163   **'This is Castro':** Ibid.

163   **travel to Rome by train:** Ibid., p. 471.

163   **'look inside people':** Ibid., p. 453.

163   **'Via Castro Pretorio':** Ibid., p. 472.

164   **caked with pollution and graffiti:** Observations taken during site visit in June 2021.

164   **drowned off the Italian coast:** 'UNHCR Calls for Urgent Action as Hundreds Feared Lost in Mediterranean Boat Sinking', UNHCR, 20 April 2015.

164   **'We will not forget you':** Message posted by 'Castro' on his personal Facebook page.

164   **flight to Beirut:** 'Indictment, Operazione Stammer', p. 478.

19: 'Mustafa Badreddine is Present'

165   **their commander's dead cousin:** Anne Barnard, 'Hezbollah Deploys Weapon, a Press Tour, on the Syrian Front', *New York Times*, 16 May 2015.

165   **a fifth of its territory:** While the Assad regime had lost significant geographical territory by this point it still controlled most of Syria's largest population centres. Laila Bassam and Tom Perry, 'How Iranian General Plotted Out Syrian Assault in Moscow', Reuters, 6 October 2015.

166   **launched an assault:** 'Syria Military Resists Major Rebel Assault in Aleppo', BBC News, 3 July 2015.

166   **turn the regional balance of power:** 'Lebanon's Hizbollah Turns Eastward to Syria', Crisis Group Middle East Report, No. 153, 27 May 2014, p. 6.

166　　**burned, shot and castrated:** Liam Stack, 'Video of Tortured Boy's
　　　　Corpse Deepens Anger in Syria', *New York Times*, 30 May 2011.

166　　**'the time has come':** 'Syria Unrest: World Leaders Call for Assad
　　　　to Step Down', BBC News, 18 August 2011.

166　　**demand the Syrian dictator went:** Jonathon Burch, 'Turkey Tells
　　　　Syria's Assad: Step Down!', Reuters, 22 November 2011.

167　　**regime's security apparatus:** 'Syrian Army Defectors Hit Intel
　　　　Complex – activists', Reuters, 16 November 2012.

167　　**coordination meetings:** 'Treasury Sanctions Hizballah Leaders,
　　　　Military Officials, and an Associate in Lebanon', US Department
　　　　of the Treasury, 21 July 2015.

167　　**obituaries:** 'Hezbollah Military Commander "Killed in Syria"',
　　　　BBC News, 2 October 2012.

168　　**fresh graves:** Martin Chulov, 'Syria Bomb Blast Kills Hezbollah
　　　　Operative', *Guardian*, 2 October 2012.

168　　**'jihadist duty':** 'Hezbollah Military Commander "Killed
　　　　in Syria"'.

168　　**'Mustafa Badreddine is present':** 'FSA: Mustafa Badreddine
　　　　Leading Hizbullah Operations in Qusayr', *Naharnet*, 20 May 2013.

168　　**'a defence of Lebanon':** Ali Hashem, 'Nasrallah on Syria: "This
　　　　Battle is Ours"', *Al-Monitor*, 26 May 2013.

168　　**'a field [of] such importance':** Nasrallah quoted in Hearing
　　　　Transcript, Special Tribunal for Lebanon, 31 May 2016, p. 54.

169　　**cut telephone lines:** 'The Battle for al Qusayr, Syria', Complex
　　　　Operational Environment and Threat Integration Directorate,
　　　　2013, p. 6.

169　　**hit-and-run tactics:** Ibid., p. 7.

169　　**killing and wounding:** Ibid., p. 9.

169　　**excavating tunnels:** Nicholas Blanford, 'The Battle for Qusayr:
　　　　How the Syrian Regime and Hizb Allah Tipped the Balance',
　　　　CTC Sentinel 6:8, Syria Special Issue (August 2013).

170　　**had been surrounded:** Ibid.

170　　**urban warfare:** Ibid.

170　　**supplies dwindling:** Ibid.

170　　**taken by surprise:** Christopher Phillips, *The Battle for Syria:
　　　　International Rivalry in the New Middle East*, 2nd edn (New Haven:
　　　　Yale University Press, 2020), p. 158.

171   **Timber Sycamore:** Mark Mazzetti, Adam Goldman and Michael S. Schmidt, 'Behind the Sudden Death of a $1 Billion Secret CIA War in Syria', *New York Times*, 2 August 2017.

171   **'something we don't know':** Erica Solomon, 'Syrian Intelligence Tsar Takes Assad Secrets to the Grave', *Financial Times*, 3 May 2015.

171   **secretly flew:** Bassam and Perry, 'How Iranian General Plotted Out Syrian Assault in Moscow'.

20: *TG NIKE*

172   *TG NIKE:* The boat departed the port of Turbo on 2 August 2015 and docked sixteen days later. 'Indictment, Operazione Stammer', Fermo di indiziato di delitto del pubblico ministero, Procura della Repubblica di Catanzaro, Direzione Distrettuale Antimafia. Proc. Pen. N.9444/14 R.G. notizie di reato/Mod. 21 DDA, p. 701.

172   **210-metre:** The length and flag of TG NIKE is taken from the boat's entry on www.vesselfinder.com

173   **he realised the complexity:** 'Indictment, Operazione Stammer', p. 730.

173   **only more bananas:** The description of banana-printed foil and boxes is taken from photos in ibid., p. 782.

174   **twenty-three kilograms:** Ibid., p. 770.

174   **Antonio pleaded:** Ibid., p. 731.

175   **'lose €1.2 million':** Ibid., p. 733.

175   **'if he is even coming':** Ibid.

175   **'which one is ours':** Ibid.

175   **'I could be shot':** Ibid.

176   **'tomorrow night':** Ibid., p. 734.

176   **large belly bulging:** A picture of Jhon waiting at the arrivals gate from ibid., p. 748.

176   **cowboy shirt:** A picture of Jota walking through arrivals gate is in ibid.

176   **white beach shorts:** A photo of Antonio and the car from ibid., p. 750.

176   **Rome–Florence motorway:** Ibid.

176   **another car pulled up:** Still CCTV images from ibid., pp. 751–2.

176 **a lone woman:** Still CCTV images from ibid., pp. 752–6.

176 **floating on a lake:** Description of the inside of the bar taken from ibid., p. 756.

177 **nine hours:** They left the cafe at 3.25 a.m. and arrived in Calabria at 12.15 p.m. Ibid., p. 760.

177 **began to be unloaded:** *TG NIKE* docked in Livorno at around 12.30 p.m. Ibid., p. 762.

178 **'another shipment':** Ibid., p. 765.

178 **'directly from us':** Ibid.

178 **'different types of fruit':** Ibid., p. 766.

179 **rip off the boxes:** Photo of containers from Ibid., p. 763.

179 **exact weights:** Ibid., p. 770.

179 **'Is it good':** Ibid.

179 **'time and money':** Ibid.

179 **'you will know everything':** Ibid.

179 **sixty-three bricks of cocaine:** Ibid., p. 779.

179 **anti-scanning foil:** Ibid.

180 **Romain Jerome:** Ibid., p. 783.

180 **During the raid:** 'Detienen a 57 presuntos integrantes del "Clan Úsuga" en Antioquia', *Vanguardia*, 12 March 2015.

180 **second-in-command:** 'Roberto Vargas Gutiérrez, alias "Gavilán"', *Insight Crime*, 9 January 2017.

181 **fearing arrest:** 'Indictment, Operazione Stammer', p. 790.

181 **'the newspapers':** Ibid., p. 776.

21: Terror Control

182 **sitting in his office:** Interview with Iain Edwards.

182 **the first time:** 'About the STL', Special Tribunal for Lebanon, accessed at [https://www.stl-tsl.org/en/about-the-stl].

183 **had been charged:** 'Warrant to Arrest Mr Mustafa Amine Badreddine Including Transfer and Detention Order', Special Tribunal for Lebanon 28 June 2011.

183 **to retake Aleppo:** Tom Perry, Laila Bassam, Suleiman Al-Khalidi and Tom Miles, 'Hezbollah, Other Shi'ite Allies Helped Assad Win in Aleppo', Reuters, 14 December 2016.

183 **masterminding the bombing operation:** Indictment, The Prosecutor v. Mustafa Amine Badreddine, Salim Jamil Ayyash,

Hussein Hassan Oneissi and Assad Hassan Sabra, Special Tribunal for Lebanon, 10 June 2011.

183   'cut off the hand': 'Indictments Come at Key Moment for Hezbollah's Nasrallah', *Der Spiegel International*, 17 July 2011.

183   since the Nuremberg Trials: 'Appeals Chamber Dismisses In Absentia Appeals', Special Tribunal for Lebanon, 1 November 2012.

184   'green network': Indictment, The Prosecutor v. Mustafa Amine Badreddine, Salim Jamil Ayyash, Hussein Hassan Oneissi and Assad Hassan Sabra, p. 12.

184   adopted aliases: Ibid., p. 13.

184   Mitsubishi truck: Ibid., p. 11.

185   final instructions: Ibid., p. 19.

185   Ayyash received: Ibid.

185   the last calls: Ibid.

185   under the microscope: Interview with Iain Edwards.

185   'leaving no footprint': Robin Wright, 'The Demise of Hezbollah's Untraceable Ghost', *New Yorker*, 13 May 2016.

186   'Western intelligence organizations': All of the following references to Terror Control are taken from www.stop910.com. References to the timing of the articles are taken from the Internet Archive's Wayback Machine.

22: A Family Crisis

188   scrambling: 'Indictment, Operazione Stammer', Fermo di indiziato di delitto del pubblico ministero, Procura della Repubblica di Catanzaro, Direzione Distrettuale Antimafia. Proc. Pen. N.9444/14 R.G. notizie di reato/Mod. 21 DDA, p. 907.

188   over a million euros: Ibid., p. 733.

188   precautionary measure: Ibid., p. 810.

189   The Colombian refused: Ibid., p. 821.

189   improvised submarine: Ibid., p. 809.

189   she hated: Ibid., p. 983.

189   'the newspaper': Ibid., p. 810.

189   'work hard for this': Ibid.

190   raise new funds: Ibid., p. 803.

190   peaceful again: Ibid., p. 843.

190   'You have to pay': Ibid., p. 829.

190　　a concrete shopping centre: Ibid., p. 1426.

191　　'Are you sure': Ibid.

191　　twenty-three-year-old: Sentencing, Operazione Stammer 2, La
　　　　Corte d'Appello di Catanzaro, Seconda Sez. Penale, N. 1964/20,
　　　　19 November 2020, p. 4.

191　　bail them out: Ibid., p. 235.

192　　told the doctors: Ibid., p. 234.

192　　ten years younger: Sentencing of Alex Pititto, Tribunale per i
　　　　Minorenni di Catanzaro, N. 56/18 R.G. Sent., 8 June 2018, p. 1.

192　　'breaking my balls': 'Indictment, Operazione Stammer', p. 1430.

193　　told his mother: Ibid.

193　　Salvatore had called: Ibid., p. 1426.

193　　always a risk: Pasquale Pititto was sentenced to twenty-five years
　　　　in prison in Operation 'Tirreno' for the murder of Pietro Cosimo
　　　　but has served much of his sentence under house arrest for medical
　　　　reasons. See ''Ndrangheta: l'ergastolano di Mileto Pasquale Pititto
　　　　passa ai domiciliari', Il Vibonese, 13 June 2022.

194　　lined with wild trees: 'Indictment, Operazione Stammer', p. 896.

194　　ambush his enemies: Interrogatorio di Iannello Michele, Procura
　　　　della Repubblica presso il tribunale di Catanzaro, 24 January
　　　　2002, p. 48.

194　　watching them: 'Indictment, Operazione Stammer', p. 895.

194　　'Jhon, stay here': Ibid.

23: 'Very Important Russians'

195　　due to fly: Information from US and European law
　　　　enforcement sources.

197　　Badreddine's brother: 'Treasury Targets Hizballah Financial
　　　　Network in Africa and the Middle East', US Department of the
　　　　Treasury, 2 February 2018.

197　　maintaining 'direct ties': 'Treasury Sanctions Hizballah Front
　　　　Companies and Facilitators in Lebanon and Iraq', US Department
　　　　of the Treasury, 10 June 2015.

197　　ranted: Interview with Quentin Mugg.

197　　'I only coordinate': 'Cedar Judgment', Cour d'Appel de Paris,
　　　　Tribunal de Grande Instance de Paris, N° parquet 15037000675,
　　　　28 November 2018, p. 48.

197   **relaying instructions:** Ibid., p. 49.

197   **hundreds of millions:** Ibid., p. 48.

198   **working to procure:** Sworn Affidavit, United States vs Mazen El Atat, District Court for the Southern District of New York, United States, Criminal Docket No. 18 Cr. 275, 2 January 2019, p. 5.

198   **oversaw weapons procurement:** Ibid., p. 8.

198   **had been sanctioned:** Ali Al-Salim was sanctioned by the EU and the UK government in August 2011 for his role as director of the Syrian Army Supply Bureau. The Army Supply Bureau was placed under US sanctions in September 2012 for being an entity 'that supports the Assad regime's efforts to procure arms and communications equipment that contribute to the regime's violence against the Syrian people'. In July 2014 the EU sanctioned the Army Supply Bureau for being 'responsible for the violent repression of the civilian population in Syria'.

198   **Al-Salim wrote:** Sworn Affidavit, United States vs Mazen El Atat, p. 8.

198   **search warrant:** Ibid.

198   **fuses for aerial bombs:** 'Treasury Designates Syrian Entity, Others Involved in Arms and Communications Procurement Networks and Identifies Blocked Iranian Aircraft', US Department of the Treasury, 19 September 2012.

199   **attack civilian populations:** Ibid.

199   **The email:** Sworn Affidavit, United States vs Mazen El Atat, p. 8.

199   **SVD Dragunov sniper rifles:** Ibid., p. 10.

199   **sanctioned by the United States:** 'Treasury Sanctions Networks Providing Support to the Government of Syria, Including for Facilitating Syrian Government Oil Purchases from ISIL', US Department of the Treasury, 25 November 2015.

199   **deadly ingredient:** 'In Nine Years, the Syrian Regime Has Dropped Nearly 82,0000 Barrel Bombs, Killing 11,087 Civilians, Including 1,821 Children', Syrian Network for Human Rights, 15 April 2021, p. 6.

199   **DShK machine guns:** Sworn Affidavit, United States vs Mazen El Atat, p. 9.

199   **weapons procurement lists:** Ibid., p. 14.

199   **Unit 910:** See Husayn Ali Faour in 'Treasury Sanctions Hizballah Front Companies and Facilitators in Lebanon and Iraq'.

200   **trading in Iranian oil:** Mazen al-Atat was charged by the US Department of Justice with violating the International Emergency Economic Powers Act by acting in breach of US economic sanctions against Iran. Many US economic sanctions against Iran were lifted at the start of 2016 as part of the Iran nuclear deal, or Joint Comprehensive Plan of Action. In 2018 the Trump administration withdrew from that deal and reinstated sanctions against Iran. Al-Atat's French lawyer argued in his extradition hearing that his client's trading in Iranian oil was not illegal at the time under French law.

200   **one of the recorded calls:** The following conversation took place on 14 May 2015 and is taken from Exhibit 3.4.4D657/3-4 in 'Summary Memorandum for Mr Mazen Atef El Atat', US Department of Justice, p. 39. This document was submitted by his French lawyer William Julié for an extradition hearing held in Paris on 2 October 2019. The transcript of the call, translated from Arabic into French and then into English, has been edited for clarity, removing filler words and interjections. Several of the recorded calls discussing Iranian oil sales occurred before the passing of United Nations Security Council Resolution 2231, which set out the lifting of many UN economic sanctions against Iran and endorsed the Joint Comprehensive Plan of Action.

200   **Iranian oil deal:** Mazen al-Atat's French lawyer argued to the French authorities during his extradition process that the entire conversation was related to oil. The US Department of Justice, based on evidence submitted by the DEA, said that the 'huge stock' discussed was 'referring to a large cache of weapons' and that this part of the conversation took place alongside the reference to the oil deal.

201   **'Don't mess around with us':** Mazen al-Atat's French lawyer argued during his extradition hearing that this reference to Hezbollah was a joke and 'therefore not a serious threat'. The US Department of Justice said in its submission that this comment and other evidence contributed to its charging of al-Atat for conspiracy to provide material support to Hezbollah.

201 **string of messages:** Interview with Jack Kelly.

201 **three suicide bombers:** 'Paris Attacks: What Happened on the Night', BBC News, 9 December 2015.

202 **gunning down thirteen:** Ibid.

202 **Just after midnight:** Ibid.

202 **130 people died:** Ibid.

202 **returned to Europe:** Tom Burgis, 'Paris Attacks: Samy Amimour, the "Nice Guy" Who Became a Jihadi', *Financial Times*, 19 November 2015.

202 **called off:** Interview with Jack Kelly.

24: 'Your Country Has Screwed Up'

205 **windowless cell:** Interview with Adam Homsi.

205 **cleaned up:** Ibid.

206 **cook who had been seized:** Report into kidnapping of Czech nationals by National Headquarters Against Organized Crime of the Criminal Police and Investigation Service – Terrorism and Extremism Section, Reference no. NCOZ-1370/TC˘-2016-410093, 15 November 2017, p. 7.

207 **a friend of his:** Ibid., p. 4.

207 **prison phone call:** Ibid.

207 **'screwed up':** Interview with Adam Homsi.

207 **could be extradited:** 'Czech Court Nods to Extradition of Terrorism Suspects to USA', *CTK Daily News*, 14 December 2015.

208 **Khmeimim Air Base:** Christopher Phillips, *The Battle for Syria: International Rivalry in the New Middle East*, 2nd edn (New Haven: Yale University Press, 2020), p. 213.

208 **Pentagon spokesman:** 'Russia "Plans Forward Air Operating Base" in Syria – US', BBC News, 14 September 2015.

208 **end of the Cold War:** Seth G. Jones, 'Moscow's War in Syria', Center for Strategic & International Studies, 12 May 2020.

209 **ISIS had ransacked:** Phillips, *The Battle for Syria*, p. 216.

208 **'setbacks':** Simon Tisdall, 'Syrian President Admits Military Setbacks, in First Public Speech for a Year', *Guardian*, 26 July 2015.

209 **non-ISIS rebels:** Phillips, *The Battle for Syria*, p. 218.

25: Hunted Like a Dog

210   **demand money:** 'Indictment, Operazione Stammer', Fermo
       di indiziato di delitto del pubblico ministero, Procura della
       Repubblica di Catanzaro, Direzione Distrettuale Antimafia. Proc.
       Pen. N.9444/14 R.G. notizie di reato/Mod. 21 DDA, p. 1107.

210   **raced down the stairs:** Ibid.

211   **'that would be cheating you':** Ibid., p. 1101.

211   **to raise cash:** Ibid., p. 1024.

211   **the police would instead:** Ibid., p. 1083.

211   **never see again:** Ibid., p. 1107.

211   **'come for you':** Ibid.

211   **'there watching us':** Ibid.

212   **'how many photos':** Ibid.

212   **'throw away the key':** Ibid.

212   **lost shipment:** Ibid., pp. 1078–9.

212   **'How much did you give him':** Ibid., p. 1107.

212   **'I am going to kill him':** Ibid.

212   **stay faithful:** Ibid.

212   **never betray him:** Ibid.

26: The Champagne Reception

213   **they were arrested:** 'Cedar Judgment', Cour d'Appel de Paris,
       Tribunal de Grande Instance de Paris, N° parquet 15037000675,
       28 November 2018, p. 52.

213   **Rolex watch etc:** Ibid., p. 53.

213   **simultaneous European arrest warrants:** Ibid., p. 54.

214   **replica pistol etc:** Ibid.

214   **was triumphant:** From interviews with Jack Kelly, Rik Bashur
       and Quentin Mugg.

214   **'for Hezbollah for its activities in Syria':** 'DEA and European
       Authorities Uncover Massive Hizballah Drug and Money
       Laundering Scheme', Drug Enforcement Administration, 1
       February 2016.

215   **champagne reception:** Interviews with Rik Bashur, Quentin
       Mugg and Jack Kelly.

215   **called off:** The last-minute cancellation of the press conference
       was confirmed by three independent sources from both countries.

216 'try and fix this': Interview with Jack Kelly.

216 first visit to Europe: 'Iran's Rouhani to Visit Italy, France Next Week, First Europe Trip After Sanctions Lifted', Reuters, 18 January 2016.

216 'a glorious victory': Saeed Kamali Deghan, 'Sanctions Against Iran Lifted After Compliance with Nuclear Deal', *Guardian*, 16 January 2016.

216 118 aircraft: 'Airbus Signs $25bn Deal to Sell 118 Planes to Iran', BBC News, 28 January 2016.

217 'Hezbollah-affiliated money launderers': 'Treasury Sanctions Key Hizballah Money Laundering Network', US Department of the Treasury, 28 January 2016.

217 'working closely with foreign counterparts': 'DEA And European Authorities Uncover Massive Hizballah Drug and Money Laundering Scheme'.

218 sped away: Interview with Adam Homsi.

218 sliding down the hill in fear: Ibid.

218 'What the hell happened to you': Ibid.

218 plane to Prague: Report into kidnapping of Czech nationals by National Headquarters Against Organized Crime of the Criminal Police and Investigation Service – Terrorism and Extremism Section, Reference no. NCOZ-1370/TCˇ-2016-410093, 15 November 2017.

219 'encourage criminal groups and terrorists': Hana de Goeij, 'Missing Czechs Return Home in an Apparent Swap Deal', *New York Times*, 6 February 2016.

219 did not negotiate with terrorists: Karel Janicek, 'US Embassy Condemns Czechs for Not Extraditing Suspects', Associated Press, 4 February 2016.

219 signed 'MALEM': Report into kidnapping of Czech nationals by National Headquarters Against Organized Crime of the Criminal Police and Investigation Service – Terrorism and Extremism Section, p. 14.

27: 'A State and Condition of Death'

220 snoozed in a maternity ward: Interview with Iain Edwards.

220 'have a look at this': Ibid.

220 'the martyrdom of the commander Mustafa Badreddine':
Al Manar news report cited in official transcript of open session,
Special Tribunal for Lebanon, 31 May 2016, p. 15.

221 'partner in jihad': Ibid.

222 women in black veils threw confetti: Descriptions taken from
footage 'Hezbollah Mourns Top Commander Killed in Syria',
Associated Press, 13 May 2016. Accessed at [https://www.youtube.
com/watch?v=WyD_ympaVDo].

222 Abdallah Safieddine: Official transcript of open session, Special
Tribunal for Lebanon, 31 May 2016, p. 33.

222 sanctioned as a Hezbollah financier: 'Treasury Targets
Hizballah Financial Network in Africa and the Middle East', US
Department of the Treasury, 2 February 2018.

222 Rawdat al-Shahidayn cemetery: Official transcript of open
session, Special Tribunal for Lebanon, 31 May 2016, p. 40.

223 'Sayyed Mustafa': Ibid., p. 51.

223 hindered his ability to walk: Ibid., p. 52.

223 'inside Syrian territories': Ibid., p. 54.

223 would have to be closed: The transcript of the debate below is
taken from ibid., p. 93.

224 the same person: 'Public Redacted Version of Annex G to F0257,
Prosecution's Submission Pursuant to Rule 91(Part 4) and the
Corrigendum for the Annexes A and H to F0246 – Corrected
Version of the Pre-Trial Brief', Special Tribunal for Lebanon,
2020, p. 97.

224 'in fact dead': Official transcript of open session, Special Tribunal
for Lebanon, 31 May 2016, p. 93.

225 'whether you are satisfied': Ibid.

226 questions were beginning to be asked: 'Experts Doubt
Hezbollah's Account of Commander's Death', Reuters,
14 May 2016.

226 'in the investigation soon': Anne Barnard and Sewell Chan,
'Mustafa Badreddine, Hezbollah Military Commander, is Killed
in Syria', *New York Times*, 13 May 2016.

226 quickly pulled its article: Bassem Mroue, 'Top Hezbollah
Military Commander Killed in Syria', Associated Press,
13 May 2016.

226   **Mustafa's demise:** 'Press Briefing by Press Secretary Josh Earnest', The White House Office of the Press Secretary, 13 May 2016.

226   **no further details:** *Al Manar* report cited in official transcript of open session, Special Tribunal for Lebanon, 31 May 2016, p. 41.

226   **seven kilometres away:** Sammy Ketz, 'Badreddine: A Hezbollah Chief Mysterious in Life and Death', AFP, 13 May 2016.

226   **claimed credit:** 'Syrian Rebels Deny Hezbollah's Military Commander Killed in "Artillery Shelling"', *Long War Journal*, 14 May 2016.

226   **'There is no truth':** SOHR statement on Facebook, accessed at [https://www.facebook.com/syrianhroe/posts/ pfbid02zasjCYL3Uv3t7xbwcCnAZAzmndhbMdYF4sD7TJ1 pTcV9TXTJqXWs6qwsBpW6yhWrl].

227   **no damage to the building:** 'Al Arabiya investigates: Who Really Killed Hezbollah's Mustafa Badreddine?', Al Arabiya News Channel, 8 March 2017.

227   **'with our assessment':** 'Israel: Hezbollah Commander Mustafa Badreddine "Killed by Own Men"', BBC News, 21 March 2017.

227   **'a leadership crisis':** 'Israel's Army Chief: Hezbollah Commander Mustafa Badreddine Killed by His Own Men', *Haaretz*, 22 March 2017.

227   **hothead and a womaniser:** Yossi Melman, 'Why Syria Isn't Firing Its S-3000 Missiles at Israeli Jets', *Haaretz*, 15 May 2020.

227   **cannon fodder:** Shimon Shapira, 'Mustafa Badr al-Din ("Zulfiqar") and the Ansariya Operation', Jerusalem Center for Public Affairs, 13 May 2019.

227   **strategic direction of the war:** This version of Mustafa Badreddine's death is recounted by Yossi Melman in 'Why Syria Isn't Firing Its S-3000 Missiles at Israeli Jets'. It should be noted that, in an article published four years earlier, immediately after the Damascus airport explosion, the same author had considered the possibility that rumours of Badreddine being killed by his own side was 'disinformation being spread by some intelligence agency's psychological warfare department'. See: Yossi Melman, 'Intelligence Agencies Succeeding in Penetrating Hezbollah', *Jerusalem Post*, 15 May 2016.

227   **resolve their differences:** See also a tweet published by the

then spokesman of the Israeli Defence Forces in 2020 accusing Qassem Soleimani of killing Badreddine, quoted in Al-Masdar, 'Israeli Army Spokesman Accuses Nasrallah, Soleimani of Killing Hezbollah Commander', *Syrian Observer*, 15 May 2020.

228 **midnight ceremony:** Shimon Shapira, 'Iran and Hizbullah Mourn Mughniyeh and Plan Revenge Worldwide', Jerusalem Center for Public Affairs, 1 February 2015.

228 **Mustafa's father:** Ibid.

228 **shot Mustafa:** Melman, 'Why Syria Isn't Firing Its S-3000 Missiles at Israeli Jets'.

229 **'cogent and reliable evidence':** 'Public Redacted Version of Badreddine Request for Lifting of Suspensive Effect in re. Interlocutory Appeal of the Interim Decision on the Death of Mr Mustafa Amine Badreddine', Special Tribunal for Lebanon, 30 June 2016.

28: No Options Left

230 **lie down on her bed and pray:** 'Indictment, Operazione Stammer', Fermo di indiziato di delitto del pubblico ministero, Procura della Repubblica di Catanzaro, Direzione Distrettuale Antimafia. Proc. Pen. N.9444/14 R.G. notizie di reato/Mod. 21 DDA, p. 1575.

230 **'I don't throw it at you':** Ibid., p. 1574.

231 **'I have to leave again tomorrow':** Sentencing, Operazione Stammer 2, La Corte d'Appello di Catanzaro, Seconda Sez. Penale, N. 1964/20, 19 November 2020, p. 141.

231 **'You don't have to go':** Ibid.

231 **'Because they will kill me':** Ibid.

231 **get Antonio to look after her:** Ibid.

232 **'you won't find me when you come back':** Ibid., p. 142.

232 **'then you won't be able to go':** Ibid., p. 143.

232 **'to provide a future for you':** Ibid.

232 **'what you are doing':** Ibid.

232 **caught a ferry to Albania:** Ibid., p. 147.

232 **Salvatore was nervous:** Ibid., p. 149.

233 **a pouch on his lap:** Ibid., p. 151.

233 **'you are at home here':** Ibid., p. 150.

233 **'neither a thief nor a crook':** Ibid.

234 **'I will tell him that':** 'Indictment, Operazione Stammer', p. 1281.

234 **only one of them was going to survive:** Ibid., p. 1283.

235 **'Here is your bed':** Ibid., p. 1282.

235 **'why did you tell me the Colonel is dead':** Ibid., p. 1283.

235 **'I really don't':** Ibid., p. 1282.

236 **raided the banana plantation:** 'Incautan en Colombia el cargamento de cocaína más grande de la historia: 8 toneladas', *El Confidencial*, 16 May 2016.

236 **an underground bunker:** 'La policía colombiana decomisa 8 toneladas de cocaína en Urabá', *Euronews*, 16 May 2016. Video accessed at [https://www.youtube.com/watch?v=KQJUo1scC5Y]. Also 'Incautan en Colombia el cargamento de cocaína más grande de la historia: 8 toneladas', *El Confidencial*, 16 May 2016.

236 **359 white tarpaulins:** 'Un policía se infiltró en Turbo para ubicar caleta de "los Úsuga"', *El Tiempo*, 16 May 2016.

236 **lined up one by one:** 'La policía colombiana decomisa 8 toneladas de cocaína en Urabá'.

236 **tweeted his congratulations:** Tweet sent by Juan Manuel Santos on 15 May 2016 from @JuanManSantos: 'Felicitaciones @PoliciaColombia: operativo en Turbo incautó la mayor cantidad de droga en la historia. Golpe contundente a criminals.'

236 **as much as $250 million:** Niraj Chokshi, 'Colombian Authorities Seize a Record 8 Tons of Cocaine on a Banana Plantation', *Washington Post*, 16 May 2016.

236 **posing as a day labourer:** 'Un policía se infiltró en Turbo para ubicar caleta de "los Úsuga"'.

236 **drop coded messages:** Ibid.

236 **keep its staff quiet:** Ibid.

237 **Four days before Christmas:** 'Indictment, Operazione Stammer', p. 1581.

237 **had a bad feeling:** Ibid., p. 1586.

237 **dull yellow beams:** Ibid., p. 1588.

238 **295.7 grams of cocaine:** Ibid., p. 1587.

29: The Retirement Party

239 **DEA headquarters:** Except where separately noted, the account in this chapter is taken from interviews with Jack Kelly, Derek Maltz, John Fernandez, Jimmy Grace and Rob Zachariasiewicz.

240 **bring in fresh faces:** Zachariasiewicz v US Department of Justice, United States District Court, E.D. Virginia, Alexandria Division, Case no. 1:19-cv-00055 (RDA/JFA), 8 July 2019.

240 **rock stars:** Nick Miroff, Scott Higham, Steven Rich, Salwan Georges and Erin Patrick O'Connor, 'Cause of Death: Washington Faltered as Fentanyl Gripped America', *Washington Post*, 12 December 2022.

241 **shifted to a field group:** Zachariasiewicz v US Department of Justice.

242 **leaving it rudderless:** Miroff et al., 'Cause of Death'.

242 **a string of departures:** Ibid.

242 **fentanyl epidemic:** The US Centers for Disease Control and Prevention estimates that there were 100,306 drug overdose deaths in the United States during the twelve-month period ending in April 2021. See: 'Drug Overdose Deaths in the US Top 100,000 Annually', Centers for Disease Control and Prevention, 17 November 2021.

242 **sex parties:** Lauren French and John Bresnahan, 'DEA Agents had "Sex Parties" with Prostitutes, Watchdog Says', *Politico*, 27 March 2015.

242 **failed to effectively monitor:** 'DOJ OIG Releases Audit Report on the Drug Enforcement Administration's Headquarters-Based Oversight of its Supported Foreign Law Enforcement Units', US Department of Justice Office of the Inspector General, 26 August 2021.

30: 'My Name is Oksana'

245 **began to speak:** Interview with Camillo Falvo, public prosecutor of Vibo Valentia.

245 **a trickle of words:** Statements of Oksana Verman, 'Verbale riassuntivo di interrogatorio di persona sottoposta ad indagini', Procura della Repubblica di Catanzaro, Direzione Distrettuale Antimafia, N. 9444/14, 9 February 2017, p. 1.

245 **'I want to change my life':** Statements of Oksana Verman in 'Verbale illustrativo della collaborazione', Procura della Repubblica di Catanzaro, Direzione Distrettuale Antimafia, N. 9444/14 RG Mod. 44, 15 June 2017, p. 6.

245   **tears streamed down her face:** Interview with Antonia Condemi, Oksana Verman's lawyer.

246   **Oksana was exhausted:** Statements of Oksana Verman, 'Verbale riassuntivo di interrogatorio di persona sottoposta ad indagini', 8 February 2017, p. 9.

246   **Three other men:** Ibid., p. 1.

246   **protected the prisoners:** Italian Ministry of Justice, Paliano Prison, 10 March 2020. Accessed at [https://www.giustizia.it/giustizia/it/dettaglio_scheda.page?s=MII179331#].

246   **told the prosecutor:** Statements of Oksana Verman in 'Verbale illustrativo della collaborazione', p. 6.

247   **physically sick, shaking with fear:** Interview with Antonia Condemi. Statements of Oksana Verman, 'Verbale riassuntivo di interrogatorio di persona sottoposta ad indagini', 9 February 2017, p. 2.

247   **'constant panic attacks':** Statements of Oksana Verman in 'Verbale illustrativo della collaborazione', p. 28.

247   **'killed various people':** Statements of Oksana Verman, 'Verbale riassuntivo di interrogatorio di persona sottoposta ad indagini', 9 February 2017, p. 2.

248   **arresting fifty-four people:** Gianluca Prestia, 'Operazione Stammer, disposto il giudizio immediato per 54. La decisione del gip, prima udienza fissata in autunno', *Il Quotidiano del Sud*, 12 July 2017.

248   **final piece of the investigation:** Interview with Camillo Falvo.

248   **showed her pictures:** Statements of Oksana Verman in 'Verbale illustrativo della collaborazione', p. 13

249   **slipped the secret phone:** Statements of Oksana Verman, 'Verbale riassuntivo di interrogatorio di persona sottoposta ad indagini', 8 February 2017, p. 2.

249   **'Salvatore had lots of debt':** Statements of Oksana Verman in 'Verbale illustrativo della collaborazione', p. 9.

249   **allowed to go:** Ibid., p. 49.

250   **an unexpected visitor:** Philip Pullella, 'Pope Makes Easter Visit to Fortress Prison Holding Ex-Mafiosi', Reuters, 13 April 2017.

250   **'we are not like God':** Quotes from Pope Francis' Easter sermon at Paliano taken from 'Pope Francis'

Holy Thursday Homily at Paliano Prison', Salt +
Light Media, 14 April 2017, [https://slmedia.org/blog/
pope-francis-holy-thursday-homily-at-paliano-prison].
250   she felt free: Interview with Antonia Condemi.

31: The Speech at the Stone

251   ten years younger: 'Indictment, Operazione Stammer', Fermo
       di indiziato di delitto del pubblico ministero, Procura della
       Repubblica di Catanzaro, Direzione Distrettuale Antimafia. Proc.
       Pen. N.9444/14 R.G. notizie di reato/Mod. 21 DDA, p. 4.
252   smoking joints and eating pizza: Sentencing of Alex Pititto,
       Tribunale per i Minorenni di Catanzaro, N. 56/18 R.G. Sent., 8
       June 2018, pp. 16–17.
252   his girlfriend Noemi: Ibid., p. 17.
252   make him jealous: Ibid., p. 18.
252   becoming increasingly paranoid: Ibid., p. 9.
252   drop them all home: Ibid., p. 7.
252   a popular and handsome boy: Pietro Comito, 'La Procura
       di Vibo riapre le indagini sull'omicidio di Francesco Prestia
       Lamberti', Il Vibonese, 17 September 2020.
252   something special he had hidden: Sentencing of Alex
       Pititto, p. 8.
252   asked Alex for a cigarette: Ibid., p. 10.
252   Alex told Domenico: Ibid., p. 19.
253   running towards the car: Ibid., p. 8.
253   wasn't picking up his phone: 'Le Iene: Ucciso da un coetaneo a
       15 anni', Mediaset, 30 October 2018.
253   'I killed him': Sentencing of Alex Pititto, p. 11.
253   'Where is my son': 'Le Iene: Ucciso da un coetaneo a 15 anni'.
253   a terrible accident: Sentencing of Alex Pititto, p. 5.
253   lunged at his friend: Ibid.
253   into a bramble hedge: Ibid.
254   slumped on the ground: Ibid., p. 6.
254   metal detectors and sniffer dogs: Ibid.
254   mourners were arriving: Ibid., p. 8.
254   walking alone on Corso Umberto: Ibid., p. 21.
255   beating them with an iron bar: Ibid., p. 12.

255 'too many things going on': Ibid., p. 15.

255 started to swear: Ibid.

255 'what are you going to do': Ibid.

256 who to believe: Ibid., p. 16.

256 nothing to fear: Ibid.

256 'capacity to understand': Ibid., p. 28.

257 Francesco's nickname: Ilaria Lenza, 'L'ultimo saluto di Mileto a Francesco: "Il tuo ricordo ci renda tutti migliori"', *Zoom 24*, 1 June 2017.

257 hundreds of mourners: Details of Francesco's funeral taken from the video 'L'ultimo saluto a Francesco Prestia Lamberti', *La C*, 2 June 2017.

257 doused with petrol: 'Calabria: Incendiata porta abitazione sacerdote di Mileto', *Il Lametino*, 1 November 2013.

257 'today you unite us': Lenza, 'L'ultimo saluto di Mileto a Francesco'.

257 blue and white balloons: 'L'ultimo saluto a Francesco Prestia Lamberti'.

257 high towards the heavens: Ibid.

Epilogue

259 only going to be for a few months: This account is taken from interviews with Jack Kelly.

260 store uranium ore: Ronald Smothers, 'Three-Acre Legacy of the A-Bomb; A Pile of Radioactive Dirt Awaits Cleanup in New Jersey', *New York Times*, 27 October 1998.

260 sealed off to be decontaminated: 'Fact sheet – Middlesex Sampling Plant, NJ', US Army Corps of Engineers, New York District, 5 January 2022.

260 'I cannot say': Rachel Binhas, 'Le Hezbollah tisse sa toile en France', *Le Point*, 14 June 2021.

261 'linked to the Lebanese Hezbollah group': 'A View from the CT Foxhole: Gilles de Kerchove, European Union (EU) Counter-Terrorism Coordinator', *CTC Sentinel* 13:8 (August 2020).

261 nobody knew where he was: Interview with al-Atat's French lawyer, William Julié.

262 continued to deny: 'Sayyed Nasrallah Says STL Decisions Mean Nothing to Us: I Tell Those Who are Betting on Them "Don't

Play With Fire!"', *Al Manar*, 26 August 2018 and 'Hezbollah
Denies US Accusations of Drug Trafficking', Reuters, 19
January 2018.

262　**'the leader of both the preparation and performance of the
conspiracy':** 'The Prosecutor v Hassan Habib Merhi Hussein
Hassan Oneissi Appeal Judgment', Special Tribunal for Lebanon,
10 March 2022, p. 224.

262　**sanctioned Mustafa Badreddine's brother Mohamed:** 'Treasury
Targets Hizballah Financial Network in Africa and the Middle
East', US Department of the Treasury, 2 February 2022.

263　**followed his father and uncle:** 'State Department Terrorist
Designations of Ali Damush and Mustafa Mughniyeh', US
Department of State, 9 January 2017.

263　**killed in a US drone strike:** 'Qasem Soleimani: US Kills
Top Iranian General in Baghdad Air Strike', BBC News, 3
January 2020.

263　**sentenced to eighteen years:** Operazione Stammer – Corte di
Cassazione, Penale Sent. Sez. 3, Num. 1555, 21 September 2021.

263　**sentenced to four years, Giuseppe nine:** Ibid.

263　**Gianluca was sentenced:** 'Narcotraffico: condanna definitiva in
Cassazione per i Pititto di Mileto', *Il Vibonese*, 27 May 2022.

263　**sentenced to fourteen years:** Sentencing of Alex Pititto, Tribunale
per i Minorenni di Catanzaro, N. 56/18 R.G. Sent., 8 June 2018.

263　**reduced to three years and eight months on appeal:**
Operazione Stammer – Corte di Cassazione, Penale Sent. Sez. 3,
Num. 1555, 21 September 2021.

263　**The men from the Colombian cartel:** Gavilán, the Clan del
Golfo second-in-command who Italian police believed ultimately
owned the cocaine Salvatore was trying to buy, was killed in a
shootout in August 2017 in a joint Colombian police-military
operation. Otoniel, the Clan del Golfo leader, was captured in
Colombia in October 2021 and extradited to the United States
in what the country's president described as the most significant
blow to drug trafficking in his country since the demise of Pablo
Escobar almost thirty years before.

263　**a scam involving construction contracts:** 'Falsos funcionarios de
Embajada sueca detenidos en Colombia', *DW*, 29 January 2016.

263   **whom she named Nicholas:** Reginald Green, '"The Nicholas Effect" 25 Years Later: After We Donated our Son's Organs, Italy was Never the Same', *Los Angeles Times*, 29 September 2019.

263   **passed away in 2017:** Rory Cappelli, 'Roma, morto il giovane che ricevette il cuore di Nicholas Green', *La Repubblica*, 9 February 2017.

264   **'Lebanese Hezbollah Transnational Organized Crime':** Award citation seen by author.

Index

Page numbers in *italic* refer to images

Picture Credits

Associated Press/Alamy Stock Photo: 3
Sipa/Shutterstock: 4, 87
Jack Kelly: 11
Reuters News Agency: 20
Alain Nogues/Getty Images: 49
Procura Della Repubblica Di Catanzaro: 60, 151, 153, 177, 180, 238
Balkis Press/ABACA/Shutterstock: 112
Nabil Mounzer/EPA/Shutterstock: 221
Tousssaint Kluiters/EPA/Shutterstock: 262